A CONCISE HISTORY OF THE BRITISH EMPIRE

G. DURAND

A CONCISE HISTORY OF THE

BRITISH EMPIRE

GERALD S. GRAHAM

with 250 illustrations

THAMES AND HUDSON · LONDON

To My Grandchildren
Who never knew the British Empire

Frontispiece: *Britannia and her boys*,
from the *Illustrated London News*, 1885.

Reprinted 1972

Printed in Great Britain by Jarrold and Sons Limited, Norwich

ISBN 0 500 45007 2

Contents

Preface

This book attempts to describe, within restricted limits, the origins and growth of the British Empire from the end of the fifteenth century to the period beginning with the First World War. The subsequent transition from Empire to Commonwealth has been summarized in an epilogue, which is of necessity impressionistic. The task of bringing any kind of unity to so untidy and diversified a theme has been almost insuperable. Indeed, it could only be attempted by taking metropolitan London as a base, and holding tightly to the reins that guided British activity and British policy round the world. Until the beginning of the twentieth century, the British Empire was, generally speaking, within London's grasp and comprehension; imperial history remained essentially European history. Most areas of the earth were, both for good and evil, within the orbit of Europe's political systems. In the words of Ramsay Muir: 'Five great world-States divided between them more than half the land surface of the globe, and the fortunes of all the other peoples depended in no small degree upon the relations of these five.'

Within this global context, the British Empire represented one very substantial sample of European expansion. But the 'span' in terms of time and space is immense, and any author, like any teacher, is bound to acknowledge some lack of authority when contemplating certain periods and places, and to admit the provisional character of many of his conclusions. It has been argued that individual studies confined to an area or region would be equally useful, less liable to error and far more manageable than a world-wide mosaic within a single framework. Yet such a piecemeal approach, by ignoring the broader setting, might lose rather than gain in value as an intellectual exercise.

7

The results of British expansion have been very different in different climatic and geographical zones; the repercussions of European affairs on these same parts of the overseas world have been similarly varied. British imperial history reveals not only developments common to all areas within the Empire; it demonstrates the special problems that can crop up in various guises in various regions, whether tropical or temperate, primitive or highly civilized, problems which have perplexed and at the same time stimulated generations of British administrators and students of administration to the present day. In fact, the relationships between Britain and her colonies, by providing an unrivalled source for the study of political experience, constitute one of the grand and central themes of modern history. Started in the sixteenth century, chiefly for purposes of trade, the Empire gradually evolved into a complicated international laboratory, whence new nations activated by the old were precipitated into independent existence.

Edmund Burke was probably the first to proclaim that discontinuity in history is an illusion; that it is impossible to disinherit the past. Certainly the history of British overseas expansion is the outstanding illustration of his doctrine of continuity in change, and change in continuity. Burke saw the British Empire as the epitome of a long and continuous process of building and consolidating laws, customs, institutions and traditions, all of which contributed to the form and content of colonial offshoots in different parts of the world. Whatever the influences of geography, whatever the revolutions in political history, these could not obscure the constant overlapping of ideas and habits, transferred through a succession of new structures which inevitably embodied living elements of the old. In short, Burke saw human society as, 'a partnership not only between those who are living, but between those who are living, those who are dead, and those who are to be born'.

In the case of the British Empire, once Burke's doctrine of continuity is ignored, the basic patterns of colonial development are lost, and British colonial history is in danger of breaking up into a series of important, manageable but unrelated regional segments. Indeed, national studies may well suffer from such a separation unless students are invited at an early stage in their careers to view and appraise the processes of British expansion as a whole, and to appreciate their ramifications in politics and ideas. Otherwise, for example, how many Ghanaians will recognize in 1975 that their independence came about, not simply through Nkrumah and the accelerating influences of post-war nationalism, but also through an active and continuing tradition of constitutional evolution and democratic practice reaching from Ottawa round the world to New Delhi. And how many Indian students, in five years' time, will be able to compare, say, indirect rule in Africa under Lugard, with indirect rule in India under

Munro, or to appreciate that their constitution of 1950 owes its foundations to the same British liberal philosophy that is embodied in British political conventions and institutions.

Curiously enough, one still hears the vapid argument that since European imperialism is outmoded, British imperial history belongs to the lumber-room of obsolete books and lost causes. Admittedly, history has its fashions, but the lust for new horizons of learning should not be allowed to force history into regional or national strait-jackets, when that same history may have been, for one, two or even three centuries, inextricably mixed up with British policies and practices. The living roots of many new nations lie deep in a British past, and, as Stubbs remarked in the preface to his *Constitutional History of England*, '. . . nothing in the past is dead to the man who would learn how the present comes to be what it is'. To summon the past does not mean, however, that one hankers after lost greatness; nor does it imply a craving for the pleasures of self-reproach: I am averse to contemplating the imperial past as something to be atoned for.

The substance of this book has been drawn from accumulated lecture notes built up over the last twenty-three years. In the course of revising, excising and adding to the lectures, one cannot now be sure how much of the final product is the author's own, and how much is the work of his colleagues in this country and in other lands. I am especially indebted to Professor Peter Marshall of McGill University, who read the completed manuscript and saved me from errors of omission as well as fact; to Professor John R. Alden of Duke University, North Carolina, who brought his wide knowledge to bear on the American colonial period; to Professor W. N. Medlicott who tenderly, yet incisively, gave of his wisdom within the field of nineteenth-century British imperialism. My colleague in King's College, Dr Peter Marshall, with characteristic scrupulousness, reviewed the highly compressed sections on India. I am also grateful to my secretary, Mrs Marjorie Sutton, who sustained the ordeal of many revisions without loss of gaiety. But in no way can these generous allies be held responsible for the angularities and faults of a book which is not intended as a symmetrical outline of the history of the British Empire, but as an individual synthesis that may conceivably serve as a bridge to more substantial and sophisticated studies.

G.S.G.

King's College
University of London
February 1970

Chapter One: Introduction

Modern colonization may be said to date from the explorations of the sixteenth century, and to have evolved as a result of the demands of trade. The main thread in the history of English expansion is entwined with the history of over-seas trade routes; indeed, they are the constant elements in British imperial growth until the end of the nineteenth century. Up to the middle of the fifteenth century, the world in European eyes was a confined and conjectural entity whose centre of gravity was the Mediterranean Sea. Trade routes from the Red Sea and the Persian Gulf and from south-east and central Asia converged at its eastern extremity, but the areas round and beyond these ancient corridors lay in the mists.

When Marco Polo made his astonishing journey across central Asia in the thirteenth century, contemporary maps were apt to be a wild confusion of mis-applied scriptures. Later on, after he had dictated his travels, Polo's embroidered story of the fabulous court of Kublai Khan provided the first full account of the Chinese East the European world had ever had placed before it. It was a good book and it broke fresh ground, but nothing of its content can explain its subsequent influence on world history, which was so out of proportion to its literary quality and historical substance. This volume of travel, describing golden cities and strange customs, possibly had more influence on world history than any other book except for the Bible, the Koran or Adam Smith's *Wealth of Nations*. When Columbus sailed westward he was looking not for America, but China and the Indies. And long after Columbus, the romance and wealth of the East drove explorers east, west and south-west in search of the land of the Great Khan and Chinese trade.

Logically, the first colonizing and exploring powers should have been England and France. Both were strategically placed in relation to Atlantic

11

◀ The circumnavigation of the globe: the voyages of Francis Drake (1577–80) and Thomas Cavendish (1586–88) on a map of *c.* 1590.

routes. Both had royal revenues and kings whose ambitions were certain to focus on outside adventure. But at the critical moment for both nations, the Hundred Years War began. The battles of Crécy and Poitiers, and the exhausting campaigns which followed, cost both England and France the lead as exploring and colonizing countries, while in England the Wars of the Roses added a further agonizing handicap. Consequently, at the time when Columbus discovered America and da Gama rounded the Cape of Good Hope, neither England nor France had become maritime powers of sufficient strength to challenge either Portugal or Spain. Both Iberian nations were resolute to find new trade routes; both of them sought connections with the East. And the whole of modern history gathers in a large degree about their grand adventures.

The Portuguese and Spanish discoveries had a momentous revolutionary effect on the economic outlook of Europe. They initiated an era of acquisitive capitalism which was to change the face of the globe. After 1450, slaves and gold, pearls and ivory were among the new incentives that were to spur Western endeavour. Portugal started first, partly because she was first freed from the menace of Moorish invasions, but chiefly because a great ruling house, in the fifteenth century, produced two distinguished men of thought and action, Henry the Navigator and Emmanuel the Fortunate.

The seafaring impetus acquired under Henry the Navigator and his school continued after Henry's death, and led to the achievements of Diaz and da Gama in the decade between 1488 and 1498. Thanks to the absence of any strong Asian naval power (save only the Chinese, whose isolationist rulers had deliberately turned their backs on maritime expansion before the end of the fifteenth century) the Portuguese were able to secure the mastery of the Indian Ocean with astonishing speed. Goa, a land-locked island, became the headquarters of their Eastern empire. The capture of Malacca by Albuquerque in 1511 secured a central emporium for the spice trade, as well as the strategic key to the trade of the South China Sea and the Indonesian Archipelago. With the seizure of Hormuz in 1515, Portugal obtained control of the Persian Gulf and one of the two routes by which the spice trade was carried on with the Levant. Albuquerque attempted to block the alternative Red Sea route by taking Aden. Although he narrowly failed, the Portuguese could, none the less, enter the Red Sea at will, even though they never succeeded in closing it to the Moslems.

The Portuguese were enterprising sailors, but their kingdom was almost enveloped by the land frontier of Spain, and therefore too vulnerable to thwart Spanish ambitions even on water. By 1585 they had capitulated, and for more than half a century remained an annex of Spain. Admittedly, Portugal had acquired Brazil, which she was able to retain under the Papal division line of 1494. But Brazil was a possession held on sufferance and left largely to manage its own affairs; it was always at the mercy of the major power. During the greater part of the sixteenth century, the course of events in the New World that Columbus had revealed after 1492, was shaped by Spain, because Spain held command of the sea without serious competitor. Absorbed in the Indian Ocean, Portugal was never a serious Atlantic rival.

Spanish colonization may be dated from 1492 when Columbus touched the island of San Salvador in the West Indies. Between that point and 1531, there began an epoch of imperial expansion so extraordinary that fiction cannot keep pace with fact in the Spanish history of these years. In 1498 Columbus touched the mainland; in 1512, the Spaniards concluded that there was an ocean between the New World and Asia; in 1513, Balboa actually saw the Pacific Ocean; in 1519 Magellan started on his great voyage which proved that too-far east was to be west and vice versa. Between 1518 and 1521 Cortez invaded and conquered Mexico and in 1531–32 an even richer country was discovered by Pizarro – Peru. Spain now possessed two American empires.

During 5000 years of Mediterranean history the Americas had been protected by Atlantic and Pacific; that isolation was now at an end. The barrier of the Atlantic had been their sole guarantee of an independent existence. When that obstacle had ceased to be insurmountable, the end of the first American civilization known to history was inevitable; a new era in the history of Europe had begun.

Meanwhile, as the Portuguese followed da Gama's track round the Cape of Good Hope to India and the spice islands, the Spanish confirmed their claims to the gold and silver empire that Columbus had discovered. They planted substantial populations of settlers in their new Caribbean domain, of which Florida may be regarded as a part, but they ignored the less congenial eastern mainland of North America. From the evidence available, it would appear that until nearly the middle of the sixteenth century, Spain made no serious effort to stop expeditions directed to the northward of the continent. Jacques Cartier's first voyage up the St Lawrence River in 1534 seems to have caused the Spanish court no more concern than did the earlier explorations of Cabot and Verrazzano. A perfunctory effort was made to catch Cartier and Roberval on the last expedition in 1541, but failure occasioned no sense of alarm. Indeed, the abandonment of the French settlements before they had taken root, rightly suggested that the north-eastern elbow of North America would remain a remote and untenanted zone of fishing activity. Almost a hundred years were to elapse between the first discovery of the St Lawrence by Cartier and the establishment in Canada of permanent colonization.

Without naval support from home, France was in no position either to break or infringe the Spanish monopoly in the Caribbean. The extinction of

Mariner's astrolabe, *c.* 1588.

Sir Francis Drake.

the short-lived French post, Fort Caroline, in Florida in 1565, demonstrated how precarious were rival colonial establishments that encroached upon or brushed the claims of Spain in the New World.

A relatively poor and equally distracted England required no such lesson on the perils of challenging the world's leading sea power. There was no thought of a major confrontation with Spain; English projects were deliberately designed to avoid competition and conflict with Spanish overseas territories. English adventurers, such as Hawkins and Drake, might win glory and booty by coastal raids, or find cold security in the hidden recesses of Newfoundland, but, like France, England could not afford to stake out even modest settlements on the Atlantic coastline without ensuring her maritime connections with Europe. Until 1588 she was in no position to challenge Spanish-Portuguese hegemony in the New World, and the sixteenth century closed without a single English colony in North America.

Despite her insular situation, Tudor England, like pre-1914 Serbia, was essentially a small agricultural country, continental in outlook rather than sea-faring and expansionist. Unlike the Norsemen, and contrary to general belief, Englishmen had no deep-rooted tradition of the sea. Apart from the Crusades and the occasional private expedition to Africa, their pretensions to sea suprem-acy had been confined to the Channel, which was regarded as a part of the feudal domain connecting them with their possessions in France.

Until Elizabeth's reign, interest was chiefly landward. While English soldiers fought to conquer Scotland or France, Dutch, German and Venetian sailors carried the bulk of English wool to Flanders, almost all the wine from France, the spices from the Levant, and even the fish from Iceland and the Grand Banks. Henry VII had given some slight encouragement to the Cabots, but subsequent failures dampened the enthusiasm of a still turbulent and almost bankrupt England. Doubtless other adventurers after Cabot's time continued to visit old fishing grounds and search for new routes to the riches of Cathay but whatever the object of the voyage, to avoid trespass on Spanish or Portuguese lanes of commerce English ships were almost bound to seek a detour either by the north-east round Norway or by the north-west round Newfoundland.

A London merchant by the name of Robert Thorne, who had lived for some years in Seville, the seat of the Spanish school of navigation, was probably the first Englishman to promote a northern expedition. There was no doubt, he told Henry VIII in 1527, 'that sayling Northwards and passing the Pole, descending to the Equinoctiall lyne, we shall hitte these Islands, and it would be [a] much shorter way than eyther the Spaniardes or the Portingals have'. But Thorne's appeal bore little fruit until 1553, when far-seeing London merchants prepared to pool their capital. Together they hired ships, bought provisions and enlisted professional sailors of varying capacities and loyalties. The result was a joint-stock company, which was responsible for the first effort to reach Asia by the north-east.

Between 1553 and 1559 Sir Hugh Willoughby, Richard Chancellor, Stephen Borough and Anthony Jenkinson tried to break the barriers. Willoughby and Chancellor followed the same route as the Second World War convoys round the North Cape to Russia. They were separated by storms, and Willoughby's men were later found by Lapps, dead from starvation and cold. But Chancellor reached the White Sea and present-day Archangel, whence he travelled to Moscow by sledge and met Ivan the Terrible, returning to England in 1554, not with silks and spices of the Orient, but with humdrum articles like beeswax, hemp and flax. Jenkinson too pursued the northern trail, reaching as far as Bokhara in Persia. But the road through central Asia was both tedious and dangerous, and increasing tribal anarchy was subsequently to make the overland route through Persia to the Indian Ocean as treacherous as the ice-packed stretches leading to the White Sea. It was still a far call to the golden roofs and balmy breezes of the spice islands.

Drake's expedition attacks the Spaniards of St Augustine, Florida. This engraving (1588) is believed to be the earliest view of a town in the United States.

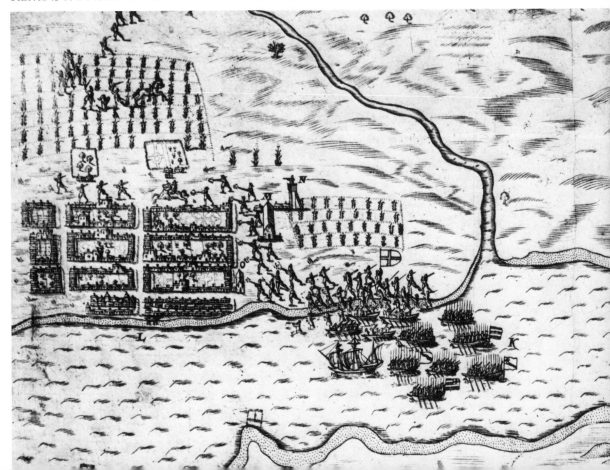

Sir Humphrey Gilbert.

Then followed the attempted breakthrough by the north-west route, equally compounded of hardship and tragedy. In 1567, Humphrey Gilbert, one of the first to suggest colonization as well as trade and exploration, posed the problem of finding 'a passage by the Northe to go to Cataia [Cathay], and all other east partes of the worlde'. It was his *Discourse of a Discoverie for a New Passage to Cataia* that first predicted a clear passage round Newfoundland to China and the spice islands, and laid down rules for the equipment and financing of expeditions with a colonizing objective. After him came the greatest explorers of the age – men like Martin Frobisher, who just missed finding a through-route to Hudson's Bay; and John Davis, the finest English sailor and navigator of the century, whose name is perpetuated in Davis Strait between Greenland and Baffin Land. Each made three voyages to the Arctic, voyages which stimulated Richard Hakluyt to write the glorious saga of the first explorers.

But little came of these undertakings, other than the final discovery of the Hudson Strait, and the painful conclusion that a road to the East, at least by the north-west or north-east, was for the time being too costly in terms of life and money. It was left to Drake in 1577 to find a route to the Moluccas by the south-west. In the process he became the first Englishman to circumnavigate the globe.

Meanwhile, attempts to found English settlements on the mainland of North America failed tragically and sometimes mysteriously. Between 1585 and 1587, three expeditions, the first led by Sir Richard Grenville, landed settlers on the coast of present-day North Carolina, but all of them failed, the last one disappearing without trace. All told, only about 250 settlers were involved. Entirely apart from insecure communications with the mother country, limited colonizing resources doomed English colonial projects to the same failure as French enterprises in Brazil and Florida. Capital for prospective plantations might be supplied by plundering raids on the Spanish merchant fleet, as Grenville and subsequently Sir Walter Raleigh demonstrated, but the close association between colonization and privateering meant that untrained crews and rapacious passengers lacked the discipline so necessary for community existence. England's potential settlers preferred piracy and easy money to prosaic farming and village life. No settlement could be established on a firm economic basis when both skills and resolution were lacking. Lack of agricultural knowledge, as we shall see, came close to finishing the famous Jamestown colony. As late as 1607, the administrators of the Virginia settlement had not learned the lessons that had been taught by English failures in the 1580s. For a colony to succeed without continuous support from the homeland, it had to be strong enough to provide for its own defences against native and European enemies, and possess the manpower, the organization and the experience to enable it to live off the land.

Sir Martin Frobisher.

Encounter with eskimoes, a drawing
after John White, *c.* 1610.

Sir Richard Grenville.

Sir Walter Raleigh with his son.

17

Flood at the mouth of the Orinoco, encountered by Raleigh's expedition in 1595.

In a symbolic sense, the first British Empire began with Humphrey Gilbert. Gilbert's formal gesture of taking possession of the island of Newfoundland in August 1583 endorsed the old Cabot claim of eighty years previously. His dramatic death on the return voyage was an accident which scarcely affected the future of a colony whose fate was foredoomed. Once again resources, in terms of men, money and tools, fell far behind grandiose conception. Gilbert's half-brother, Sir Walter Raleigh, was in a stronger position. He was close to the great queen. Whether or not he was, as he claimed, Elizabeth's lover, is irrelevant; suffice it to say, his position at court enabled him to find state as well as private support for his projects, and he was fortified in his appeals by the most influential scholar of his day, Richard Hakluyt, whose epic tales of English navigation provided thrilling incitement to adventure overseas. Hakluyt's *Discourse on Western Planting*, which was presented to the queen in 1584, stressed the prestige element in national expansion, the need to combat Iberian Catholicism by the introduction of Protestant settlers in new lands, and the economic and strategic advantages of obtaining bases of attack against the possessions of Spain.

Like Cecil Rhodes, Raleigh was empire-intoxicated, but far more than Rhodes, he let his dreams run away with his judgment. He lacked both his mistress's political and business acumen. In Guiana he hoped to found a colony at the expense of Spain, and his *Discovery of Guiana*, written after his return from the Orinoco in 1595, reveals the naïve emotions and ideals of a poet to whom glory was probably more important than profits. It may be that his hatred of Spain provided the imperialist compulsion which in the end led to the scaffold. No one made greater personal sacrifices to create the beginnings of an anti-Spanish empire, and no one knew less about the actual work of colonization. His gamble failed, but like so many proud men in that brutal age who had made a mess of their lives, he 'knew with assurance how to die'.

The art of colonization had yet to be learned by England; on the other hand, exploration, privateering and trade were becoming for the first time national enterprises. Hawkins, Drake and their confrères may have been smugglers, slavers and perhaps pirates, but they were also popular idols. In all probability, however, their personal appetites inclined more towards riches than national uplift. 'We find it in daily experience', wrote Raleigh, 'that all discourse of magnanimity, of national virtue, of religion, of liberty, and whatsoever else had been wont to move and encourage virtuous men, hath no force at all with the common soldier in comparison of spoil and riches. . . .'

Indeed, the glamorous achievements of the early adventurers tended to obscure an evolving national purpose that lay behind individual efforts to trace and maintain sea routes to the spice islands, the West Indies and the Grand Banks. Under cover of widely advertised privateering, buccaneers and merchants were pointing the way to a new form of commercial rivalry. In the past, territorial expansion founded on military force had been the principal issue of European rivalry; in the seventeenth-century era of transatlantic colonization, competition on the seas gradually superimposed itself on the traditional pattern of continental relationships. A new element had entered into the international equilibrium, namely, sea power. If colonial trade was an essential constituent of a country's prosperity and strength, it was soon apparent that the wealth of colonies could only be garnered by those nations that possessed military power at sea. The North Atlantic and the Indian Ocean were to be new European battlefields; command of the sea implied the ability to maintain trade routes.

The Drake Cup, presented to the adventurer by Elizabeth I on New Year's Day 1582.

English settlers arrive in Virginia.

Chapter Two

THE EXPANSION OF ENGLAND

VIRGINIA AND THE CARIBBEAN

From the beginning of the century English colonization did not, as in France, depend chiefly on the stimulus of a monarch or a royal minister; it was more often the by-product of commercial enterprise, represented by independent companies like the East India, the Levant or the Virginia. The Virginia Company, which in 1606 sent three ships loaded with settlers to America, announced its objective three years later as, first, the propagation of the Gospel, secondly, the export of 'the rankness and multitude of increase in our population', and thirdly, profit.

Undoubtedly, in the beginning, government saw the prospective colonies as useful dumping-grounds for the unemployed, paupers and felons, but there can be no doubt that both promoters and settlers were guided primarily by economic considerations, and occasionally, for example, in the case of New England or New Zealand, by religious or even philanthropic motives. Just as the early history of exploration was linked with the search for Eldorado, so were the first phases of English colonization dominated by the continued search for gold and silver and precious stones.

As the seventeenth century advanced, however, wealth was judged to consist not simply of precious metals and precious stones but of essential commodities, such as naval stores, timber, dyes, salt, saltpetre, spices and fish – staples of trade heretofore largely supplied by the foreigner. Such resources were constituents of national strength. Hence, the concept of a European balance of power was soon to include overseas colonies as bases of trade, and, before the end of the seventeenth century, English colonization can be regarded as almost incidental to commercial expansion. One may 'well and truly conclude with reason and authority', wrote Hakluyt, 'that all the commodities of our olde decayed and dangerous trades in all Europe, Africa and Asia haunted by us, may in a short space and for little or nothinge, in a manner be had in that part of America which lieth betweene 30 and 60 degrees of northerly latitude'.

Coat of arms of the Virginia Company, an engraving of 1633.

Although North America was subsequently to reveal great wealth, its eastern coastline was not easily opened to settlement. In the Caribbean the Spaniards had found comparatively pleasant conditions. They suffered strange diseases, but the climate was genial, the products of the soil were readily procured, and, compared with those of the northern mainland, the natives were docile. The men who first settled in North America (and particularly in New England) faced a rigorous winter, a population of bellicose Indians, and, because neither gold nor for the moment any alternative trading commodity was available, they found themselves struggling for existence.

Their situation in the beginning was appalling; they suffered fevers, pneumonia, lack of proper food through lack of skills – the Jamestown settlers were much more interested in mining than in farming; only the threat of starvation drove them to the scrubby fields – and finally troubles with the Indians which threatened their extinction. Up to this point every English colony had been a failure; for a time it seemed that the new effort would fail because of actual casualties. Between 1606 and 1618, some 1800 colonists had arrived; by 1618, 600 were alive; between 1619 and 1620, 1200 set out from England; by the end of the latter year only about 200 were alive.

The battle against odds continued until 1624. In the meantime, the man who did most to make the colony stick was Captain John Smith, best known in popular history as the wilderness knight rescued by the 'fair lady' Pocahontas. He remains a controversial figure, but despite romantic embroideries, there is more common sense in his writing on colonization than in those of almost any other pioneer essayist. His mind was restless, as befitted an adventurer and soldier of fortune, but he had all the aggressiveness and self-confidence that was to

Colonial defences: two early seventeenth-century forts.

Title-page of
Captain John Smith's
*The Generall Historie
of Virginia . . .*, 1624.

mark the successful nineteenth-century American capitalist. He realized at once that a colony could not be founded by debauched convicts and enfeebled paupers; and when New England got its start it may well have owed something to Smith's vigorous judgment: 'All you can expect from them, must be by labour.' He swept away illusions about gold and the search for a route to China just over the horizon. He called for labour on the land, and in times of crisis he taught men how to hold on to life.

His successors until 1618 were soldier-governors who enforced rigid discipline in the interests of survival. Sir Thomas Dale (governor, 1611–16) literally chilled the settlement into order, and a kind of martial law became the rule until the institution of an assembly in 1619. The Virginia assembly was the first 'free parliament' in all America, and even after Virginia became a royal colony in 1624, it continued in practice to enjoy most of its earlier liberties.

The attractions of *Nova
Britannia* across the
Atlantic.

James I was too lethargic, too provincial to be an assertive imperialist, and although Virginia passed out of Company hands, the assembly remained and slowly developed a life of its own.

But constitutional liberties could not guarantee survival; 'freedom of the individual' was no substitute for either 'guns or butter'. Despite the defeat in 1588 of the Armada, the Spaniards were still powerful enough to wipe out the anaemic colony, just as in the past they had dealt with neighbouring French settlements. Indeed, Spanish reconnaissance vessels watched the early progress of the English colony, and were able to report growing weakness and debility. Why not let the Indians and the fevers finish the job? In any event, the settlement in no way endangered Spanish trade; there was no gold, no silver; England would soon tire of profitless colonization.

Spanish forbearance was vital to survival, and peace was made with Spain in 1604. Yet what put the first English colony on its feet was neither Spanish restraint nor English political wisdom, but tobacco smoke. Leaf tobacco seems to have been first grown by John Rolfe in 1612; by 1619 tobacco plantations extended along the banks of the James River, both above and below Jamestown. The plantation system, based on indentured white labour, had begun. Not until the end of the seventeenth century did Negro slavery begin to replace the indentured servant, bound to work for four years or thereabouts in payment of his passage. But Virginia was not always a land of great plantations administered by wealthy leisured aristocrats. The majority of owners started with fifty acres, and scarcity of labour in the seventeenth century limited growth; at no time was more than one-eighth of the population subject to rules of indenture.

Meanwhile, attention had been drawn to the Bermudas, where Sir George Somers, in company with the first governor, Sir Thomas Gates, was shipwrecked in 1609 *en route* to Virginia. As a consequence, Bermuda came under the control of the Virginia Company, and so remained until a separate company was formed, known as the Company of the Plantation of the Somers Islands. Settlers were recruited, and eventually tobacco plantations worked by slave labour were developed.

But far more energy was directed towards colonizing Caribbean islands, many of which, it was discovered, could produce not only tobacco, but sugar and cotton. The most prosperous of the English islands was Barbados, which had been occupied in 1625, although substantial settlements grew on the Leeward chain, extending from the Virgin Islands to Martinique, and including St Christopher (1623), Nevis and Barbuda (1628), Antigua and Montserrat (1632). In 1638 a small plantation took shape on the mainland of Honduras. Seventeen years later, Cromwell's expedition, under Penn and Venables, aimed at the heart of Spanish Caribbean power, and captured Jamaica. As

Colonial trade: detail from Henry Popple's map of North America, 1733. Note especially the tobacco.

with the Atlantic colonies, representative government was the significant feature of existence that distinguished even slave-worked islands from the overseas settlements of other nations. When they submitted to the Commonwealth in 1652, the Barbadians managed to retain their assembly, asserting with Royalist boldness that it was 'the ancient and usual custom here'.

THE PURITANS

Once the foundations of a Virginia settlement were laid, London buzzed with colonization plans. Liverymen, fishmongers, politicians and publicans talked about England's national interest and the need for national effort. Yet emigration to the New World started slowly in the wake of the Jamestown pioneers. From 1620 onwards, it took on strength, growing in volume until the Civil War temporarily put a stop. Between 1620 and 1642, the West Indies and Bermuda received about 40,000 colonists, of which nearly half went to Barbados. The continental coast took fewer than 30,000, of which nearly half went to Massachusetts.

25

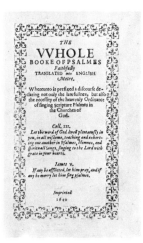

Title-page of the *Bay Psalm Book*, 1640.

The *Mayflower*, a contemporary representation on a Dutch tile.

Why did so many men leave their homeland? According to Francis Bacon, from the beginning the prime mover in the Virginia Company, it was not the propagation of the Christian faith that motivated the discovery and plantation of the New World, 'but gold and silver and temporal profit'. Admittedly, the wars of Elizabeth had linked national loyalty with national faith. Yet, as Hakluyt had pointed out, while the Spaniard had been busily converting 'many millions of infidells', English Protestants had done nothing. It was high time, he urged his countrymen, to link colonization with conversion, and to instil into the parched minds of the heathen, 'the swete and lively liquor of the Gospell'.

As a positive argument for colonization, this much-advertised duty to christianize the Indian can be ignored. The English colonizers of North America had none of the missionary zeal manifested so violently by the Spanish and so heroically by the French. The English paid lip-service to an obligation that was rarely performed. On the other hand, the religious motive, operating by repulsion, was important. Suffering from the restrictions and tyrannies of a state church, many Protestants and Catholics sought to escape into the freedom of distant and unknown lands. Their impulses as well as their doctrines led to the foundations of New England.

These dissenters were not all bitterly uncompromising; the Congregationalists, for example, were willing to uphold the king's authority in all matters agreeable to God's word, but they wanted self-governing congregations without bishops or prelates of any sort. Ritual was to be simplified and based on sound Evangelical doctrine. In brief, they demanded liberty to worship as they pleased. Unfortunately, in so doing, they found themselves acting against the laws of England. Hence a large group, the nucleus from Nottinghamshire, escaped across the North Sea in 1607–08 to Holland, where they found toleration not obtainable under the early Stuarts. They were still English, but English exiles; and, their leaders were soon considering the prospect of emigration to North America where they might establish their church under the English flag. They sought a settlement with James I, and to do him justice he was willing to connive with them provided they carried on peaceably. They made a good bargain in their first dealing with the Virginia Company; indeed, the negotiations suggest considerable business sense.

The *Mayflower* set sail from Southampton in early September 1620, and landed 101 passengers, men, women and children, at Plymouth in December. Happily they did not, as they had once contemplated, go to Guiana. There were Caribbean plantations bidding for Puritan emigration and it is conceivable that the tropics might have received the first Nonconformist immigration and engulfed it. But the landing on Plymouth Rock – if it was the Rock – occurred outside Virginia Company territory, and in 1621 a new patent of settlement had to be secured. In the bitter cold of winter, which took toll of half the arrivals, the most remarkable experiment in the history of English colonization had its beginnings.

Plymouth was founded by what might be called the upper working class – humble folk, farmers, mechanics, craftsmen; neither their piety nor their standards were those of the governing classes. But some of their leaders were men of education, for example, William Brewster, a postmaster, and William Bradford, who became their historian. Bradford's history of the Plymouth plantation, with its moving account of 'Why the Pilgrims left England for Holland', told the whole human story of relentless determination and sacrifice. This great chronicle of events between 1620 and 1646 was not published in full until 1856, but various pamphlets and relations revealed to the English-speaking world the possibilities of establishing semi-religious colonies in America. The humility with which most of them were written impresses one as genuine; these people were not a stiff-necked, sullenly narrow type. On the other hand, they did not intend to establish toleration as we know it; anyone in Plymouth who wished to lead a normal life had to join the Congregational Church. Their Puritanism had no connection with democracy; their leaders aimed at a state purged of old England's corruptions, legal, religious and commercial. In short, the Pilgrims were as Puritan – if anything, more so in their discipline – as were the middle-class Englishmen who came to Massachusetts Bay in 1630.

The departure of the Pilgrims from Delft Haven in the *Speedwell* to join the *Mayflower*; from a painting of the period by Adam van Breen.

The intricate negotiations which eventually enabled the New England Puritans to get control of their own destinies are not fully known. Suffice it to say that a colonization company called the Dorchester Adventurers had bought the Pilgrims' right to a fishing station at Gloucester on Cape Ann, and started a settlement in 1624 under patent from the council of New England. A similar series of small settlements took shape along the coast of Maine. The Cape Ann foundation was not a success, partly owing to the poor quality of the settlers, and when it broke up, a reorganized association managed to secure another patent, and in 1629 received a charter creating the Massachusetts Bay Company. In form, it was another Muscovy Company. As it happened, however, the charter was vulnerable in that it did not specify either London or the New World as the site of Company headquarters. It did not state that a general court meeting had to be held in London: why not, therefore, in the colony itself, free from all government interference except that of a king some 3000 miles away? Such questioning led to a unique event in the history of colonization – the migration overseas of an entire English company, and, vested within it, the entire powers of local management. At a time when other colonies, Spanish, French and Portuguese, were being governed from Europe, the colony of Massachusetts was literally governing itself.

The transfer of the charter did protect the colony from the close attentions of the English government; it also provided a notable precedent for American institutions, that is, a written document with limits on the ruling authority. The vital feature was the annual election of governors and assistants, not by outside authority as in Virginia, but by the freemen voters in the colony who met four times a year as a general court. It is well to note, however, that although the scope of company government in Virginia was more restricted, the inhabitants probably enjoyed a more liberal democracy than those in New England. In Virginia, almost every landowner had a vote; in New England, because of the difficulty of coming up to church requirements (freemen had to be communicants), it was scarcely more than one in five.

The Puritans who settled the villages in and about Boston were largely yeomen and small country gentlemen. Unlike Plymouth, Massachusetts had the advantage of being peopled not merely by religious Nonconformists, but by an enlightened and industrious society, headed by learned ministers and gentlemen trained in the arts of government. It was the age when the lower gentry of England had come into their own; indeed some of the greatest names in the struggle against Charles I belong to that class – Eliot, Pym, Hampden, Cromwell.

Politically and socially, the Massachusetts colony was not a democracy; inevitably it became a theocracy. And within this monolithic Bible common-

The Massachusetts Charter, 4 March 1629.

wealth, a rigorous church discipline was bound to lead not only to strict regulation of manners, dress and amusements, but to the severe treatment of those
unwilling to abide by the rules. The very men who had fled from the harsh
restrictions of the Church of England were themselves unwilling to tolerate
variations in their own established form of worship.

Equality of all men was not, therefore, a basic tenet of the Massachusetts
constitution; the slavery of lawful captives was permitted – indeed, of any
strangers willing to sell themselves. Climate and soil, not morality, explain the
absence of plantation slavery in the north. Although it can scarcely be argued
that the Puritans misapplied the Scriptures, certain inhumanities in administration suggest a leaning towards Mosaic law. But if their principal failure was to
confuse crime with sin, they were probably more merciful in general outlook
than any other group of colonists of the time. The death penalty was used far
less freely than at home; there was no imprisonment for debt; civil marriage was
legal, and on the whole women had a far better standing in law than they had in
England. Probably the most odious phase of the colonists' history was the period
which saw the persecution of Quakers and witches; to these they were merciless.
It is well to remember, however, that in England between 1647 and 1661, some
6000 Quakers were put in prison, and nearly 500 suffered death by violence.

In its beginnings, the New England theocracy was bigoted and sometimes tyrannous in policies and practices. Yet, the Puritan form of Calvinism was in so many ways peculiarly suitable for a pioneer society. The modern American philosophy of 'making good' or 'climbing to the top' owes much to the Calvinist creed. Men could best serve God through hard work, and those who were successful had a sense of having fulfilled some particular destiny. They belonged to the elect, most of them secure in the knowledge of their future salvation. This doctrine of the elect, along with the strict moral code, helped to build the New England conscience. Of course, in its lowest form, such a doctrine could be translated into a mere taboo on pleasure, as subsequently applied by 'Watch and Ward' societies. Even May Day frolics were resented as sources of immorality, and while the average Puritan detested cruelty to animals, it may well have been that, like Macaulay's fastidious Englishman, they were less concerned about the baited bear than about the pleasure his sufferings afforded to the spectators.

In many respects a rigid code of faith and conduct is an advantage to pioneers. Since this world has been largely shaped not by moderates, but by extremists, at the start of English colonization an extreme Protestantism was not a disadvantage. However narrow their religious views, the Puritans were men of independence, drive and initiative. Their morality was fierce, and in organization, autocratic. Yet, with all the terrors of the moral law, there was stability of domestic life; they were fathers and mothers, not adventurers, striving to carve homes in the wilderness. And although they who had been persecuted, persecuted in their turn, all the forces of frontier life pressed in the direction of freedom. Paradoxically, this strait-jacketed community became a seedbed of religious toleration.

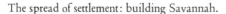

The spread of settlement: building Savannah.

The Wonders of the Invisible World:

Being an Account of the

TRYALS

OF

Several Witches,

Lately Excuted in

NEW-ENGLAND:

And of several remarkable Curiosities therein Occurring.

Together with,

I. Observations upon the Nature, the Number, and the Operations of the Devils.

II. A short Narrative of a late outrage committed by a knot of Witches in *Swede-Land*, very much resembling, and so far explaining, that under which *New-England* has laboured.

III. Some Councels directing a due Improvement of the Terrible things lately done by the unusual and amazing Range of Evil-Spirits in *New-England*.

IV. A brief Discourse upon those *Temptations* which are the more ordinary Devices of Satan.

By COTTON MATHER.

Published by the Special Command of his EXCELLENCY the Govenour of the Province of the *Massachusetts-Bay* in *New-England*.

Printed first, at *Boston* in *New-England*; and Reprinted at *London*, for *John Dunton*, at the *Raven* in the *Poultry*. 1693.

Above: Cecil Calvert, second Lord Baltimore, founded Maryland, which received its charter in 1634.

Top left: Puritan intolerance: Cotton Mather's account of New England witch trials.

Left: self-portrait of a seventeenth-century American, Thomas Smith, who lived for a time in Boston.

Enduring European colonies have rarely been created by adventurers in search of glory or gold; nor was state paternalism alone sufficient to make a European settlement live and grow. During the first half of the seventeenth century, it was the good fortune of the United States that men and women better fitted in body and spirit as colonizers than any similar company in the world, were forced to cross the Atlantic.

What was the relation of the colonies to the mother country? There was no Colonial Office. The royal power granted charters, and continued to exert its authority through and about those charters. The royal power also granted territories to individuals. Naturally, it intervened to send governors (although Connecticut and Rhode Island were able to escape such attentions for a considerable period). But little real control of colonial government was exercised from England because the distance was great, and because kings were too busy with other things. However, in 1634, Charles I, through Archbishop Laud, tried to intervene in Massachusetts. His first objective was to control emigration, and then revoke charters surreptitiously obtained. He appointed a council called the Lords Commissioners for Plantations, corresponding to a Colonial Office, and these commissioners demanded a proof of Massachusetts' claims by 'quo warranto'. The rights of the Massachusetts Bay Company were obviously to be taken into the king's hands. Things looked very black for New England.

What Richelieu had done in France, Charles meant to do in England. He dismissed Parliament, and raised money without a grant. But Charles was no Richelieu. He had no ready-made army, no surplus revenue, and he had a reforming party to fight in England, as well as a battle with the Scots on whom he tried to force episcopacy. So the Massachusetts men, isolated by 3000 miles of ocean, simply sat tight and did nothing. By letting well alone, they delayed a decision, and then the Civil War which started in 1642 saved them.

There is no more remarkable chapter in colonial history than the expansion of settlement in North America. During the years of *laissez-faire*, the Puritans blossomed out into a series of little states. Between 1635 and 1636, John Winthrop Jr and the Reverend Thomas Hooker withdrew from the parent colony to found settlements which eventually became the united colony of Connecticut. In a sense the emigrants represented the vanguard of the great pioneering processions that were to travel westward during the next two centuries. Within two or three years, Hartford, Windsor and Wethersfield took shape. Like Plymouth, the new settlements in the wilderness lay outside the organized jurisdiction of the crown or any existing corporation, and as at Plymouth each little group of settlers at first provided for the maintenance of law and order by a 'plantation covenant', establishing government of a simple kind resting upon the consent of the settlers themselves.

For its first quarter-century of existence, Connecticut remained a 'squatter' colony with no other sanction for powers that it exercised than the compact provided by the 'fundamental orders'. The civil wars and the confusion of the Interregnum in England tended to prevent application for recognition, but it is by no means certain that a population adhering to the compact theory deemed such a recognition necessary, except as a prudential measure to establish status in the king's eyes.

Rhode Island dates from 1636, the year of the founding of Providence by Roger Williams, an extreme separatist, who was the first notable to be expelled from Massachusetts. Perhaps because Williams was so radical in his own views, he felt the need for toleration. Unless he left others alone, he could not ask to be left alone himself. Hence Rhode Island became, curiously enough, a tolerant settlement. 'Within the Congregation there shall be absolute strictness', but outside the Congregation men might think as they pleased. Although his stature as a leader and thinker has been questioned in recent years, in many respects Roger Williams emerges as a greater man than any of the leaders of

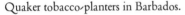

Quaker tobacco-planters in Barbados.

Massachusetts Bay. He was in the truest sense a pious man, but his religious zeal never eroded his humanity. He was the apostle of religious liberty in New England.

Anne Hutchinson was a cat of a different colour. A vigorous fighter for freedom against the stiff theocracy, Mrs Hutchinson had a restless energy which was only partially consumed by a raft of children, and, in the scant intervals between births, by her devotions to the sick and sorrowing. Her claim to be favoured by Divine revelation frightened the New England Puritans, who possessed what they assumed to be 'a gentleman's religion'. And they saw the doughty Anne, whose devotees were growing, leading the colony into Holy Roller antics and frenzies, or whatever other form the spirit of God took in ignorant rather than educated people – although, admittedly, one of her first converts was Sir Harry Vane, who was for a short time governor of Massachusetts.

The leaders of the colony were anxious to avoid the wilder extravagances of Protestantism, and while Mrs Hutchinson's banishment in 1638 may have been a defeat for freedom and a victory for intolerance, it has to be remembered that she was a fearful busy-body, undermining the authority of the minister, the governor and the magistrates; and it is also as well to note that a few years after her departure she was raising the devil in tolerant Rhode Island.

The Reverend John Davenport and Theophilus Eaton were annoyed by the Hutchinson controversy. Finding Massachusetts too quarrelsome and worldly, they determined to establish an independent state on a scriptural model. New Haven was founded as a theocracy in 1639 and absorbed by Connecticut in 1664. In New Haven the meeting-house was the town hall, and the Bible was the textbook not only for church, but for state. Yet like the other new towns, it developed a vigorous democratic constitution. All had a governor, usually elected; all had magistrates, not unlike Presbyterian elders; and as the little towns multiplied into larger settlements, each township sent its deputies to the little state assembly – all of them remarkably Puritan in temperament, and democratic, but only in name.

One must, however, guard against overemphasizing the colonial Bible phase and its narrowing effects on men and institutions. The vital thing in the history of these small English settlements was the habit of forming, by mutual agreement, associations for any common purpose. Regardless of creed, the Anglo-Saxon throughout history set up these homespun types of government whenever it seemed necessary. The constitutional history of New England is essentially the history of governments owing their origins to agreements made voluntarily by the people. That such governments derived their powers from the consent of the governed was not a theory but a reality.

Despite the intrusion of serious constitutional issues which left little time for overseas administration or the formulation of new principles of empire, the pursuit of 'closer control' from England following the end of the Cromwellian régime gives a kind of unity to Restoration colonial policy. Between 1676 and 1688 the effort was made to bring the colonies more tightly under royal super-vision, and by the time of the Revolution of 1688 the character of almost every North American settlement had been challenged in law. Those that remained intact did so only because, in the last days before the Revolution, the king's ability to mould events was petering out.

In 1660 Massachusetts escaped, but her conduct was becoming increasingly scandalous; she had even denied Parliament's right to regulate the trade of the Empire. This was a challenge that England could not ignore. In 1683 proceed-ings were initiated against the Massachusetts charter, and in 1684 it was annulled. Two years later, the frigate *Rose* arrived in Boston harbour bearing Joseph Dudley, president of the newly created Dominion of New England. In May 1686 the old general court of the Charter held its last meeting; self-government had departed from Massachusetts, only to be restored ninety years later.

The Dominion of New England (at first consisting only of Massachusetts) was subsequently expanded to all New England. In 1688, it was extended to New York and the Jerseys, thus bringing eight jurisdictions into a single province – an immense dominion stretching from the Delaware River to the St Croix – an administrative monster, quite unworkable in terms of communica-tions and government. There was no general legislature, no assembly; the governor was ruler, assisted by a council appointed by the king. The seat of government lay in Boston. Meanwhile, legal proceedings were taken against the proprietary authority in Maryland and the Carolinas. These attempts to annul charter government seem to have been the first major step towards a general plan of political reorganization. Undoubtedly it was the intention of James II to create a second dominion based on Virginia.

The Dominion of New England had many good features, but it was bound to be a failure because of the king's arbitrary method of dealing with a people who had been more or less independent of England for more than half a century. James was scarcely the man to build the unified edifice that the colonies them-selves failed to construct some sixty-five years later. None the less, it was a grand concept – almost unique in British imperial history. Although a doctrinaire administrator, it is well to remember that in spite of his admiration for Louis XIV, James II never stood for any extension of French power in America. In the long run it was as much his hostility to New France in America, as his love of centralization for its own sake, that led him to take away individual

New Amsterdam in 1626. The town's name was changed to New York after its capture by the Duke of York's troops in 1664.

charters and erect what amounted to vice-royalties under centralized government.

The colonies had been proud of their separate individuality – each unit had its local pride; the new union obliterated all differences, as well as entangling the provinces once again with the laws of England. Consequently, when news of the Revolution of 1688 reached America, the New Englanders acted decisively and like statesmen. They immediately arrested their governors, and, disclaiming mutinous intentions, maintained that they were constitutionalists resisting an illegal government. It was the first example in colonial history of the rewinning and securing of liberties without violence, although it is true that circumstances in Britain favoured this essentially irregular and spontaneous act.

Pennsylvania and New Jersey owed their origins to Quaker action, demonstrating again that religion in terms of repulsion continued to be a creative force in colonization. The Quaker sect had spread throughout Europe, but the chief concentrations were in Germany. In 1652, when Quakers first appeared in the American colonies, they were tortured, whipped and hanged. In the long run,

36

by passive resistance, they won toleration of a sort, and in England they finally obtained a recognized, if not a legal, position. By about 1670 they were becoming respectable, and sooner or later were bound to contemplate organized overseas settlement. The first opportunity presented itself in 1675. In 1664, the Duke of York had given land west of the Hudson River, between the Hudson and Delaware rivers (New Jersey), to Lord Berkeley and Sir George Carteret. At the end of the Third Dutch War, Berkeley sold out West New Jersey to Quakers seeking a refuge in America, and two years later the first shipload arrived. Four years later (1681), William Penn, who had a claim on the king, obtained a charter for a region extending some 5 degrees west from the Delaware River, and he tempted many of these Quakers into his new domain.

Penn's father was an admiral who had distinguished himself during the assault on Jamaica (1655) and in the Dutch War of 1662–64. He himself began as a rebellious young buck. Expelled from Oxford for Quaker leanings, then ousted from home, he was sent to Paris to expend his wild oats. When he returned in 1664 he became a Quaker permanently. His friendship with the Duke of York was a curious but enduring relationship. He probably attributed to that gentleman more virtues than he ever possessed. Certainly, after James ascended the throne, Penn was misled by his indulgent policy towards Catholics and Quakers, and he continued to think well of the king even after his expulsion in 1688.

Penn had all Sir Walter Raleigh's adventuresomeness with a more stable and persevering character. His writings may still be read with profit. A thinker with considerable insight into human nature and politics, he was the first Englishman to propose a league of nations, urging the creation of a sovereign parliament in Europe before which all disputes, justiciable or otherwise, should be brought. In being ahead of his age, he was, however, inevitably out of touch with it.

Pennsylvania was a proprietary colony, and Penn regarded it as an English estate. Its liberties were the gift of the proprietor; it was not, like a New England colony, largely its own master. On paper, Pennsylvanians had considerable freedom, as their charter bears out, but generally speaking when Penn was on the spot, the government was a benevolent dictatorship. Admittedly, the assembly was freely elected. All who confessed and acknowledged God became full citizens with all the rights and privileges of free-born subjects of England; yet offices of any importance were given only to bona fide Christians. On the other hand, it is worth remembering that Pennsylvanian criminal law was wiser than that of England. The object was reform rather than the infliction of punishment for its own sake. In addition, Pennsylvania had the best record of any colony in its dealings with the Indians.

John White's drawing of an Indian in body paint, 1577–90.

Because it was a Quaker colony, it was pacifist in outlook. None the less, since it had a long frontier, it was attacked frequently by the Indians, and in times of stress it was often difficult for a Quaker at Philadelphia to reconcile non-aggression with the needs of frontier defence. William Penn saw to it that his governors were fighting-men; but these deputies sometimes found vital supplies difficult to obtain. The Quaker assembly resisted plans for offensive operations – even for adequate military safeguards. While New England, after 1689, was being hacked about by bloodthirsty Indian allies of the French, Pennsylvania tended to watch and wait.

The Quaker ideology did not adapt comfortably or logically to colonial life and practice. Yet Quakers themselves possessed a mixture of common sense and Godliness that was useful in a new land; theirs was a philosophy of steady toil and sound family life. But in no way did it inhibit literary and cultural development. Two great intellectual centres grew up on the eastern seaboard, Philadelphia and Boston, the city of the Quakers and the city of the Puritans. Philadelphia soon outstripped both Boston and New York in the liberties, arts and graces of existence. Hence, eighteenth-century English philosophers were interested in Pennsylvania, as were philosophers like Voltaire, a contemporary of Benjamin Franklin, who saw in cosmopolitan, not Quaker, Philadelphia a seedbed of American civilization, a 'microcosm of America-to-be'.

Penn makes a treaty with the Indians, November 1682.

When the East India Company was incorporated on the last day of the year 1600, Moslem power in India was reaching its zenith under the Moguls. A century earlier, these invaders of Mongolian origin had begun to press through the passes of the North-West frontier into the plains below. Until their coming, no one central power had been in a position to exercise lasting suzerainty over the enormous mixture of kingdoms and feudal principalities; and as each contestant for pre-eminence declined and fell, struggles for power and readjustments of boundaries and titles followed, until the most able of the imperial dynasties – the Moguls – emerged from the chaos to establish a more enduring equilibrium. By the time the Portuguese had accustomed themselves to sailing round the Cape of Good Hope into the Indian Ocean, the whole of northern India had passed into their hands, to be hammered unevenly into an empire by a great ruler, Akbar (1556–1605).

Vasco da Gama had reached Calicut on the west coast of India in 1498. Unlike Columbus, he did not penetrate new seas; India was no *terra incognita*. Arabs, Venetians and Moors had maintained contacts with Europe for many years. None the less, da Gama's navigational achievement paved the way for British entry into the Indian Ocean, and for the British empire in India. In competition with the Portuguese, the Dutch and later the French, the well-armed ships of the East India Company rounded the Cape in search of spices, calicoes, silks, gems and saltpetre. For some time, however, the English traders could do little more than cling precariously to the coastline of India, in little factories whose existence depended on the quality of Portuguese gunnery and the favour of local rulers. In 1616 the first English post was established in a hired house at Surat on the north-west coast. Twenty-five years later, on the surf-beaten Coromandel shore, the foundations of Fort St George (Madras) were laid, despite the fact that there was no harbour to safeguard Company ships. Northward, behind a fever-ridden area of swamp and river, the eccentric Job Charnock in 1690 founded Fort William, which grew eventually into the massive capital of Calcutta. Bombay, which offered the best harbour in India, came to Charles II in 1661 as part of the dowry of his wife, Catherine of Braganza.

Meanwhile, long before French and English competitors for the spoils were prepared to launch their tiny forces against its decayed bulk, the great Mogul edifice was tottering to its fall. When the Emperor Aurangzeb died in 1707 both the power and the glory had departed. Thirty years after his death, Delhi was sacked, and the princely feudatories in the provinces, while still professing fealty to the imperial centre, had long ceased to render real obedience. India, in the first half of the eighteenth century, might be compared to Germany in

Aurangzeb.

the confused last days of the Holy Roman Empire. The way lay open for two European rivals, France and Britain, to contest the hegemony of an Eastern empire which neither Moslem nor Hindu was capable of holding intact.

Atlas maps of India rarely suggest the immensity of the country. The subjugation and pacification of a vast sub-continent by handfuls of Europeans, alien in blood, language and religion, remains one of the remarkable events of modern history. There was no sudden transformation; more than a century and a half of wars, alliances and treaties were necessary before a *Pax Britannica* was imposed on an incongruous mosaic that came to include eleven British provinces and some 500 Indian states. Addressing the House of Commons in 1833, Macaulay demonstrated, not without passion, that in the process of empire-building the sword could be mightier than the pen:

That a handful of adventurers from an island in the Atlantic should have subjugated a vast country divided from the place of their birth by half the globe . . . that we should govern a territory . . . larger and more populous than France, Spain, Italy and Germany put together . . . a territory inhabited by men differing from us in race, colour, language, manners, morals, religion – these are prodigies to which the world has seen nothing similar. Reason is confounded. We interrogate the past in vain. . . .

Admittedly the Indians were not the equal of the Europeans in arms; but unlike the natives whom Cortez faced, they knew something about guns and explosives, often used them, and certainly were not terrified of them. The two significant discoveries for conquering India, as James Mill pointed out, were the failure of native armies to stand up to European discipline, and the facility with which this discipline could be taught by European officers. Both these discoveries were made by the more imaginative French, and exploited by the English. It was victory over the French, not the Indians, that won the empire.

Starting out as clerks and mercantile agents living within the precincts of a fort or factory by permission of the local sovereign (who regarded them as we might have regarded gipsy pedlars) young Englishmen and Scots were to become the administrators of the judicial, financial and diplomatic business of provinces comprising a million square miles, and a population exceeding 120,000,000. In short, the whole business of government, commerce and defence passed into the hands of a foreign trading company, successor to a polyglot dominion once ruled by the Moslem conquerors of Hindustan. And whatever critics may say about the ruthlessness of Clive, the exactions of Warren Hastings, or the tainted fortunes made by greedy nabobs, one might argue that the integration and governance of the whole, was conducted with greater humanity and justice and accompanied by greater material improvement under the worst of the foreign, than under the best of the native administrators.

Fort St George in the late eighteenth century ▶

British factory at Surat; from an engraving of 1727.

East India Company forces at drill on Bombay
Green in 1767.

Such prodigious developments did not take place in a fit of absence of mind; the principal aim was wealth through trade. But India was valuable for much more than the wealth within its borders. Indian ports became commercial pivots for the whole of south Asia – from the Persian Gulf to Malaya, from Sumatra to Java and the spice islands. The state which could command the maritime communications between the Indian Ocean and the China Sea was in a position to monopolize practically the whole carrying trade between Asia and western Europe. Once the Portuguese had faded from the scene, the long struggle with their successors, the Dutch, led eventually to a partitioning of this Eastern commerce. While the English converged on India, the Dutch withdrew (as they did also from North America) in order to concentrate beyond the Straits of Malacca in Sumatra, Java and the myriad islands of the Indonesian Archipelago.

Within the mercantilist empire of England and of greater Britain, India fitted not perfectly, but comfortably. Since trade was the foundation of the British connection, there were no problems of population and dual adminis-tration. The members of the East India Company did not migrate in associations stimulated by religious or political fervour. As in Newfoundland, the English posts were not intended to be colonies of settlement. The country was remote, and the climate was a chronic opponent of white settlement. But the resistant quality of Indian society was a far more potent obstacle. In North America, the new settlers faced physically superb, but primitive and very thinly scattered tribes of natives, who had practically disappeared by the end of the nineteenth century. In India, the British traders and soldiers formed little oases among the growing millions, whose civilization, however decayed, stretched back beyond the Greeks, whose laws and customs had persisted through countless invasions, and whose intellectual and religious sinews, fortified by the social bonds of caste, seemed destined to withstand the philosophy, if not the technology, of the Industrial Revolution. In the words of Matthew Arnold:

> *The East bow'd low before the blast,*
> *In patient, deep disdain,*
> *She let the legions thunder past,*
> *And plunged in thought again.*

And yet, curiously, Europeans were the first to recover and make fashionable much of the learning and sacred lore that was in danger of neglect and decay. Already, in the eighteenth century, British scholars were sifting the gold grains of Hindi civilization from the dross, contributions that bore no connection with administration or trade development. Despite the heavy burden of official duties, Warren Hastings took an interest in Hindu sacred literature, and

Carousing on a terrace:
the European
through Mogul eyes.

Edmund Burke developed a respect bordering on awe for 'the piety of the Hindoos' and for 'their holy religion and sacred functions'. A young English judge, William Jones, did most to unveil the treasures of Sanskrit literature for the benefit of both Europeans and Hindus. For ten years following his arrival in India, this founder of Indology busied himself translating Hindu classics, and just failed to complete a complete digest of Hindu and Moslem law before his death in 1794.

As early as 1791, a Sanskrit college had been set up under Company auspices, but as in Africa of a later day, so in India, the native inhabitants demanded the learning of their conquerors and rulers. In some respects, Macaulay's famous minute of 1835 weighted the scale against tradition, and

1st Skinner's Horse at a durbar, *c.* 1803.

government educational funds were chiefly used, henceforward, to impart 'a knowledge of English literature and science through the medium of the English language'. By providing an escape from the babble of tongues and dialects, the decision did help to promote the unity of India, without, however, sacrificing a traditionalism that was to merge with Western knowledge and deeply influence the character of later nineteenth-century nationalism. When the Indian National Congress was organized in 1886, the discussions were conducted in English (the very same language used in the declaration of an Indian republic in 1947); but the cultural ethos was Oriental.

A common language provided no social bond. The Company traders and soldiers were visitors; grey heads were a rarity among birds of passage. None the less, before steamships began to use the short-cut through the Suez Canal, most Europeans, if they survived the lethal epidemics, were forced by time and distance to dig some kind of roots in the country. They were more than just 'tour-of-duty' men. Not all were moved by the colour and romance of their surroundings; yet long before the Mutiny had poisoned relations with its legacy of fear and hate, Englishmen and Scots entered into the life of the country to a far greater extent than was possible after the middle of the nineteenth century. There were probably not many like Colonel Skinner of Skinner's Horse, the son of a Scottish father and a Rajput mother, who lived like an Oriental prince with a clutch of wives and a regiment of servants, but there were countless men of goodwill, some of them outstanding, whose attachment had nothing to do with making money. In general, the standard of Company integrity and

44

efficiency may have been low in comparison with early twentieth-century standards. Burke's indictment of East India Company avarice and corruption contained many accepted truths. At the same time, in the eighteenth as in the twentieth century, there were soldiers, statesmen and civil servants, who, whatever their weaknesses and follies, loved India.

The original East India Company had Tory associations, and consequently lost favour after the Revolution of 1688. In 1698 a royal charter was given to a second company, and the confusion resulting from their rivalry was only resolved in 1702. The amalgamation produced a powerful association at a time when 'big business' was assuming increasing influence on government. With complete control of its own internal affairs, with fortified settlements and well-armed ships, its influence in India seemed bound to expand at a time when the central government of the Mogul Empire was beginning to disintegrate. Only two obstacles stood in the way, a natural reluctance on the part of home and Company authorities to support expensive territorial acquisitions, and more significant, the well-organized opposition of the French East India Company.

The French were the first to conceive of an Indian empire ruled by a Western people. As in North America, their principal servants showed an imperial imagination that the British usually lacked. British expansion in India was never based on a plan; indeed, there never has been in British history a consistent colonial policy. British colonial practice up to the present day has been largely a matter of meeting the needs of the day as they came, and in India the growth of the British Raj was generally the consequence of a variety of pressures and temptations that offered no alternative to aggressive action. In the beginning, the Company had been satisfied with a few coastal trading posts, and the antipathy to territorial expansion persisted until the end of the eighteenth century and after. Even when Clive had crushed Suraja Dowla at Plassey in 1757, and nine years later annexed Bengal and Bihar, his successors were sternly warned to go no further.

War and the maintenance of peace were costly operations, and the East India Company was opposed to spending money on empire-building. Commercial profit was the driving force, and any deliberate extensions were usually, at least in the initial phases, the work of individual governors bent on pacifying a frontier. In Wellesley's time, at the beginning of the nineteenth century, a conception of territorial empire began to take shape, but until the Mutiny it was regarded as a temporary, even makeshift project which Britain had undertaken reluctantly, and would eventually, it was hoped, abandon happily. Even when purposes and prospects changed in Disraeli's day, India never became a European empire; it was, and remained to 1947, an Indian empire administered by Englishmen.

Charles II receives a Barbados pineapple, the first to reach England, from the royal gardener, John Rose. From a painting of *c*. 1675.

Chapter Three

THE EXPANSION OF ENGLISH COMMERCE

Until about the middle of the seventeenth century, English and Dutch stood together against Spain. Although far from friendly in the Indian Ocean, there was a kind of tacit understanding that they would not quarrel over colonial interests in North America. Indeed, apart from two isolated river settlements (one on the Hudson and the other on the Delaware), the Dutch left the American continent severely alone, and concentrated on the tropics, especially the East Indies. In the West Indies, Dutch and English islands were unaffected by the growing commercial rivalry, although the authorities of both countries were always alert to possible Spanish interventions. But when Spain ceased to count, later English fears of the expanding Dutch empire came to the surface, and the result was a series of violent wars spread over some twenty years.

During this decisive period in English history, a commercial policy of empire evolved, referred to broadly as the Mercantile System. The basic principle of this policy was the maintenance of a favourable balance of trade in the interests of national power and military security. The attainment of this goal depended largely, it was assumed, on protecting and shaping the economic resources of the Empire to provide, as nearly as possible, imperial self-sufficiency. The active agents promoting the policy were the navigation laws. Ever since the days of Edward III in the fourteenth century, statutes designed for the promotion of overseas commerce had been accumulating, and by the end of the eighteenth century they were to reach mountainous proportions. In bulk and intricacy, this irregular and proliferating structure, representing centuries of protective legislation, was to prove as forbidding to legal reformers of the early nineteenth century as to historians of the twentieth. 'No one', wrote W. S. Lindsay, the author of a *History of Merchant Shipping* (1874), 'can rise from a study of these laws without a feeling of amazement at the trouble our ancestors gave themselves to beggar their neighbours.'

Departure of an East Indiaman, *c.* 1620.

In this pursuit of wealth and security, colonies played an important part. The trade and navigation laws were intended to secure for England not only the sole exploitation of colonial resources, but full control over the colonial import and export trade, which meant the exclusion of all foreign shipping. Colonies were required to draw their necessary manufacturing goods from England, either in English or their own colonial ships. In addition, it was expected that any imported European goods should pass through England on the way to the colonies. In the third place, colonists were expected to send their raw materials (manufacturing was not encouraged in the colonies) exclusively to England, apart from some few articles which could be exported anywhere, and these raw materials had to be sent in their own or in English ships. The object was a closed market – a monopoly of the colonial carrying trade for colonial and English ships at the expense of the foreigner, which, in the second half of the seventeenth century, meant the Dutch especially. Through a completely controlled economic system, supported by navigation laws beginning in 1650 and continued by legislation in 1651, 1660, 1661 and 1663, the colonies were to be made fruitful tributaries of the metropolitan headquarters in England.

It is interesting to consider the almost sudden and violent swing against the Protestant Dutch, because the efforts to cripple Holland reveal, as much as anything, the commercial core of British imperial policy. The Act of 1651, for example, was a piece of military preparation that aimed at protecting English shipping interests, and indirectly damaging the Dutch. 'National animosity at that particular time', wrote Adam Smith, 'aimed at the very same object which the most deliberate wisdom could have recommended, the diminution of the naval power of Holland, the only naval power which would endanger the security of England.'

S. R. Gardiner, author of the classic *History of the Commonwealth and Protectorate* (1894–1903), saw in the system the beginnings of a materialistic reaction against Puritanism. 'The new commercial policy did not profess to have any other than material aims. The intention of the framers by the nature of the case was not to make England better or nobler, but to make her richer.' According to the preamble of the Navigation Act of 1663, the ideal was one of 'maintaining a greater correspondence and kindness between the Kingdom of England and the King's plantations overseas, and keeping them in firmer dependence upon it, and rendering them yet more beneficial and advantageous unto it. . . .' In the broader sense, however, this was scarcely a colonial policy. Indeed, Charles II had no imperial policy apart from an economic policy, and for its application he depended largely on private capital and initiative.

It was inevitable, therefore, that certain private interests would benefit more than others from restrictions which canalized trade along certain narrow lines.

The *Delight*,
an East Indiaman,
in 1663.

49

The Custom House, London, 1714.

The prosperity of an increasingly large number of British merchants and industrialists was bound to depend on this system of trade protection, and national security was bound to become the catch-phrase of shipbuilders in particular, who discovered to their satisfaction that defence and opulence went hand in hand. Power and riches, as Adam Smith was to point out, were the chief ends of political economy in every country, and these objectives were not mutually antagonistic, but complementary.

In the history of the British Empire, the growth of self-government and freedom provides only half the story, and in the seventeenth and eighteenth centuries it is usually unconnected with British colonial objectives. Political growth is one thing; commercial and power policy is strictly another. The avowed object of the trade and navigation laws was to subordinate the political system to the commercial, and this in an age when there was an almost total absence of a trained civil service to enforce state action. Perhaps it was this lack of civil-service machinery that was to be responsible for the all too frequent non-enforcement of regulations – a condition which undoubtedly lessened the burden of trade restrictions or rendered them less irritating.

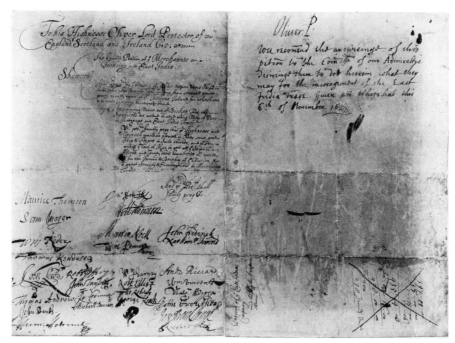

East India merchants petition Oliver Cromwell for a convoy to protect their homeward-bound ships in 1657; the Protector's favourable recommendation appears top right.

First East India House, Leadenhall Street, London.

In any event, the administration of empire was continued, however haphazardly, in the interests of commerce and national power. Colonies were expected to fulfil a double role: they would diminish England's dependence on certain foreign commodities, and those same commodities, imported from the colonies, could in turn be exchanged for home manufactures, thus increasing the volume of English exports. In addition, the foreigner would be compelled to buy various non-European (chiefly East Indian) goods from the English merchant, who thus acted as middleman.

During the seventeenth century, the main English imports, apart from the fisheries, fitted into four branches: timber, naval stores and potash from the Baltic countries; salt, wines, fruit and silk from or through southern Europe; sugar and tobacco from North America; and cotton and silk textiles, spices, dyestuffs, gunpowder (saltpetre) from the Far East. Of these commodities, wine, fruit, silk, sugar and tobacco might be called luxuries. Salt was indispensable to the fisheries, potash and dyestuffs to the woollen industry and naval stores to shipbuilding.

The argument for something like a colonial monopoly of such articles rested on the notion that a strictly confined imperial trade diminished the relative strength of rival nations. The extent of a competitor's power was assumed to depend, in part at least, on his share of a supposedly fixed total of international exports. Hence, the more colonial supplies could be made to replace foreign imports in the British market, the more would the foreigner lose in exports and consequently in relative power. Similarly, the more England's power rested on colonial supply and the less on foreign importations, the stronger and safer she would be, even though the colonial produce might be more expensive, and conceivably of lower quality.

Traders packing merchandise; from a map of the West Indies, 1700.

Tea-growing in China, 1669. The drink was especially favoured in the West as a remedy for over-eating and drinking.

But the search for controlled sources of raw materials was scarcely more important in the seventeenth century than the demand for accessible markets. The need for new markets was particularly pressing, because production, especially in the expanding woollen industry, was growing at a time when customary markets were becoming increasingly precarious under the stress of competition. Rival powers like France and Holland could curtail, if not throttle, English foreign trade simply by crimping or cutting her commercial communications with the Continent. In view of the uncertainty of the European and especially the Mediterranean trade, the possession of dependable markets outside the Mediterranean seemed vitally necessary.

All told, however, the search for colonial raw materials was the most emphasized official argument in favour of overseas colonization; and if one distinguishes the colonies of exploitation from the colonies of settlement, it is obvious that the colonies of exploitation, which alone possessed staple exports, remained, until the American Revolution, the most important parts of the Empire. They employed more shipping, produced more valuable goods and consumed more English manufactures. In North America, the chief colonies of exploitation were the sugar islands of the West Indies, and the coastal districts of the mainland as far as the northern boundary of Maryland. With few exceptions, governments disliked the northern colonies and tried to ignore them. They did consume English manufactures; but they paid for them by competing with English fishermen, building ships for sale, and trading in the West Indies or with foreign islands in time of war.

It was inevitable that English statesmen should look askance at New England. Colonists who farmed – and it was usually subsistence farming – or fished or traded, were of little use in a mercantilist empire. Indeed, like the Boers who trekked to new lands, they were not an economic asset, but a diplomatic liability. Apart from supplying a few useful articles, such as masts or ships' timber, New England was never popular. Massachusetts, remarked Josiah Child, was a community 'most prejudicial to this Kingdom'.

THE MACHINERY OF CONTROL

William and Anne gave little or no personal attention to colonial affairs, although under Anne colonial appointments were sometimes influenced by personal preferences. But on two main features, organization of colonial affairs in England and centralization of colonial administration in the colonies, their governments followed a policy of compromise. Little new administration was created, but there was a reorganization of old machinery. The colonial statutes of William and Anne were intended to secure a more effective enforcement of the system inaugurated by the Navigation Acts of Charles II, and secondly to enlarge the field in which its principles should be applied.

The general aim of the various provisions of the Trade and Navigation Act of 1696 and subsequent additions and amendments, was to bring colonial administration into harmony with that of the mother country. Vessels in the colonies were to be subject to the same regulations (for example, searches and seizures) as at home, and they were to be identified by a uniform system of registration. Any colonial laws at variance with the Navigation Acts were null and void. Additions were also made to the list of enumerated articles. Molasses from the West Indies, naval stores from New England, including hemp, pitch, tar and ships' timber, and rice from South Carolina could be shipped only to English ports. Under Anne's statute of 1705, masting-trees of a certain size were reserved for the navy and marked with the Broad Arrow.

Yet such restrictions were offset by bounties on the importation of local produce and colonial shipping was encouraged by the exemption of colonial seamen from impressment in the Royal Navy. On the other hand, to preserve colonial markets for English merchants, the colonists were not only forbidden to buy manufactured goods from foreign countries, they were ordered not to supply them to each other; hence the Woollens Act of 1698 prohibiting the carriage of wool or manufactures of wool from one colony to another.

On the whole, such measures indicated the increased importance in colonial life of political control by the mother country, and suggest that colonial trade and sources of colonial trade were now regarded as accessories of strength and elements of appreciable weight in the European balance. None the less, since the main interest in external affairs was continental Europe, colonial policy took a very subordinate place. No ministry had what one might call a distinctive colonial policy. As in Charles II's reign, there was only an economic policy.

The ministers most concerned were the two Secretaries of State, with whom the colonial governors were expected to correspond. But increasingly in William's reign, one of them took over the bulk of the correspondence, and during Anne's reign and after, colonial affairs were conducted by the Secretary of State for the Southern Department. The routine work was done by executive boards or agencies, some of which were assigned special tasks. For example, the Commissioners of Customs under the Treasury were specially charged with the enforcement of the Navigation Acts and the collection of quit rents. The Commissioners of the Admiralty, although they had a predominantly wartime function, had a continuous connection with the colonies. Among other services, they controlled the government packets sent to New York or the West Indies. Soon after the passage of the Act of 1696, courts of vice-admiralty were extended to secure a stricter enforcement of the navigation laws than could be expected from colonial courts and juries. Admiralty judges were appointed for various colonies and normally tried cases without juries. Most of them, it should be added, had strong and unpopular views on imperial control and the need for rigid enforcement of the law.

Most important, however, was the Committee of the Privy Council for Trade and Plantations, reorganized in 1689, and again in 1696 as the Board of Trade. This lasted until 1782 when, at the instance of Edmund Burke, it was abolished as a superfluous establishment, in view of the secession of the thirteen North American colonies. For long it had been obvious that some such body was needed – one that was responsible for colonial affairs and nothing else, like Spain's *Casa de Contratacion* or the French Ministry of Marine. It was, therefore, more than a mere committee of the Privy Council. It was a kind of Colonial Office, which was expected to give a close and constant attention to colonial affairs by protecting the commercial interests of the mother country, devising means to guide colonial enterprises into the right channels, and watching not only colonial trade but the processes of colonial government. The real work was done not by ministers of state, but by semi-ministerial secretaries like

Second Earl of Halifax.

William Blathwayt. With a real control over the administrative officers of the several colonies, these dexterous bureaucrats sought to build a disciplined imperial executive, capable of combining the various and disparate instruments of empire into a single, unified authority. Unfortunately, the achievement of this statesmanlike objective was barred by financial weakness, inept and indolent personnel and, above all, by the yet undeveloped state of English government.

For more than twenty years the Board did an effective job. After 1730 it lost influence, but was successfully revived in the 1750s by Lord Halifax. During the active years, a mass of material passed through its hands. It drafted instructions to the royal governors, made nominations for the colonial service, and received regular reports from the various royal governments. Colonial legislation and the administration of justice were carefully supervised. But the Board had no power to discipline royal governors. It drew up the instructions, but had no adequate means of seeing that they were enforced. Ultimate authority remained with the Secretary of State for the Southern Department. The Board could advise but not make final decisions; it could nominate officers, but not appoint them; it could remonstrate with colonial governors, but not fire them.

A significant lever in this primitive civil-service machinery was the right of disallowance. By 1692, the prerogative of the crown to disallow colonial Acts existed in the then five royal provinces of Massachusetts, New Hampshire, New York, Maryland and Virginia, and also in the proprietary province of Pennsylvania. When New Jersey became a royal province in 1702, its laws were subject to a similar veto. In 1706, a royal order annulled two South Carolina statutes. The Board of Trade, aided by its own legal adviser, was responsible for examining dubious colonial laws, frequently taking the advice of the Attorney-General and Solicitor-General; colonial Acts disapproved by the Board were usually repealed by the Privy Council.

Broad Quay, Bristol, in the early eighteenth century.

In the first decade after the Revolution of 1688, this prerogative of dis-allowance was vigorously exercised, and in Massachusetts especially, the cries were bitter against loss of usages that had been developed during the era of self-government. But the veto was generally salutary, as for example, in the disallowance of a Pennsylvania law against the theatre (Pennsylvania had 15 per cent of its laws vetoed, the general average was $5\frac{1}{2}$ per cent), or in a Connecticut Act of 1705 banishing Quakers. One significant result of this experience with objectionable statutes was the gradual addition, in the governor's instructions, of articles forbidding his approval of certain kinds of laws. Appeal was permissible, and there were some appeals, but they were not frequent chiefly because they were expensive.

Examples of military fortifications in the mid eighteenth century.

Chapter Four

THE STRUGGLE FOR TRADE AND EMPIRE
IN THE EIGHTEENTH CENTURY

Mankind has devoted an inordinate amount of time to war; interludes of peace have been almost unique and there have been centuries of history when war was almost continuous. Indeed, it was really a more normal state of life than peace. In the seventeenth century, according to G. N. Clark, there were only seven calendar years in which there was no fighting between European states; and if Russia and Turkey are counted as European powers, the seven can be reduced to three. During the eighteenth century, including the years of actual fighting that preceded formal declarations of war, there were only twenty-three full years of international peace.

The two successive wars against Louis XIV – the League of Augsburg and the Spanish Succession – started in effect some three months after the landing of William of Orange at Torbay in November 1688, when he accepted the English crown jointly with his wife Mary, daughter of James II. Following the wars against Spain and Holland, they constituted the third of the four great ordeals before the country emerged after Waterloo as the unrivalled imperial world power.

In finally eliminating Holland as a major colonial competitor (in the wars of 1664–67 and 1672–74), England had defeated a sea power more imperially minded and far more businesslike than Spain. Although their main strength was concentrated in the East Indies, the Dutch had managed to establish a port at the mouth of the Hudson River, astride the coastal communications of the English Atlantic colonies, whence they could contemplate the long inland waterway that led past Fort Orange (Albany) to the heart of Canada at Montreal. New Netherland never received the same vigorous attentions from the state as Batavia; but whether or not Holland could have succeeded in building an enduring American empire, the fact remains that a Dutch triumph

Albany factory, on James Bay.

in Europe would have greatly favoured Louis XIV's design of exorcizing English dominion from the New World. At a time when the population of the coastal colonies was small, and when existence depended completely on constant sea communication with the mother country, England's defeat would have given an immense impetus to the expansionist plans of Louis's chief minister, Colbert. Indeed, France might well have gained her cherished winter port in New York.

The War of the League of Augsburg, which began formally in May 1689, was the first in which English colonists played a concerted part in company with their mother country. For years, English, French and Indians in North America had conducted destructive and sometimes savage raiding parties on coastal or boundary settlements without the knowledge or approval of their home governments. The last decade of the seventeenth century saw the beginnings of organized effort. On their own responsibility, the New Englanders made plans to destroy the French privateering haunts at Port Royal in Acadia, and in the same year, 1690, under the leadership of an erratic adventurer, Sir William Phips, they dispatched an expedition to assault the bastion of French power in North America – Quebec. By good fortune, the attacking squadron reached its goal, but success was beyond its means and such of the ships as survived an October hurricane were lucky to return to Boston.

Thenceforward, the war became largely a matter of hit-and-run raids. In Newfoundland, the French base at Placentia became the centre for a series of pillaging forays that, by 1697, had destroyed almost every English settlement on the eastern coast. St John's was saved, but by the time the Treaty of Ryswick

(1697) had restored peace and *status quo*, the French position was stronger than it had ever been. In the long run, however, the struggle for Newfoundland could scarcely turn on a strategy of piratical raids against isolated towns and fishing harbours, however profitable. 'That place', reported the Committee of the Privy Council for Trade and Plantations in 1675, 'will allwayes belong to him that is superior at Sea.'

Similarly, in Hudson Bay, where the flags of both France and England had followed trade even to the perimeter of the Arctic Ocean, war was a matter of surprise raids against lonely posts by land and sea. In these the French put forth most of the effort and had most of the success. Like Newfoundland, the country round Hudson Bay was not a field of settlement. Acquisition was not intended to mean colonization, but merely the establishment of strategic factories or posts as bases for the pursuit of the beaver. Until the end of the eighteenth century, fur dominated the Canadian scene in much the same manner as cotton subsequently ruled the destinies of the southern United States. In fact, the northern half of the North American continent stayed in British hands chiefly

Page from the Fort York account book, 1714–15. The listing of 'ice chisels' is a forceful reminder of the difficulties faced by the early traders on the west coast of Hudson Bay.

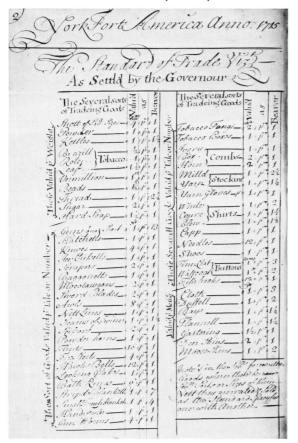

Beaver-hunting in Canada; from an engraving of 1778.

because so much importance was attached to this accessible staple. Samuel de Champlain and his successors in French Canada had followed the St Lawrence and thrust forward beyond the Great Lakes in search of beaver pelts. A half-century later, English traders, by establishing posts at the mouths of the Rupert and Moose rivers on James Bay and on the estuary of the Nelson on Hudson Bay, by-passed the rocky barriers of the Great Shield which had checked the forward progress of the French, and then, in leisurely fashion, extended their claims across the continent.

On 2 May 1670, Charles II granted about a quarter of North America to a group of London merchants and courtiers. Prince Rupert, the king's cousin, became first governor of the administering company known to this day as 'The Governor and Company of Adventurers of England trading into Hudson's Bay'. The grant covered all the land drained by the waters flowing into the Bay and the Strait, which included the huge Pre-Cambrian Shield stretching southwards to Minnesota and North Dakota. Possession of the Bay gave England not only her first substantial foothold in Canada, it gave her a strategical (although seasonal) passage into the heart of the continent, with rivers like the Hayes and Nelson to tempt her traders further inland.

The contest for command of the Bay ranged largely round the estuaries of these rivers, which drained the best beaver lands in the country. The English posts were badly fortified and poorly garrisoned, an unwise and costly neglect which was partly the result of the remoteness of this ice-bound theatre from Europe. A few trained troops would have halved the destruction wrought by French invaders from the St Lawrence Basin and occasionally from overseas. During the war of William and Mary most of the factories on Hudson Bay had remained in the hands of the French, but the end of the War of the Spanish Succession saw a major rearrangement of colonial boundaries. It was a happy coincidence that a former governor of the Company of the Adventurers, John Churchill, Duke of Marlborough, should have contributed so handsomely, by his victories on the European continent, to a peace settlement which provided for the surrender of the huge and undefined Hudson Bay area to Britain under the terms of the Treaty of Utrecht.

The War of the Spanish Succession (1702–13) had been largely a 'business-man's war', waged as much to determine the fate of Spanish trade as the destiny of the Spanish crown. The peace was naturally a 'businessman's settlement', negotiated in the interests of British maritime and commercial ascendancy. 'Of the greater part of the regulations concerning the colony trade,' wrote Adam Smith, 'the merchants who carry it on, it must be observed, have been the principal advisers.' The new Britain, which the union with Scotland had brought into being in 1707, by establishing a naval superiority over rival powers

Contemporary map of North America, 1748.

in western Europe, had now an almost unrestricted freedom to make the world her commercial oyster.

Moreover, by the Treaty of Utrecht Britain was able to extend considerably the network of naval bases which served her transoceanic communications. Apart from the Hudson Bay territories, she gained Newfoundland, with a reservation of French fishing rights on the north-west shore, Acadia (excluding Cape Breton Island), St Kitts in the West Indies and two Mediterranean stepping-stones, Gibraltar and Minorca. And by winning a sordid concession known as the 'asiento', she obtained the sole right to trade in slaves with Spanish America, thus laying the basis for her leadership in the slave trade until the end of the eighteenth century.

Meanwhile, French and British rivalry was becoming almost as acute in the Caribbean as on the mainland of North America, and here the contest was chiefly concerned with the growing world demand for sugar. It has been argued that the large-scale cultivation of sugar-cane in the West Indies under the plantation system would have been impossible without the use of slave labour imported from West Africa. Certainly, by the end of the seventeenth century, sugar had become an even more respectable and more sought-after luxury than tobacco, and the West Indian colonies pushed violently into production,

63

were soon to be regarded as the most valuable of all British possessions. Christian England – indeed Christian Europe – had no sense of shame about the iniquitous traffic on which its increasing wealth was partly built. Many of the great country-houses of England were to owe their foundations to fortunes made by nabobs of the Caribbean; and it is worth remembering that the Reverend John Newton, author of 'How sweet the name of Jesus sounds', had for some years after his conversion been the captain of a slaver.

Projects involving the transport of Negro labour to the sugar plantations were initiated shortly after the Restoration. The first English charter providing for the 'sole, entire and only trade' on the West African coast, was issued to 'The Company of Royal Adventurers' in 1663. Reorganized ten years later, the Royal African Company, until its demise in 1750, monopolized the slave trade to all the British Caribbean colonies. The Company's main trading ports were on the Gambia River and the Gold Coast. Fort St James, a sweltering, spidery little island, far up the Gambia River, was established in 1663. Some years later, the red mud-walls of Cape Coast Castle enclosed the second English depot. More than a hundred years were to elapse before the fanatical driving force of a few humanitarians like William Wilberforce and Granville Sharp began to move the British conscience and British statesmen in the direction of stopping one of the most lucrative trades in the world.

With the exception of the Spanish, the French holdings in the West Indies were larger than those of other powers, and French administrative policy was, on the whole, more relaxed. The British islands were more heavily bound by navigation laws and taxation was heavier. Jamaica was the most populous and the richest colony, and from a strategic as well as a commercial point of view, it became the pivotal base for military operations as well as inter-colonial trade. But it was long in fulfilling the expectations of British investors. Although all the British plantations suffered a bad period of depression after 1720, largely as a result of French competition, the home market continued to expand, and by 1740 the demand had caught up with the supply. The public reaction in Britain was natural. There was a loud cry for more sugar colonies, to be acquired by conquest, a demand which the planters did their best to stifle until experience finally convinced them that they had more to gain from the security afforded by strategic annexations than they would lose through increased competition and consequent lower prices.

In the years following the renewal of official hostilities in 1739, Britain tended to focus military attention on the Windward Islands, and the ensuing struggle with France for additional sugar plantations depended largely on naval performance. But the final distribution, which was not made until the end of the Seven Years War (1756–63), was the result of peace-table barter. Britain

The West African coast; from an engraving of 1745.

Above: slaves working on a plantation, 1821.

Left: sugar plantation in the West Indies, 1683.

took Grenada, St Vincent, Tobago and Dominica, leaving France with Guadaloupe, Martinique and St Lucia.

The twenty-five years that followed the Treaty of Utrecht was outwardly a period of tranquillity in so far as imperial developments were concerned. None the less, under the shelter of what amounted to an armistice, the rivalries of Britain and France grew in intensity. The explosion point came in October 1739, when Britain's declaration of war against Spain (the War of Jenkins' Ear) made direct conflict with Spain's ally, France, inevitable. Hitherto, the peace had been preserved by a kind of Franco-British *entente*. There were a few little wars, but the 'big two' were able to block any aggressive designs on the part of Spain and Austria and there were no major operations. This curious 'Indian summer' was to end with the War of the Polish Succession in 1733, when France and Spain joined together in a Family Compact that later proved to be very much concerned with questions of colonies and commerce. Under the Compact, Spain bound herself to deprive Britain of all lawful commercial privileges in America (which British and New England sea captains had been doing their best to exploit), and to transfer them to France in return for aid in capturing Gibraltar.

But Gibraltar was of minor importance in the final contest for empire. Fundamental to growing British tension after 1733 was a fear of the intentions of imperial France in North America as well as in India. By the beginning of the eighteenth century, the French administration under Colbert had transformed a feeble string of Canadian settlements along the St Lawrence Valley into a vigorous and nearly self-sustaining colony, and Louis XIV dreamed of overrunning North America as far west as the great plains and southward to the Gulf of Mexico. His project was based on the assumption that France could control the two great water routes into the heart of the continent: the line of the St Lawrence–Great Lakes running west; and, secondly, pivoting on the extremity of Lake Michigan, that of the Mississippi, which runs in a southerly direction to the Gulf of Mexico. It was a daring and magnificent conception of empire, a project first mooted by French explorers, who talked of shutting the English for ever behind the Appalachian mountain barriers. Yet, for lack of population alone, it was bound to fail. As in India, France showed imperial imagination far beyond her stolid rivals; unhappily, neither in the east nor the west were the ships or the men available to bring fantasy to life.

When the War of Jenkins' Ear merged into the War of the Austrian Succession, British statesmen became too deeply immersed in European affairs to give proper attention to the spoils that lay waiting for the victor outside the continental cockpit. The fact that the first great battle in the duel for empire

The capture of Louisbourg, the French fortress on Cape Breton Island, in 1745.

was fought far up the Rhine near the little village of Dettingen in June 1743 seemed to confirm the view of those who still believed, as in the seventeenth century, that colonial rivalries should not be allowed to complicate European policies. In any event, the protection of sea communications to the Continent and the blockade of French and Spanish ports, left few ships available for colonial expeditions on a grand scale. As a result, British strategy on the seas in India and in North America was confined almost entirely to the defensive. The War of the Austrian Succession in overseas theatres was ragged and indecisive, relieved on the British side only by one dramatic event – the capture in 1745, by an assortment of New England farmers and fishermen, of France's mighty fortress on Cape Breton Island: Louisbourg. But Louisbourg was returned in 1748, the result of a peace-table swop with France, a transaction which confirmed an unhappy stalemate that could not endure.

The Treaty of Aix-la-Chapelle, although ending formal hostilities in 1748, was founded on a settlement too unstable to be lasting. Some optimistic writers have assumed that a settlement of North American boundaries might have secured a peaceful *status quo*. This is very doubtful. The colonies, as in Anne's reign, were often more imperialistic in feelings and ambition than British

Braddock ambushed in Ohio, July 1755.

governments. There were all sorts of indications in North America that each side hoped to oust the other; there was a growing feeling that there was no room for both. A clash between the English and French colonies seemed inevitable, irrespective of what happened in Europe. On the other hand, a formal delimitation of boundaries might have prevented or reduced the guerrilla warfare, and above all the Indian savageries which were encouraged by both sides in their incessant efforts to establish new claims or wipe out old scores. Eventually, the respective home governments sent out regular troops to occupy frontier areas and to assert their claims by force of arms. The result was often violent collision in which hundreds participated, as for example in July 1755, when General Edward Braddock, the British commander-in-chief, was ambushed and killed in the backwoods of the Ohio country before war had broken out in Europe.

Fort Niagara, drawn by a member of the British force that captured it.

This kind of irregular warfare was to become endemic. Forts were erected by the French on every position of strategic importance along the whole inland border of the British colonies, from the St Lawrence to Lake Michigan and thence into the Ohio and Mississippi valleys southward to the Gulf of Mexico. All these were utilized as starting-points for forays into British-claimed territory and as barriers to close every natural route for traffic through the river and lake systems of the central and western parts of the continent.

On the British side few set defences existed; the French military organization was by far superior, chiefly because all control in Canada was vested in a central authority with dictatorial power, free from the interference of locally elected councils and civil officials. Some historians, including French scholars, have taken the view that if the ruling power in France had displayed sufficient inclination to support the ambition and military enterprise of its colonists, French dominion would have been secured. The golden opportunity, they say, was lost through lack of home interest in colonial affairs and the clash of personalities at court, which sometimes led to the betrayal of distinguished colonial governors and generals.

The argument is partly sound. The only real hope for the French empire overseas lay in putting sea power and western colonization ahead of European ambitions, a course of action urged by some very able men in French councils. But this was asking too much. Such a policy would have meant diverting heavy military expenditure to naval purposes and for a continental country such a division of expenditure was not practicable. Having no protective moat like the English Channel, France had to be a strong military power, and with all her great wealth she could not afford a first-class navy as well as a first-class army. Britain was torn by no such impelling conflicts of interest. In the eighteenth century she could afford to neglect her army and build up a fleet capable of seizing and occupying transoceanic regions and holding them.

For Britain, the colonial wars were part and parcel of the war in Europe; and once English sea power had survived the ordeal of strenuous Dutch rivalry, French dominion in North America and French gains in India were bound to exist on sufferance. After what proved to be the decisive Battle of La Hogue in 1692, the Royal Navy was in a position to deny the French colonies continuous help from Europe. British detachments could seal up the St Lawrence River at almost any time the Admiralty wished. Quebec had been twice threatened – in 1690 and 1711; Nova Scotia had been lost and Newfoundland had fallen into British hands. Louis XIV had himself been warned that nothing could save Canada if communications with France were not sustained. If the British squadron cruising between Ushant and Finisterre picked up a French convoy, French settlements in North America might have to do without the needed grain and salt fish; similarly, they might have to make their own shot and mix their own powder. By comparison, the British colonies could call at will on all the resources of their mother country and the neutral world.

The war for empire with France had begun in 1689 and went on until 1815; but, as we have seen, up to the end of the Austrian Succession war, overseas engagements were usually indecisive. A few pieces of land changed hands, but the effects were of a purely local nature. None the less, it would be a mistake to say that no progress had been made towards the British conquest of Canada and India. By mid-century, the sea power of France showed signs of serious erosion; the navy had lost half its ships of the line and more than half the merchant fleet had fallen to the enemy. On the other hand, the French colonial domains remained outwardly intact; much that had been lost had been regained at the peace-table in Aix-la-Chapelle.

Although the French and Spanish navies more than doubled during the short years of truce after 1748, they did not begin to equal the Royal Navy in ships of the line. By the beginning of the Seven Years War, Britain had a comfortable superiority over the combined French-Spanish fleets, with the additional advantage of unified command. In short, the rivals for world empire were unequally matched. England had 130 ships of the line; France 63, of which only 45 were in fair condition; Spain could contribute 46, but these were in poor shape. French morale was bad; the men were undernourished, rarely paid and there were many desertions. In 1755, 700 officers out of 900 served on land, quarrelling with each other or their commanders; ratings were sometimes taken to the ports in chains. It is significant that at the time when the Royal Navy was the strongest fighting force in the world, Britain in 1759 could afford to send to Quebec no less than a quarter of her full war establishment. The official complement of crews serving under Admiral Saunders was 15,000 men; the grand total for service at large in 1759 was 60,000.

As for bases, Britain had Bombay, then the best port in the East, and a number of good Atlantic ports – New York, Boston, Philadelphia, Portsmouth, Salem, Marblehead, Cape Ann, Ipswich and Newbury – which received about 1400 vessels annually. France had only Cape Breton, with an average annual entry of about 150 ships; Quebec was far up the St Lawrence and of little value as a base for operations. Nevertheless, France possessed an army of 300,000 trained soldiers; the British peacetime army numbered only about 40,000 horse and foot. French Canada had, moreover, the advantage of a closely knit hierarchical administration, compared with the divided colonial segments that composed the British domain on the Atlantic coast. The British colonies had nothing to match Canada's autocratic organization, professional soldiery and militia. Yet in the final rounds of a struggle for world empire, it is doubtful, as Admiral Richmond put it, 'whether in any contest of like magnitude and significance, two less evenly matched powers ever have faced each other'.

In British North America the war was carried through under the Old Colonial System. For example, the British commander-in-chief could not obtain colonial money without the consent of the assemblies. Rhode Island and Connecticut, because of their peculiar constitutional status, suffered no clashes between executive and assembly, and Rhode Island contributed effectively for its size. In practice, however, the assemblies in all the Royal and Proprietary colonies were reluctant to contribute money or troops, and often held up business by delaying tactics – pushing off discussions to committees, a system quite contrary to the instructions of the Board of Trade.

Pennsylvania was the scene of the bitterest struggle; there, the proprietor's representatives and the assembly were equally obstinate. Both sides preferred democratic rights to defence needs; most Quakers refused to take up arms. Only after Braddock's defeat was the stalemate temporarily broken. Maryland followed the Pennsylvania line. Virginia, which was to produce the greatest military figures, looked very unmilitary at the beginning of the war. There was no active militia and little prospect of getting one. In October 1754, with the French and Indians already on the frontier, the assembly passed a Militia Act permitting the drafting of all vagrants and vagabonds. One year later, the New York assembly refused to vote a penny towards military expenses. North Carolina was torn by factional quarrels; South Carolina did little more than defend her own frontier. In 1755, four years after she had become a royal province, Georgia's militia force consisted of some forty men. In June 1754, a general convention at Albany empowered a joint committee to draw up a plan of union. It was a well-constructed project of union, largely the work of Benjamin Franklin, but the colonial assemblies refused to touch it.

On the other side – in Canada – the French needed no plan of association; Canada was a unit within a pyramidal structure of government that reached to Paris. By comparison with the British, however, the population of the French colony was tiny. Indeed, it is easy to forget how small the numbers actually were. From the founding of Quebec in 1608 to the coming of Frontenac in the last quarter of the seventeenth century, not more than 10,000 French men and women had established themselves on the banks of the St Lawrence. By the time of the cession in 1763, the population was less than 60,000. In the circumstances, the great French empire stretching from the Gulf of Mexico to the valley of the St Lawrence and Hudson Bay was scarcely more than a precarious option which the government in Paris had no real chance of confirming. When the final struggle began, the French could only fight for time, and hope that a successful war in Europe might in the end, once again, weight the scales of barter in their favour.

WILLIAM PITT AND THE SEVEN YEARS WAR

The Seven Years War marked the beginnings of a fundamental shift in British imperial strategy. During the War of the Austrian Succession, the issue of colonies as areas of settlement was never the predominating one. Governments were not interested in adding to the territorial domain by conquest. The trade and navigation system had been developed through the years to control an empire of commercial entrepôts, whether on the coasts of India or West Africa, or along the Atlantic seaboard of North America. There was no comprehensive imperial policy before 1759, only an economic policy; the basic factor influencing the choice of a colony (if there was a choice), or its value, was accessibility by sea. The founders of the navigation system and their successors frowned on projects involving inland expansion. 'Colonization upon the Continent of America', declared the Board of Trade in a retrospective review following the end of the Seven Years War, 'had for its object to extend the Commerce, Navigation and Manufactures of Great Britain; and for these Salutary purposes, it has been the policy of this Kingdom to confine her settlements as much as possible to the Sea Coasts.'

Since 1629, when David Kirke had captured Champlain's feeble settlement, two attempts had been made to recapture Quebec; but these carelessly planned and abortive expeditions of 1690 and 1711 were no more than half-hearted efforts to whittle down French power in the New World. British governments were not interested in a land empire. No more than in 1763, after the surrender of Canada, did they relish the task of administering an inland colony. Indeed, the short-lived project to win Quebec in 1746 was intended chiefly to strengthen bargaining power before the impending peace conference. In brief, British imperial strategy was negative or defensive to the extent that Britain's treasure through trade could be obtained most easily and at least cost from colonies which had a frontier on the sea. The law-makers of Charles II and William and Mary, whose prescriptions guaranteed a seasoned navy, believed that the flow of such riches could be best controlled in the national interest from bases embedded in salt water.

Although hostilities had been proceeding informally in America and in India for two years, war proper (as legally declared) did not break out until May 1756. In Europe, two small countries, Britain and Prussia, were faced with the greatest military empires then existing, and the opening phases suggested that the smaller powers were doomed. In India, England seemed to have lost her vigour. Dupleix had won over many of the native rulers, and although he had been recalled, these French allies were still intent on thrusting the English into the sea. In the west, Braddock had been cut to pieces in the North American backwoods; in Canada, to all appearances, General Montcalm had things well in hand. Worst of all, England seemed to be losing her control of the seas; Admiral Byng failed to relieve Minorca and was executed, 'pour encourager les autres'. The Duke of Cumberland surrendered with his whole army in Germany and Frederick the Great of Prussia found both his rear and flank exposed to attack.

Then occurred a remarkable change in popular temper. The British people became concerned about the menace of the expanding French empire, as well as apprehensive about their own home security. They communicated their fears successfully to an eccentric and extraordinarily dynamic leader, William Pitt, who undertook not only to defeat France in Europe, but to conquer and possess vast stretches of her overseas lands. Imperialism, in the territorial and prestige sense, was now to be an important adjunct of imperial trade policy; and the quest for colonial estates to be occupied, ruled and exploited in the name of empire was soon to rival, if not displace, an almost rigid national concentration of the balance of power on the Continent.

It was almost a one-man affair. This titan won the people's confidence, and, above corruption, backstairs influence and royal intrigue, led them to un-dreamed-of heights. Within four years England was raised to a position such that she had never held before and was never to reach again. Pitt has frequently been a subject of contention among historians and there are as many interpreta-tions as there are students of the man's life. Years ago Van Ruville tried to make him small and mean and ordinary. But frail humans who strike at greatness they cannot understand, often reveal more of their character than that of their sub-ject. Pitt was a miracle, and until physicists or metaphysicians come closer to revealing the riddle of life, who is fitted to dissect his peculiar genius?

Outwardly and superficially, he had all the shortcomings of his time. He made his under-secretaries stand in his presence, but was so obsequious before the king that he would kneel for hours on end if necessary. He was verbose and pretentious. Burke spoke of 'some significant, pompous, creeping, explanatory, ambiguous matter, in the true Chatham style'.

It is useless to look for balance and consistency in the life of a genius. Pitt's mannerisms and poses, his studied arrogance and carefully adjusted bandages, his inconsistencies – all these weaknesses were of little account in comparison with the supreme fact that he succeeded in completing the first British Empire. He is the perfect example of the hour bringing forth the man. For good or ill, a single man transformed the world. In four years he not only restored, he multi-plied the empire of Elizabeth and Cromwell.

Like Lloyd George and Churchill, he had erratic impulses, and often in times of crisis, the erratic impulse could explode in flashing inspiration. This curious kind of eccentric strength seemed to run throughout the Pitt family; when they were great they were odd. William Pitt, Earl of Chatham, was anything but the average man; his son, William Pitt the Younger, was an infant phenomenon. Chatham's sister had all the eccentricities and few of the virtues of the *grande dame*. Pitt's grand-niece, Hester Stanhope, lived a good part of her life among the Arabs in Syria, less decorously than Gertrude Bell. They were all a little mad, and if they were not mad, they were merely commonplace, like Chatham's father.

Brian Tunstall has diagnosed Chatham's mental trouble as manic-depressive insanity. His contemporaries had no such phrase, but they recognized that his energy and fire came from an abnormality, which was also responsible for long periods of seclusion and despair. In 1754, he married the beautiful Lady Hester Grenville, a union which, besides giving him a valuable connection with an influential family, seems to have effected a cure, for until 1761 he was at his full powers. It has been suggested that without his wife, Pitt's genius never would have ripened. This is going too far. By the time of his marriage it had all but matured. What was required for the ripening was not a wife, but a war.

Pitt made his start as a troublesome orator opposing Walpole, but after 1754 he found himself more and more in difficulties. He had alienated the king by his attacks on Hanover, and the old conservative Whigs by the violence of these attacks. He lost his job in 1755 because he insisted on attacking his fellow ministers in Parliament. He did not come to power until December 1756, after Newcastle's failures abroad. He was out of office in April 1757, and was called back in June in alliance with the Duke of Newcastle. Pitt had the brains and principle, Newcastle took care of political organization.

Rhetoric was one of his chief weapons. He belonged to the Commons in its great age of oratory. Government in fact was conducted by oratory. Votes were changed by speeches; men could be fused together in unanimity or urged to higher purpose by them. Pitt had all the characteristics necessary to make a great orator. His speeches were based on knowledge, knowledge condensed into powerful paragraphs, for example, Pitt on the peace treaty, on the navy, or on the American colonies. They were not general and shallow appeals, but frequently learned treatises on the subject at hand.

In the House of Commons, his physical qualities were conspicuous – commanding height, the noble hawk-like head, the flashing eye; even the gout was an impressive aid. Men watched in awe as Pitt was carried into the Commons, his legs swathed in flannel. His strong moral character told enormously. Both Chatham and his son had faults, but they were saints compared with most other politicians. Chatham's self-confidence was of immense importance. His knowledge and mastery of men gave him a control of the House that no one else possessed. Regarded as a political fact, Pitt's eloquence was a substantial and effective instrument of government.

The majority of the English people at this time had no votes. Popular feeling manifested itself only indirectly; but at certain moments of crisis the flood-gates could break. Pitt knew the fundamental soundness of his country – its wealth, patriotism, endurance and fighting qualities. He believed that little groups of corrupt politicians were flinging away the mastery of the seas, the American colonies and India, as well as betraying their Prussian ally. He saw that the one salvation lay in clearing away the political obstructions and letting the people have their will by making him their leader. Pitt became the first modern English statesman who in some uncanny fashion got the nation behind him.

He set himself to concentrate all national influence in one place. He allowed Newcastle to carry on the administrative routine; he allowed the king all the state dignity he wanted. But Pitt himself became a virtual dictator. He made England into an *ad hoc* despotism, crushing ordinary discussion in Parliament. He bullied his colleagues into doing his will, sometimes frightening subordinates out of their lives. When opposition arose, he quelled it by authority not by argument. A crisis had arisen. Victory for Britain could only come through effective central action and Pitt compressed all the scattered ineffective parts of the constitution into an instrument that would beat the French.

Hitherto, the British parliamentary system had not been famous for knowledge or wisdom, except in financial matters. William III was a great diplomatist, but there were few men, Marlborough excepted, to follow him. Pitt brought to British government the knowledge, the diplomatic skill and the military capacity that had been absent since Marlborough died. He was engaged in a world war when communications were fearfully slow – six months to India, six weeks to New England. He studied geography; he knew the Empire, and above all he showed an astonishing knowledge of the best men in the services. He promoted according to merit, not birth, and he carried on operations regardless of cost. In short, he invested in Empire, and British foreign trade began to catch up with the Dutch. On his statue in the Guildhall are the meaningful if mournful words: 'He made commerce to flourish by war.'

Indeed, war seems to have released latent volcanic forces which he was unable to control; having entered into a world-wide conquest of empire, he was determined to hold what he had won. In the long run, such imperial megalomania could be dangerous. Hatred of France, combined with pride of empire, made him incapable of realizing that retention of all the winnings would breed bitter jealousy and nourish the spirit of revenge among defeated rivals.

Before Mahan wrote his *Influence of Sea Power on History*, knowledge of the doctrine of sea power was the prerogative of a very few statesmen and sailors. Pitt was one of this privileged group, as Mahan's own chapters reveal. Command of the sea, as Pitt saw it, was essential to victory. The strategical function of the navy was, above all else, to ensure secure passage of troops and supplies, and to furnish cover against escapes from Brest or Toulon. But once operations were under way, Pitt was slow to realize that the striking force was the army, that

Pitt attacked: a cartoon published by Lord Bute's party in 1762.

Pitt remembered: the monument to him
in Westminster Abbey, 1784.

in Canada and in India the decision had to be sought on land. While he made first-rate appointments in the Admiralty (where Anson had laid the groundwork), in the army, a good many blockheads were allowed to hang on. Moreover, he made the mistake of trying to direct military operations from London. After 1757 he still made the plans, decided the number, character and distribution of the troops and arranged their equipment, but it took him almost two years to weed out the poor generals like Abercromby and apply new methods to wilderness warfare. Indeed, on land, Britain began an offensive war for which she was unprepared, and she took a long time to win it. By 1757 she should have been in a position to end the war within two years; it dragged on for four.

The delay was partly owing to French defensive strategy, the result of the comparative numerical weakness of the French navy. Instructions to French commanders were often marked by directions to avoid risk of losses and such advice was bound to induce caution and cripple initiative. On the other hand, such a strategy could and did prevent the British from securing quick, positive or decisive results. By so procrastinating, the French were in a position to make military gains in Europe, which might be used as trading pawns in time of peace. In fact, by avoiding offensive operations likely to lead to a decision at sea, and by confining themselves to a defensive role, the French were able, in the course of five campaigns, to prevent Britain from conquering Canada, which was one main object of the war. Had they staked the issue on one fleet action during the first campaign and lost, Pitt could probably have achieved his objective in half the time.

In Canada the nerve centres were Montreal and Quebec. The only artery of supply from home was the St Lawrence River, and the only means of access from the British colonies were two waterways – one by Lake Champlain and the Richelieu River, the other by the Upper Ohio, Lake Ontario and the Upper St Lawrence. Those two waterways the French could control by a series of

North America in the eighteenth century.

	British possessions before 1713
	Territory ceded to Gt. Britain in 1713
	Territory ceded to Gt. Britain in 1763
	Spanish territory in 1763
	French fishing rights in 1783

The capture of Quebec in 1759.

forts, strategic outposts of Canada itself, and each fort was in easy communication with the centre. For defence, therefore, Canada was superbly equipped. The only unimpeded entry by water lay up the St Lawrence itself, and for the protection of Montreal and Quebec, the French relied not only upon their base at Louisbourg, but on the hazards of the river navigation (which they exaggerated) and upon the impregnability of Quebec itself.

The French hoped, as has been remarked, to defer the conquest of Canada until the issue had been fought out in Europe and the diplomats had saved the day. Every move was a move for time. With the British, it was necessarily a strategy of offence – the conducting of a siege of Canada, which had to be regarded as one vast fortified network. They had to seize the interior approaches, proceeding fort by fort until they reached the heart of French power on the St Lawrence. This involved setting on foot at least two inland expeditions during each campaign to prevent the French from concentrating at a single point, and secondly, blocking incoming supplies and reinforcements from France, thus diminishing Canada's powers of resistance.

Some of the failures were undoubtedly owing to an inheritance of inferior commanders; but by 1758, Pitt's own men began to score – Boscawen, Amherst, Wolfe. In July, Louisbourg fell, the French east flank was bare, and the British fleet prepared to enter the St Lawrence. On the west flank there were fumblings, but eventually forts Duquesne (Pittsburgh) and Frontenac (Kingston) were reduced. In the centre, Abercromby's check at Ticonderoga was unfortunate, and the failure nearly spoiled Wolfe's success at Quebec. Not until 1759 was the Champlain route cleared; but Amherst had no time to take Montreal and go to help the besieged Quebec garrison, isolated from November until May 1760 by the frozen river.

The assault on Quebec in September 1759 was planned as an amphibious operation, involving far more naval assistance than was required for a straight-forward landing operation, such as at Louisbourg. In consequence, Montcalm was quite unable to find out what Wolfe was doing behind the impenetrable screen of British ships, and his men were worn out in the vain attempt to keep up with the transports and anticipate the movements of the landing parties. Including the crews of all supply and transport vessels, there were three times as many seamen as troops. Wolfe's little army, as William Wood put it, was essentially 'a most efficient landing party from an overwhelming fleet'.

Yet the victory on the Plains did not secure Canada or even clinch Quebec. Not until the decisive Battle of Quiberon Bay, in November 1759, was the French power of intervention finally extinguished. Wolfe's victory was 'glorious' because it came with all the drama of death and triumph after a long series of set-backs and defeats; but the honour which posterity properly bestowed on a reckless and talented soldier has, until recent times, served to cloud the signifi-cance of Admiral Hawke's success at Quiberon Bay and shadowed the per-formace of Charles Saunders, whose skilful seamanship brought an armada of 277 sail up the tortuous St Lawrence to the heart of New France. In comparison with the *annus mirabilis*, the triumphs of succeeding campaigns came as something of an anti-climax. In the spring of 1760 Quebec was relieved and, with the surrender of Montreal in September, the conquest of Canada was complete.

James Wolfe.

The Battle of Quiberon Bay, November 1759.

Meanwhile, as French and British clashed in the Ohio Valley, Hindu Marathas and Afghans fought over the disintegrating empire of the Moguls. In 1755, no one could have foreseen that the future of India lay in the hands of two European trading companies whose fortified factories faced the sea in widely separated crannies and corners of the sub-continent. The British East India Company, as has been noted, held three main trading stations, Calcutta, Madras and Bombay, each independently managed through presidents and councils, which reported separately to the directors in England. Each was responsible for its own internal management and defence – all the normal responsibilities of self-government that an American colony possessed. Few of the directors had any first-hand knowledge of the country, and even had they understood Indian geography and politics, their decisions would have suffered as much from delay as ignorance. The average sailing time between London and Calcutta was six months, and a year or more might elapse between a request for guidance and the reply. And since long periods of suspense could be hazardous, a good deal of initiative had to be left to the men on the spot.

The French possessed only two main factories, Pondicherry, south of Madras, and Chandernagore, to the north of Calcutta. Both were supported

British officer in a procession, late eighteenth century. His only concession to Indian custom is the jewelled aigrette he wears in his hat in preference to the usual military plumes.

East India Company officer smoking a hookah; a late eighteenth-century Indian painting.

by the naval base of Mauritius, where an enterprising governor, Mahé de La Bourdonnais (1735–46), raised a squadron of considerable strength and efficiency. Unlike the British, the French East India Company (founded in 1664) was closely connected with the home government. It farmed monopolies, received treasury grants and subsidies, and dealt in loans and lotteries; it was usually deep in debt to the crown and at its mercy. Under good officials this worked well, but under bad, patronage and bribery were ruinous. Years later, when India was lost, French Company officers were to declare that interference from Paris was the cause of all their misfortunes.

Even before the war for India began in 1744, François Dupleix, the enterprising governor of Pondicherry, was looking ahead to the duel and had started negotiations with native rulers. His object was to entrench the Company within the political system of the country. Unfortunately for France, the final result did not depend on the genius of French diplomatists or soldiers or small naval battles off the Coromandel coast, or even on some successful alliances with Indian princes. The issue was largely determined by the struggle for supremacy in the English Channel.

The whole structure of Indian commerce was based on secure trade communications with Europe; the security of coastal factories and bases depended ultimately on winning and holding command of the sea. When hostilities opened, Britain had no squadron in East Indian waters; hence, the early success of La Bourdonnais off the Coromandel coast, leading to the capture of Madras in 1746. But as soon as Britain was in a position to assert her naval supremacy, it was impossible for the French to send adequate reinforcements to India. Dupleix, however, was able to play local politics and the British Company tried, not so successfully, to follow suit. Dupleix got his candidates on the thrones both of Hyderabad and the Carnatic. By 1750 French prestige in India had reached a new peak.

Yet the dominating position of the French Company was coming to an end; Dupleix was recalled in 1754 and the dream of a French empire in India seemed to have collapsed with his departure. For a few years he had come close to success; by his system of alliances he had given France a complete ascendancy in southern India, and had, indeed, taught the British how a Company empire could be created by princely allies and small bodies of European-trained troops.

Robert Clive's victory at Plassey in June 1757 was a rout rather than a battle and it delivered Bengal to the East India Company. In January 1760 Eyre Coote, one of Clive's men, fought the decisive Battle of Wandewash, and a year later, Pondicherry, the focal point of French power and influence, fell to Company troops. The genius and daring of Clive in holding Bengal, and at crucial moments sending reinforcements southward out of Bengal, influenced the final result, but in the last resort Hawke's destruction of the French fleet in Quiberon Bay settled the issue in India, as it had in North America. After the first general action near Pondicherry between the British and French squadrons in April 1758, the Royal Navy gained command of the Bay of Bengal and never lost it. Because the French Atlantic fleet had been reduced in importance, no aid from home could be expected to help reverse the balance. From 1759 until the end, bereft of their native allies, the half-starved French forces struggled heroically but in vain. In defence of their trade, the British East India Company had been drawn into a costly war, only to find themselves by 1761 saddled with the responsibilities of an unwanted empire.

In the meantime, in October 1761, Pitt had resigned office and three months later, as he had predicted, Spain entered the war as France's ally. But the lethal machine which he had created still moved relentlessly. The year 1762 saw the final ruin of the Spanish and French empires. An expedition under Rodney captured Martinique, Grenada, St Lucia and St Vincent without difficulty; Havana, the capital of Cuba, fell to an amphibious force; Manila came next, a victory which forced the surrender of all the Philippines.

Britannia made to vomit up the territories won during Pitt's administration; a cartoon of December 1762.

The stern architects of the Peace of Paris, 10 February 1763, have often been unfairly compared with the abstemious Castlereagh and his colleagues at Vienna in 1814–15. It is well to remember, however, that Pitt would have taken everything, and risked the world's reaction; his successors in 1761, eager to end the war, and perhaps more conscious of the dangers of monopoly, prescribed a more moderate peace. Their disposition of such vast and varied conquests is without precedent in modern diplomatic history. They refused to take Louisiana and the French West African settlements, and they refused to exclude France from the Newfoundland fisheries or the trade with India. In North America, Canada and all the territories east of the Mississippi, except New Orleans, became British; France retained only two little island fishing bases, St Pierre and Miquelon, off the south shore of Newfoundland. In the West Indies, she was allowed to regain her most prosperous sugar islands – Martinique and Guadaloupe. Only in India was British supremacy made almost absolute; apart from a few minor trading posts, France kept only two of her historic coastal settlements, Pondicherry and Chandernagore.

83

Shah Alam grants the fiscal administration (*diwani*) of Bengal, Bihar and Orissa to Clive in August 1765.

When the recently ennobled Lord Clive came back to India as governor of Bengal in 1765, the East India Company held controlling authority in the province he had so brilliantly safeguarded, and its prestige and influence in other parts of India had been greatly enhanced. There was as yet no thought of ruling India. Indeed, events over the next few years suggested that Britain's role as conqueror and peacemaker might well be approaching a dismal conclusion. Indiscipline and greed infected many of the Company's servants; nawabs were being mulcted or muzzled, and to make matters worse, during a famine in which a third of the population was dying of starvation, the ravaging Marathas were again threatening Bengal. It was a gloomy anti-climax to the exhilarating triumphs of the Seven Years War.

At this desperate moment, when the first British Empire was disintegrating in North America, India was saved by the courage and diplomatic skill of Warren Hastings, whom Parliament had appointed governor-general in 1773. Against a confederation of the strongest powers in India, backed by the arms of France, Hastings, with the help of a few British regulars, held his own. He himself made no wars of conquest, but he began the process (as Dupleix had attempted for his country) of making the British Raj the centre of a system of alliances with the chief Indian states. And near the end of his term of office, after cleansing the Augean stables of Company government, he was to witness the first major step in the transfer of political power from the Company to the crown. By the Act of 1784, all political instructions and dispatches addressed to the Company's offices in India had to be submitted to a supervisory body called the Board of Control, which could amend or reject them as it saw fit. Henceforward (as Hastings had wished), the final voice in the affairs of India was not the Company's board of directors, but the British government, exercising its responsibility through an appointed agency of its own making.

Warren Hastings.

The cruel and unjust impeachment of Hastings for gross misgovernment and corruption began in 1788, and the proceedings stretched on for seven years. No doubt this unusual man, perhaps the greatest governing mind that Britain produced in the eighteenth century, was guilty of wrong-doing, but his administration was an improvement beyond calculation on previous régimes. The rancour and venom with which Burke and Fox pursued him, recoiled on the Whigs even at that time. Burke called him the 'common enemy and oppressor of all', 'the human tiger', who had 'laid waste the plains of Bengal'. 'If a man will appear extravagant,' remarked Dr Johnson to Boswell, 'it is no wonder that he is represented as mad.'

Burke has more than once been described as the greatest political thinker whose thoughts are expressed in the English language. But unlike his speeches on the American colonies, many of his later diatribes against Hastings reflected something like acute hysteria. Burke was using inexcusably bitter, personal quarter-truths to expound the loftiest of political principles: that the Indian people should not be at the mercy of a commercial company and its patrons, that empire was a trusteeship to be administered with impartial justice, and that the British name should not be tarnished by any suspicion of oppression in the governing of dependent subjects.

Edmund Burke.

Burke erred deeply in particulars and in the savagery with which he pursued them, but there can be little doubt that the long ordeal endured by Warren Hastings did help to familiarize the British public with the new concept of trusteeship. The trial, which wasted seven years of a brave man's life and left him broken in health, though by no means impoverished, not only served to awaken a new public sense of duty towards Asian subjects; its lessons were expanded to include African slavery (the agitation for abolition of the trade was running concurrently with the trial) and finally all backward or primitive peoples.

Interior of the Lutheran church in York, Pennsylvania, 1800.

Chapter Five

THE IRREPRESSIBLE CONFLICT

At the close of the seventeenth century, the old Puritan order was still deeply entrenched in New England. Church membership qualifications for voters had been superseded by property qualifications, but the Puritan clergy still exerted a strong influence on the conduct of public affairs. None the less, as Massachusetts developed closer commercial and political relations with the outside world, the exclusive supremacy of Puritan ideals was seriously shaken by liberal movements within the church. In his *Magnalia Christi Americana* (1702), Cotton Mather wrote: 'The old spirit of New England hath been sensibly going out of the world, as the old saints in whom it was, have gone; and instead thereof the spirit of the world, with a lamentable neglect of strict piety, has crept in upon the rising generation.'

By the beginning of the eighteenth century, Quakers, Baptists and Anglicans each had a regular organized church in Boston. King's Chapel in Boston had grown to almost fashionable Anglican respectability. It had the prestige and patronage of the crown and most of the crown's representatives in Massachusetts attended its services. The burial-ground beside the church bears eloquent testimony to the many distinguished citizens who were its obedient adherents. By the time of the death of Anne in 1714, there was talk of organizing a colonial episcopate, a subject that continued to be discussed over the tea-cups until the Revolution came. But, in general, ecclesiastical controversies played only a very minor part in widening the gap between colonies and mother country. Provincial jealousies and competitive self-governing ambitions made illusory any serious consideration of an American Church of England. Although frequently narrow and parochial in outlook, above all else the assemblies stood for the principle of colonial autonomy as against any form of official, imperial policy.

It was the crown, not the English Parliament directly, which shared in the internal political life of the colonies, and the link between crown and colonial subjects in the royal colonies was the governor, who was appointed by the king. His powers and duties were defined by his commission and instructions. He possessed ordinary executive powers of appointment and military command, and, with limitations, power of pardon. With the help of his council, he appointed judges and influenced certain judicial functions; for example, royal governments could act as courts of appeal in civil cases. But a very significant part of the governor's duty was to prevent the local legislature from acting contrary to British policy; for this purpose he could, as has been noticed, exercise the veto.

The office of governor was not a particularly lucrative job and the salary was rarely paid on time. William Shirley of Massachusetts, at the beginning of the 1740s, was the first incumbent to get £1000 at the beginning of each year, and such punctuality was owing to the fact that he was liked. The home government sometimes appointed American-born men to the highest administrative posts (Massachusetts, under the charter of 1691, was governed for more years by natives than by Englishmen); but such indulgence made little difference to success. Home-grown products, like Dudley, Belcher and Hutchinson, were not very effective and scarcely conciliatory; the most popular governors were importations such as Bellomont, Shirley and Lewis Morris.

The salary question was really linked up, as in Canada a century later, with the question of popular control. The royal governors were instructed to get a fixed salary voted, but most of the assemblies, especially Massachusetts, refused because they wanted to hold the governor as hostage. In Virginia, a fixed salary was eventually secured, but not in many of the others. Indeed, there was a growing tendency to pass all monies in itemized detail for limited periods, thus enabling the assembly to exert additional pressures on the governor to carry distinctively popular measures. In the assembly's view, money raised by public taxation belonged to the people, and the representatives had a right, therefore, to say how it should be spent.

By the beginning of the eighteenth century, every province had its representative assembly: Virginia, a house of burgesses; South Carolina, a commons house of assembly; Massachusetts, a house of representatives. Representation was based chiefly on property, but was not restricted to freeholders as in English counties. With few exceptions, by the close of Anne's reign, the assemblies were enforcing their claim not merely to impose taxes and determine expenditure, but also to appoint the chief financial and administrative officers.

All this meant controversy carried overseas. There was a need, therefore, to guard colonial interests through colonial agents. Until nearly the end of the seventeenth century, these were *ad hoc* appointments. After 1688, it became the custom for each colony to maintain standing agencies in London. At first they were appointed by act of assembly, requiring the consent of the governor and council (in Massachusetts, the choice was practically that of the house of representatives). In this manner, colonies which could afford the expense were able to exert considerable influence in Westminster.

But zealous colonial agents failed to budge the Navigation Acts; neither did they succeed in softening the laws governing colonial manufactures. The general policy remained restrictive. In 1732, for example, Parliament prohibited the inter-colonial trade in hats, and restricted their manufacture in America. A similar policy regarding iron manufactures was urged and an Act was passed in 1750 forbidding the erection of any additional slitting, plating or steel mills. The Molasses Act was the harshest and most important. In 1733, after two years of talk, prohibitive duties were imposed on molasses, sugar and rum imported into the continental colonies from the West Indian colonies of other countries than Britain. The Act was intended to encourage the British West Indies as against the Dutch and French, but it was not effectively enforced.

Inevitably, colonial grievances, existing or declared, were chiefly economic, but they were not deeply disturbing. There was some disposition on the part of colonists to deny the legality of trade regulations, although the practical necessity for an overall superintending power was recognized, however grudgingly. During the first twenty-five years after the Treaty of Utrecht, the home government had made considerable progress in reconciling local governments with imperial administration. Obviously, there was a need for uniformity in matters affecting the colonies generally, for example, postal and currency regulations, Indian relations, local defence and war. The colonial American knew that the powers of his own government were limited; and he was becoming accustomed even to having his own laws disallowed.

By the 1740s, it was widely assumed that colonial governments were subject to a paramount law – not merely charter authority, but a vague body of rules that one might call Imperial Law. Had there been aggressive imperial action during the early decades of the eighteenth century – for example, the imposition of a stamp tax – discontent and scepticism might have crystallized much earlier. Meanwhile, it was generally admitted that the King, Lords and Commons were supreme; there was no attempt to draw up any theory of colonial rights. On the other hand, it was equally clear that any direct taxation by a British Parliament would be regarded as a violation of colonial rights and tradition.

In general, by the mid eighteenth century imperial controls had tended to tighten, but they were being countered by strong independent tendencies within the colonies. There was no disloyalty in the sense of treasonous talk and agitation, but the connection was growing thinner. The problem of reconciling imperial authority and colonial self-government was coming to the political surface. In retrospect, the situation might suggest that the battle of royal prerogative versus local self-government was already a losing one. At the time, this was not so considered. If there had been more governors like Shirley, Wentworth, Dinwiddie or Spottswood, it is possible that British colonial history might have taken a different course.

THE AMERICAN REVOLUTION

In April 1775, British troops marching by the little village of Concord, Massachusetts, were fired upon by colonial militia. This was the famous shot that 'rang around the world' (actually the first shot was fired at Lexington, but no one knows who fired it). Within a year Britain found herself committed to a struggle far from her own shores, and against 2,500,000 people who could draw supplies from within or without their own territories. The long and complicated story of rebellion ended with the Anglo-French naval action in Chesapeake Bay. The Royal Navy lost control of the sea just long enough for Washington, by a swift concentration of available French and American troops, to corner a British army of 7000 men under General Cornwallis on the peninsula of Yorktown, and to force their surrender on 19 October 1781.

It has been said that French intervention in North American waters was decisive. In a sense this is true; Yorktown sealed American independence. But to suggest that only French intervention could have won independence for the Thirteen Colonies is an over-simplification. Bereft of all allies – the only major war she has ever fought without allies – and occupied with three powerful enemies in other parts of the world, Great Britain could scarcely, after 1778, have found the resources and the men to subdue a quarter of a continent, 3000 miles away.

Within the last generation the Revolution has come to be studied both in the United States and Britain with resolute objectivity. Historians are still not agreed on all the causes, but pride of nationality rarely affects their scholarship. Today, it is generally accepted that the outbreak was not the spontaneous uprising of an aggrieved majority; rather, like all revolutions, it was the work of an aggressive minority with strong minds and good organization who carried along a more numerous body of less active participants. It can be considered, indeed, as a great civil war, involving a gigantic social upheaval, with an aftermath of persecution, deportations and confiscations of property.

Economic exploitation has been largely rejected as a major cause of rebellion. Needless to say, the obvious charge has often been made that the trade and navigation laws represented a one-sided system imposed in the interests of the

◀ The skirmish at Lexington,
19 April 1775: the Lexington militia
disperse after a volley from
Major Pitcairn's advance guard.

Cornwallis writes to Washington
asking for a cease-fire, 17 October 1781.

York, Virginia 17th Octr. 1781

Sir

I propose a cessation of hostilities for Twenty four hours, and that two Officers may be appointed by each side to meet at Mr Moore's house to settle terms for the surrender of the posts of York & Gloucester. I have the honour to be

Sir

Your most obedient & most humble Servant

Cornwallis

His Excellency
General Washington
&c. &c. &c.

mother country alone; that Britain valued her colonies for what she could get out of them and did her best to restrict colonial trade and prohibit colonial manufactures. Incomplete and unreliable statistics make any final conclusion an impossibility. That the object was the exploitation of the colonies, there can be no doubt; *empire* in the eighteenth century meant exploitation. On the other hand, Britain, in the interests of a self-sufficing empire, was prepared to make certain sacrifices – in other words, some of the benefits arising from enforced regulations were mutual. Certainly, the discontents – in Virginia there had been loud complaints about the injuries suffered by the tobacco trade – were not long lasting. Up to about 1763, when the real troubles began, the colonists took things pretty well for granted. No doubt serious protests would have arisen had the Molasses Act of 1733 been enforced against the illegal import of foreign molasses. But the act was not enforced, and only New Englanders might have denied the present-day assumption that the system worked to the benefit of both sides. Despite spasmodic friction, it did not directly contribute to the secession of 1776.

British commercial measures may have been generally acceptable in colonial eyes; none the less, the technique of administration was clumsy and British reforming zeal came at the wrong time. By the conquests of the Seven Years War, the British Empire had been enormously enlarged and in North America consolidated by the conquest of Canada; but no new theories or methods of administration had been conceived to meet the problem of the maturing white colony that had outgrown traditional tutelage and subordination. Between 1760 and 1776, Great Britain had not reached a stage (as she had in 1931) when it was possible to remodel the Empire as a kind of federation of self-governing nations under the crown. Until the famous Durham Report of 1839, there was no thought of reconciling British supremacy and colonial self-government. Men of sympathy and imagination like Burke and Pitt thought only of remedy-ing grievances, not of changing the system of British ascendancy to permit colonies to govern themselves. The Commonwealth ideal was still outside the minds of the great English liberals of that generation, although some colonials, such as Benjamin Franklin, did have glimmerings of a federal empire.

At the end of the Seven Years War, British statesmen were guided by the necessity of tightening up their overgrown Empire and making it a more businesslike organization. With vast new territorial responsibilities, and with a heavy debt, it was assumed that the grateful American colonies – thankful to have the menace of French Canada removed at last – would help to foot the war bill. Apart from a few percipient pamphleteers, no one bothered to ask whether the withdrawal of France from Canada, by reducing the colonies' military dependence on the mother country, would produce a less pliant

Colonial trade and manufacturing flourished despite heavy taxes, as this engraving of 1770 indicates.

Planter selling tobacco; from a map of 1775.

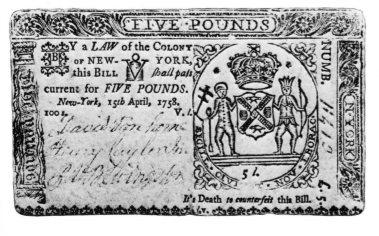

Five pound bill, New York, 1758. Much ill-feeling resulted from British efforts to curb the over-issue of paper money in the colonies.

Colonial reaction to the Stamp Act.

Sam Adams.

attitude towards authority. Freedom from fear sharpened sensitivity and encouraged defiance. Consequently, when a succession of unprecedented but perfectly legal measures – the Sugar Act, the Stamp Act, the Townshend Acts – were passed with the object of getting more revenue from the colonies, a challenge was inevitable.

Had British governments been as resolute as their legislation suggested, they might well have won their case and re-established their sovereign prestige. But instead of taking a stand and sticking to it, they withdrew, or whittled down, each irritating measure before each cry of anguish, thus encouraging colonial leaders to make new and greater demands. Although the Stamp Act may have been a common abomination, not all the colonies were irritated by every measure; the degree of feeling varied. Yet each colony, as time went on, developed a sense of local grievance which, added to the general vexations, enabled it to agree with the complaints of others, as skilfully blended by political agitators like Sam Adams of Boston. In this manner, a community of antagonisms was developed which helped to break down the old provincial rivalries and jealousies that had for so long promoted division and even hostility among neighbours on the Atlantic coast.

In retrospect, one can see a clash of principle emerging – colonial self-government versus British supremacy. On the other hand, the average colonial of that day, while he may had some knowledge of John Locke's *Treatises of Government* and been aware of Rousseau's *Social Contract*, in the beginning at least, held a considerable affection for men like William Pitt and even for George III. Moreover, by 1772 many people were tiring of violence and the demagogic appeals of rabble rousers such as Sam Adams. Conceivably the whole business might have blown over – perhaps for years; certainly the great bulk of the population was against war. Then came the Boston Tea Party of 16 December 1773, when various malcontents disguised as Indians threw a cargo of East India Company tea overboard in Boston harbour. Sam Adams had a talent for dramatizing political issues. Even with the threepenny Townshend duty, this cut-price East India Company tea would have put the smugglers out of business. Once the tea had been landed, and people had realized how cheap it was, agitators would have found it a difficult task to stir up the lukewarm embers of colonial discontent. Sam Adams undoubtedly devised the Tea Party to enrage the English, and his scheme worked, for, next to the monarchy and the constitution, the Englishman cherished his tea. Who knows – the British public might not have risen in wrath, if the Adams gang had thrown overboard anything other than tea!

This episode led to the punitive policy that Adams and his colleagues were aiming at. Once the British government had decided to be firm and to enforce

A society of patriotic ladies
in North Carolina
signs a declaration
to boycott tea and other
English imports, 1775.

the principle of central control, as exemplified in the right of taxation, blood was bound to be shed, and after that appeasement became futile. Further acts of contagious violence were followed by the so-called Coercive Acts – the closing of Boston port, the withdrawal of Massachusetts charter rights, the trial of certain classes of crime in Britain. Messages of sympathy poured in to Massachusetts from the other colonies; urgent petitions to the crown defining colonial rights crossed the sea, only to be rejected. Such were the events that kindled passions and led to the shots at Lexington and Concord, the denial of the legislative power of the British Parliament, renunciation of allegiance to the king, and finally, the Declaration of Independence on 4 July 1776.

The result was a great civil war; between a quarter and a third of the total population in the colonies hated the idea of revolution, and remained loyal to Britain. At a guess, half were Patriots, a quarter remained Loyalists and a quarter stayed neutral, or nearly so. No precise figures are available; it is impossible to draw clear-cut divisions of affiliation. Suffice it to say, the Continental Congress which declared for independence was bitterly torn even at the last between decisive action and further mediation.

95

As in the case of the English Civil War, the American Revolution was the work of a minority who knew their own minds, and they were clever and unbending minds. Perhaps no minority in history (except in Russia after 1917) ever forced itself so strongly and successfully on a majority as did the minority of Patriots in 1775–76. And because the Revolution was a civil war, the consequent social upheaval was considerable. Possibly as many as 80,000 unrelenting colonists stayed by the mother country to the last. Most of them were driven into exile and their property confiscated. This was a social revolution not unlike that which saw the exodus of the Huguenots from France; the loss to the United States of a significant conservative element may have been equally serious. Some 40,000 of the Loyalists crossed the border into British territory, and within the space of three or four years the old French colony of Canada, which had been acquired by Britain in 1763, was turned into a land of two nationalities – an unhappy division which remains to this day.

George Washington.

Once the minority had won, the colonies faced insuperable difficulties. They were still a weak conglomeration of jealous units. Indeed, the Revolution might have been a failure had it not been for the character and quality of George Washington, who must rank with the greatest leaders of all time. There have been greater field generals; Washington was a confident but rarely brilliant strategist and tactician. There have been greater statesmen; he remained in many respects the slow and sober country squire, without intellectual pretensions. None the less, Washington's leadership – the leadership of a phlegmatic but dependable man – was perhaps the supreme achievement of the war. In the manner of Pitt, he pulled together by sheer force of character a divided country, and in the process welded something like a nation.

It would, however, be a mistake not to recognize, before 1776, the growth of what one might call a separate American feeling, the development within the separate colonies of political self-consciousness and self-dependence, a spirit that had been stimulated by the struggle for self-government, the subtle, re-moulding influences of the frontier, and by the need for common exertions against the enemy during the Seven Years War. By mid-century, the third or fourth generations of colonial-born were beginning to feel that they were different from Englishmen or Scots; that they were a distinct people who had managed to govern themselves by means of British institutions for many years, and who had their own rights as much as any Englishman. This is not to suggest that a national feeling was being generated; there were too many regional and inter-state antagonisms, and only the genius of Washington, the energy of the Patriot party, and the propaganda of a few idealists who saw 'a new Heaven and a new Earth' were sufficient to bring them together.

If British governments had possessed the wisdom and vision which they revealed in the time of Lord Durham in the nineteenth century, they could have faced the issue of Home Rule; evolution, not revolution, would have been the key to an unfolding Commonwealth in 1776 rather than in 1839. But it is easy to be patronizing in retrospect and one has no right to ask too much of Britain's obtuse rulers. One can only say that the loss of the Thirteen Colonies at that time was not inevitable; the really significant objectives of the colonists could have been obtained within the Empire, as they subsequently were elsewhere after 1839, with a minimum of cost and trouble. In short, there was no 'irrepressible conflict'. If matters in dispute could have been patched up by wise men of goodwill, the subsequent growth of free trade ideas might well have postponed a crisis until the nineteenth century. 'We might', wrote Thomas Jefferson in the first draft of the Declaration of Independence, 'have been a great and free people together.' Jefferson had to delete that last somewhat nostalgic sentence, but he may have been right.

Thomas Jefferson.

Loyalist settlement at York in Upper Canada, 1804.

Chapter Six

THE SECOND BRITISH EMPIRE

CANADA

The immense conquests of the Seven Years War saw the culmination of the first British Empire. Twenty years later that Empire had been broken by the successful revolt of the American colonies and not only petulant cynics believed that Britain's day was over. The feeling of depression was general. With few exceptions, political observers in Britain and on the continent of Europe believed that the War of Independence had decided the fate of Britain. Some years after the event, Dean Josiah Tucker satirized the popular opinion of the day in the manner of Macaulay's New Zealander.

Nay, those patriotic worthies, the news writers, not only proclaimed the Downfall of the Commerce of this opulent kingdom, but also ventured to foretell that a set of Ciceronis would appear in a century or two, who were to conduct inquisitive strangers over the ruins of our once great Metropolis. 'Here, Gentlemen, stood Westminster Hall and adjoining to it was the Parliament House. Let us now go and view another famous ruin. Here, Gentlemen, was a place called the Royal Exchange, where merchants used to meet, when merchants used to live.'

With the loss of the Thirteen Colonies, the immediate need for a radical revision of colonial policy disappeared. Had the rebels been defeated and made to return to the imperial fold, it is almost certain that the Old Colonial System would have undergone a considerable overhaul. Many of the more restrictive navigation laws and some of the irritating revenue laws would probably have gone the way of the old tea tax. But once the colonies were on their own, the need for immediate reformation vanished. Although no further attempts were made to benefit the British Treasury by means of internal taxation, henceforward colonial affairs were subjected to a more watchful and stringent supervision from London. Too much freedom, it was assumed quite sensibly, had nourished the seeds of discontent that had blossomed at Lexington and Bunker Hill.

99

There was little comfort in the knowledge that the three northern colonies on the Atlantic coast had remained loyal. The fishing base of Newfoundland, the oldest British overseas settlement, inevitably belonged to the power that held command of the seas. Nova Scotia, isolated from the Thirteen Colonies by a stormy arm of the Atlantic, had rid herself of most of the Acadians by the deportations of 1755 and had become essentially British in character. Almost as a matter of course, she received the familiar representative institutions that had been developed further south. New Brunswick had yet to be established as a province of American Loyalists (1784), but Prince Edward Island in the Gulf of St Lawrence had been given a separate government in 1769, with an assembly of its own.

As for Canada, it is doubtful if the British government in 1783 regarded the country with any more favour than in 1761, when the Board of Trade declared that Newfoundland, 'as a means of wealth and power', was worth more than Canada and Louisiana put together. Indeed, most statesmen shared Samuel Johnson's vision of a cold, uncomfortable land of furs and fish, 'a place fit only to send exiles to, as a punishment for their ill-spent lives'. Until the arrival and settlement of the American Loyalists, colonies which had a frontier on the sea held a much more imposing and useful position within the British Empire than those situated inland.

A Canadian settler talks with Indians, 1833 ▶

Quebec; from an engraving of 1761.

Fisherman and trapper on the shores of
Davis Strait, 1680.

Nova Scotia, apart from the value of Halifax as a naval base, had a definite commercial importance because of its accessibility and the opportunities it offered as a colonial entrepôt. Admittedly, Quebec was a seaport, the head of ocean navigation; but a long and hazardous journey from the Gulf of St Lawrence made it relatively remote, and during the winter, the ice-bound river barred all connection by sail. The only argument that carried any weight was that which stressed the advantages of exploiting the inland fur trade. But a valuable part of the trade had been lost as a result of the American boundary settlement, and it was seriously questioned whether the returns in the future would balance the expense of government and defence. 'It would be an insult', declared a jaundiced pamphleteer, 'to ask the projectors of the Upper Canada scheme, what good this Colony was to do us. A man of delicacy would as soon ask one afflicted with the gout, what good his pain could do.'

Above all, the task of governing a conquered European people of differing religion, language and customs was not of a kind to excite the rulers in Westminster. Parliament's cool reception of the conquest in 1763 had shown little of the imperial spirit that had been kindled by Pitt during the Seven Years War. With the exception of 300 or so traders, mainly from New England, who had settled in Quebec and Montreal after the conquest, a French population of about 60,000 had no experience of self-government. The bulk of the population was peasant or habitant, and little concerned with politics, which had been the preserve of the ruling class of seigneurs, the majority of whom had left the country. Between the fearful habitant and his foreign conqueror stood the priest as guardian and confessor.

French-Canadian Sulpician of the late eighteenth century.

In 1763 the British government had issued a proclamation providing for the establishment of representative assemblies and the introduction of English law. For the untrained and Catholic French who were barred by religious tests, this was obviously unjust, and the first governors pointed out the absurdity of such an attempt to apply the customary measures in a predominantly un-English colony. But ten years of confusion and discussion ensued before Lord North's government found a compromise solution. The Quebec Act of 1774 annulled the proclamation of 1763, recognized the Roman Catholic religion, and restored French law and custom in all civil matters. English criminal law, which was somewhat more lenient than the French, was not affected.

Essentially, the Quebec Act was an act of appeasement, an effort to hold what had been won, regardless of the low commercial value attached to the new possession. Indeed, the Act may be regarded as an expedient to save Canada at a time when colonial agitation to the southward had become threatening and when war with France was regarded as more than a possibility. As it happened, the Act (which extended the boundaries of Canada to include

Four bishops, holding hands in the form of a cross 'to show their approbation and countenance of the Roman religion', dance a minuet round the Quebec Bill. Lord North (second left), the author of the Bill, directs the dance, with the Devil hovering over him.

the fur country north of the Ohio River) gave great offence to sensitive Americans, especially in New England, and did nothing to win over the French-Canadians, most of whom remained sullenly neutral. The Americans had counted on a Canadian uprising and as late as 1781 left the door open for the fourteenth colony; but both seigneurs and clergy scorned a mixed marriage with the old frontier foe. Probably fewer than 400 French-Canadians fought on the British side; a much smaller number joined the rebels.

Eventually the Quebec Act was to be recognized as the bastion of French-Canadian liberties and the foundation of French-Canadian nationalism. The clauses which settled the status of the Roman Catholic Church by granting Catholic emancipation (half a century before it was achieved in Britain) attracted the loyalty of the clergy; the legal provisions which prescribed French civil law, subject to amendment by governor and council, won the approval of the seigneurs. Nevertheless, it was clear from the beginning that the entire restoration of French civil law, much of it obsolete even in France, was absurd, and the governor, Sir Guy Carleton, was instructed in 1775 to maintain the old French laws only until altered by ordinances of the legislative council. The task of knitting French and English law in a manner acceptable to both races would have been difficult under any circumstances. In the face of threatening rebellion to the south, Carleton wavered. Fearful of offending the French by making apparent concessions to the handful of British settlers, and dominated by the thought that Canada must forever remain a predominantly French province, he concealed his instructions, thus leaving the small minority of British merchants for some years without the benefit of *habeas corpus* and jury trial for civil suits, and without the protection and the incentives provided by English commercial law.

Such was the situation in the years 1783–84, when some 7000 British Loyalists, either through conviction or fear, crossed the Upper St Lawrence River as refugee immigrants. Most of the newcomers resented the restrictive bonds of the Quebec Act, which had been intended solely for a French community. Such an attitude was natural for people trained in the arts of self-government, but it was bound to excite nervous French-Canadians. Suspicious of the new invaders, who appeared to be more British than the British, and dreading the possibility of changes in law which might undermine their religion, language or customs, they sought refuge behind the Quebec Act, and transformed what was intended to be a temporary 'halting ground' into a preserve of French-Canadian rights and privileges. In making Canada a land of two nationalities, the American Revolution was thus responsible for the birth of a bitter and uncompromising spirit of race nationalism.

For the next few years, two distinct societies – the French in the Lower St Lawrence Valley and the Loyalists along the Upper St Lawrence, west of the Ottawa River – lived uneasily side by side under the government provided by the Quebec Act. It was clear that the recent immigrants deserved a measure of the self-government to which they had been accustomed, but it was equally clear that the French-Canadians had little or no knowledge of the workings of a popular assembly. None the less, the British government decided to experiment, and in 1791 Parliament granted to each of two prospective provinces, Upper and Lower Canada, what its authors claimed to be a 'model' of the English constitution. The place of the king was filled by a governor, with subordinate lieutenant-governors in each province. The House of Lords was paralleled by two small legislative councils appointed for life by the crown, and the House of Commons was represented by two legislative assemblies elected every four years.

Unfortunately (but understandably at this moment of disillusionment and postponed hopes of reform), no provision was made for making the governor and his ministers responsible to the will of the assembly. Almost inevitably, therefore, members of both assemblies came to regard themselves as a permanent opposition, whose object was a continuous assault on the authority and independence of the executive. Not for another decade or more did the French-Canadians begin to appreciate the value of the new and unaccustomed instrument as a means of bolstering and preserving 'la nation canadienne'. In Upper Canada, the end of agitation was essentially political reform for its own sake; in Lower Canada, it was race domination.

Medallion portrait of James Cook
by Josiah Wedgwood, 1784.

Between the Treaty of Utrecht and the outbreak of the American Revolution, few new colonies were planted; from the time of William Dampier, who coasted along the west coast of Australia in 1699, to the age of Cook, Byron, Wallis, Carteret and their French contemporaries, the historian of maritime exploration has little to record. Only the interminable world wars between France and Britain offered evidence that expanding empire was still important to European nations of the mercantile faith.

Not until the end of the Seven Years War did the Admiralty dispatch two expeditions to the south Pacific. That of John Byron (1764–66) attracted immense public interest by its reports of encounters with 'giants' in Patagonia; in 1766–67, Samuel Wallis and Philip Carteret rediscovered the terrestrial paradise of Tahiti and explored the Solomon Islands and the New Guinea coasts. But the most remarkable voyages in the history of exploration began on 25 August 1768, when Lieutenant James Cook set sail from Plymouth for Tahiti in command of the barque HMS *Endeavour*. It was the first fully organized scientific expedition supported by the Royal Society and was accompanied by scientists and scholars, the most distinguished of whom was Joseph Banks. At Tahiti, Cook was ordered to record the transit of Venus on 3 June 1769, an astronomical measurement which would help to determine the distance of the earth from the sun. Thereafter, under secret instructions from the

Admiralty, he was ordered to hunt for the elusive southern continent which was assumed, both in France and Britain, to lie in the sub-tropical latitudes of the south Pacific.

Cook's fruitless search, a romantic errand which had lured explorers for more than 200 years, finally disproved the existence of any southern continent in latitudes north of 40° South. He then circumnavigated New Zealand, defined it as two islands, and thence explored the unknown eastern coast of Australia for 2000 miles before turning home by way of the Torres Strait and Batavia. In two further voyages, 1772–75 and 1776–79, he charted most of the main island groups in the Pacific, penetrated the ice-floes of the Arctic as far south as 71° 10', surveyed the west coast of North America as far as the Bering Straits, and then met a tragic and unnecessary death in the Sandwich Islands. Only Columbus and possibly Magellan can approach Cook in courage, stamina and navigational genius; 'for variety of experience', wrote J. C. Beagle-hole, his achievement 'transcends most other voyages ever made'.

Not until twenty years after Cook embarked on his first voyage of discovery did Europeans settle on the continent of Australia. In January 1788, a thousand or so convicts, soldiers and officials were removed from the swampy shores of Botany Bay to Sydney Cove. As compared with the American continents or even New Zealand, the penetration of Australia by Europeans is unique, chiefly because Australian history began with an almost empty continent. In North America, from the Gulf of Mexico to Hudson Bay, it was impossible to ignore the Indians, whose existence profoundly affected the character of European settlement as well as the fortunes of rival powers. The importance of the Indian was not only political and military (during the first half of the eighteenth century the Iroquois either held or greatly influenced the balance of power between British and French), it was also economic. He had developed or dis-covered natural food products that were strange to Europe, and, whether vegetable or animal, they were highly acceptable. He also played an indispen-sable part in the expansion of the fur trade across the North American continent; his presence was vital to the early Canadian economy.

A member of Cook's crew exchanges a handkerchief for a crayfish.

By contrast, as Professor La Nauze has emphasized, the Australian aborigine provided virtually nothing. Over some 30,000 years he had managed to adapt himself to a hostile environment, but he had made no impression on it. He cultivated no plants such as potatoes, maize, tea or tobacco, and unlike the South American Indian or the African he could not even be exploited as profitable labour. The Australian aborigine only attempted to dodge or hide from the devouring invader and gradually melt away. The native animals were scarcely more helpful. One could neither milk nor even herd the kangaroo; he could jump any kind of fence the aborigine was capable of constructing. He was, of

Watering in Tolaga Bay, New Zealand, 1769; pen drawing by Cook after a drawing by Sydney Parkinson.

course, edible, but in total use-value hardly comparable to the elephant, the sledge dog or the reindeer. In short, neither indigenous man nor beast affected in any way the economic life of the European settler.

During the first half of the nineteenth century, Australia owed her invulnerable continental unity to Britain's overwhelming naval power. Without British naval superiority, not only France, but possibly other European powers, might have staked out claims. The section of Australia which Britain occupied as a convict settlement at the end of the eighteenth century was little more than a fly speck on the continental mass, and even had she wished, she was in no position to expand her claims. Not until 21 October 1805, when Nelson's victory at Trafalgar left Britain for a century practically unchallengeable at sea, was the ownership of Australia decided. Trafalgar removed all danger of serious foreign interference. There were to be threats, but the threats were unenforceable.

Unfortunately, as soon as the real or imagined fears of French interference and occupation dwindled, the colonizing energy of the governing authorities shrank correspondingly. The government had no strong political motive for

Sir Joseph Banks.

forcing matters; unlike Canada, the settlement on the rim of the continent had no harassing neighbour. There was no clashing of European colonial interests (as in Africa), or of religious or racial groups (as in Canada). Australia, by an accident of history, became a comparatively untouchable British preserve. For the whole of the nineteenth century, the country was peopled almost entirely from Britain. Moreover, Britain was the one export market and the one source of commodity imports. The separate colonial or state economies were tied, in the same way as India of that time, to a single outside economy – Britain.

But to return to the foundations. When America closed her doors in 1783, no one knew what was to be done with criminals in an age when 160 offences were punishable by death. Burke raised the question in March 1785, when many thousand offenders were liable for transportation. The Gold Coast and Gambia were both considered and it is possible that Burke's opposition helped to kill the proposals. None the less, the government was still interested in Africa and the *Nautilus* was dispatched to Walvis Bay, the site of Bismarck's first German African colony. The land seemed unutterably barren, so the Cape was considered. A settlement close by Table Bay would provide, it was argued, a useful lever in dealings with the Dutch, who were falling under French influence. But this plan too was rejected; otherwise South Africa might have become predominantly British, and – to pursue the 'ifs' of history – there might have been no Boer War, and the Pacific coast of Australia might, without competition, have gone to France.

Three men were responsible for turning the government's attention to Australia – Sir Joseph Banks, Admiral Sir George Young and a sailor called James Matra. Banks had described with enthusiasm Cook's first voyage along the coast of New South Wales and he had stressed the rich soil and wealth of vegetation around Botany Bay. This led Young and Matra to further investigation. Matra, who was a Corsican in British service, drew up a definite scheme of colonization, and in August 1783, with the support of Admiral Young, the Cabinet was informed of the attractions of a vast island in the Antipodes, as well as the strategic commercial position of the area in relation to the spice islands, India, China and Japan. It was suggested by Young that Loyalists from the lost American colonies might be induced to settle there. In April 1784, after considerable discussion, the Home Secretary, Lord Sydney, noted, as a kind of postscript to the project, the advantages of such a settlement as an open jail for criminals. On 18 August 1786, at the end of three years of fruitless searching and pondering, Sydney informed the Lords Commissioners of the Treasury that the government had decided to dump its surplus felons on territory explored by Captain Cook in 1770.

Silver kettle and spirit lamp presented to Banks by Queen Charlotte, 1813.

Convict labour on Norfolk Island, 1847.

Fair treatment for the aborigines.

Bivouac of travellers in a
'cabbage-tree forest' in Australia;
early nineteenth century.

The majority of the English and Irish prisoners were transported for a seven-year term, after which they became free settlers. But the selection procedure was not carried out in any scientific manner. The nature of the crime influenced the system only relatively. Thirty years after it had begun, a contemporary writer declared that, 'for the most trivial offences, persons of both sexes are sentenced to seven years transportation; many have actually been transported for first offences, the crime being the theft of something valued at tenpence'. The cruel inconsistencies reveal themselves starkly in the case of children and aged people. In the early years, some of those transported were seventy years of age, a few were permanent invalids, and others, boys and girls of twelve and thirteen years. Between 1812 and 1815, 396 boys and 109 girls were transported. After 1793, political prisoners swelled the totals of the largely non-criminal population. Of these, the Irish were the most numerous, the greater number arriving before 1800. All told, before the system ended, the total export of prisoners was probably less than 180,000.

It was a melancholy beginning for a great Commonwealth. The task of turning convicts into useful citizens, while not an unrelieved failure, could scarcely eliminate a taint which affected Australian life far into the nineteenth century. It should be remembered, however, that many of Britain's earliest colonists in other parts of the world, were, if not criminally inclined, at least uncultured and unreflecting rough diamonds. In the early stages of imperial development, a great deal of the dirty work, and sometimes the heroic work, was done by coarse and untutored men of stamina, scarcely capable as Gibbon Wakefield sardonically remarked, of 'bringing the light of knowledge where all had been darkness and barbarism'. 'For the growth of honour', he added, 'the colonies are not a very congenial soil.' In Australia, the convicts did at least provide necessary labour during the process of expansion coastwise and inland. With scarcely any interruption, prisoners were transported annually from 1787 to 1840, when the practice ceased in New South Wales; it continued in other parts until the final abolition of the system in 1868.

The immigration of free men made by far the greatest contribution to the Australian population. This free immigration was spasmodic until it began to receive official encouragement after the Napoleonic Wars. From 1830, it became a recognized and subsidized system, and after 1850, at the time of the gold discoveries, developed into a veritable flood, drowning the unpleasant relics of earlier days, and substantially influencing the tone and trend of national development. Between 1851 and 1861, over 500,000 colonists came from the United Kingdom.

The circumstances of early settlement differed considerably from those in the American colonies, where convicts had been handed over to plantation-owners.

Governor's house, Sydney, New South Wales, 1791.

The Australian 'dumping process' necessitated an unusual form of govern-ment. When the contractors in Britain assembled and transported the first convicts, they transferred all responsibility to the governor of the territory – New South Wales – without further compensation other than the costs of transport. In brief, the local government became the employer.

Some historians have interpreted this process as evidence of a planned colonial establishment. The early convicts, they say, were to be the nucleus of a settlement, which should, like any other British settlement overseas, observe the traditional laws relating to trade and plantations. Although the settlement might be called a penal colony, it was, none the less, part of a powerful empire, whose headquarters represented a safe market for staple exports once they were found, a source of capital and a continuing source of population, condemned or free. Of necessity, the first governors were autocratic, but sooner or later, under the inevitably haphazard control by a mother country far away, civil liberties were bound to be acquired; even if free immigration had been forbidden, freed convicts and their children were certain eventually to outnumber 'the wicked and condemned'.

Such an interpretation is compelling, at least in its conclusions. Moreover, economic forces lent weight to genetic circumstances that favoured the ultimate emergence of a true colony. By 1800, New South Wales, excluding Norfolk Island, had a population of nearly 5000, of whom 402 were settlers holding land grants totalling 44,000 acres. By that time, merino sheep had been introduced from the Cape, and shortly after Waterloo the flocks were moving slowly north and west of Sydney across the mountains to the good pastoral land beyond. The growth of private initiative and trade based on fine merino wool meant the disintegration of the purely penal colony long before the abolition of transportation to New South Wales in 1840.

SOUTH AFRICA

On the whole, the continent of Africa endures less extremes of climate than the greater part of the United States or Canada. But, if no more subject to the vagaries of weather than most regions, it has, generally speaking, been more subject to disease than any other, and probably suffered from a greater variety of damaging pests. One could write a history of Africa based on the activities of the mosquito and the tsetse fly. 'The great feat of the African', wrote Colonel W.R. Crocker, was to survive in 'this empire of insects', which in so many respects resembled H.G. Wells's 'Empire of the Ants': where forests were interminable and seemingly invincible, and where man appeared as a 'precarious intruder'.

One travelled for miles, amidst the still, silent struggle of giant trees, of strangulating creepers, of assertive flowers . . . but man, man at most held a footing upon resentful clearings, fought weeds, fought beasts and insects for the barest foothold, fell a prey to snake and beast, insect and fever, and was presently carried away.

It is doubtful, indeed, whether any race that survived so enervating and disabling an environment, would have had the vigour to concert a successful scientific attack on disease without help from Europe.

But South Africa provides an outstanding exception to such a generalization. There, colonization was a far less formidable task than in the primitive wilderness and on the plains of Australia and Canada. In the most tropical of continents, South Africa contains the largest single area of temperate climate. When the Boers trekked inland from the Cape between 1836 and 1840, they met no tumbling rivers, thick forests or arid stretches of tundra. The explorers of South Africa rarely suffered pangs of hunger and thirst, as did the white invaders of Australia; nor did they have to fight their way through barriers of snow and ice, swamp and rock, as did many of the pioneers in Canada. Not until the late seventies, when the frontiersman reached the latitude of Delagoa Bay, did he encounter the tsetse fly and mosquito that played havoc with cattle, the staple product of his labours.

The maps of the geographer, the geologist and the climatologist may well be the most significant guides to African continental history; but in South Africa,

Dutch farmers return from a day's sport, 1801.

where natural obstacles were almost non-existent, where the interior beyond the Cape beckoned with its vast plateau grasslands, the presence of the warlike and aggressive natives was the vital element affecting the progress of settlement. Far more Boer energy was consumed in battling the Bantu than any natural hazards. As Cornelius De Kiewiet has remarked, the prime key to South African history was the war for security; and this struggle helped to complicate further the tortuous route of British colonial policy.

Zulu warrior.

When Britain took permanent possession of the Cape of Good Hope in 1806 (and what was less customary in those days, paid for it handsomely), the Dutch settlers had already begun to spread inland beyond the reach of government. In the process, the struggle with native races was bound to take on new urgency. The neighbouring Hottentots had already been enslaved, the dwarf-like Bushmen to the north were nearly exterminated; but in the north-east the Boers encountered the vanguard of the Kaffir legions, tribesmen of Bantu stock who had long been pushing southwards from central Africa, men as vigorous, as disciplined and as savage as the North American Iroquois – and far more numerous. The military power of the famous Matabele was confined chiefly to the High Veld, that of the Zulus to the valleys of Natal. The strength of both rested on superb tribal organization, skilled leadership and exceptional qualities of courage and endurance. Consequently, there was no whiteman's elimination of the native as in Australia or the Caribbean. Not until after the discovery of gold and diamonds did the tribal systems break down, permitting the economic association of the two civilizations, black and white, and the beginnings of a lamentable race problem that was to divide Boer and Briton, and leave an indelible mark on Boer nationalism.

In the sixteenth century, the Portuguese had used the Cape as a repair and re-freshment station on the way to India; not until 1652 was a permanent colony established by the Dutch. Henceforward, for a century and a half the white population grew almost entirely by natural increase. In fact, Cape Colony remained a frail waif in comparison with similar European settlements in other parts of the world. In 1660, there were probably 80,000 British settlers on the Atlantic coast of North America; at that time, the Cape Dutch numbered 200. At the beginning of the Seven Years War, the white population of the thirteen American colonies was over a million; that of the Cape, about 5000. Shortly after the end of the Napoleonic Wars, this latter total had grown to about 60,000, less than 1 per cent of the white population of the new United States.

Britain captured the Cape from the Netherlands in 1795, and again in 1806, to prevent the French from using Table Bay as a base for interrupting British commerce on the way to the East. Yet the Cape remained more than a 'fortress key' to India. Although better ships and improved sailing techniques had progressively diminished its importance as an intermediate rendezvous – by the end of the eighteenth century, it could be by-passed – East India Company ships continued to use the port for rest and refitting. The only other Atlantic base on the route to India was St Helena; but apart from prevailing winds which made it an awkward port of call on the outward journey to India, it lacked sufficient food and water.

Understandably, the Cape was retained at the end of the Napoleonic Wars in the interest of India's security, and not because either Admiralty or Cabinet were attracted by its advantages as a refreshment or repair base. With few commercial assets beyond the harbours of the peninsula, the Cape was regarded as an expensive luxury and its defences were to be consistently neglected. In the dawning age of economy and *laissez-faire*, to be cherished a colony had to pay its way. Unlike Singapore, which was to be occupied in 1819, the Cape was not even a profitable entrepôt. Of the exports, only two commodities, wool and wine, developed any importance during the next forty or so years. Wool production did increase steadily, but the export total was small in comparison with that of other producers. Inevitably, therefore, British ministers regarded the Cape much as their predecessors had regarded conquered Canada in 1763, pondering with anxiety the problem of ruling a long-established colony of European settlers whose *wanderlust* and resolution were to be responsible for a succession of expensive native wars.

Until 1833, when a small nominated council was added, South Africa, or specifically, Cape Province, was ruled (as was New South Wales originally) by a governor, who was in most respects a dictator. He remained, however, subject to real restraint by the Colonial Office, and for Evangelicals like the Permanent Under-Secretary, James Stephen, or the Secretary of State, Lord Glenelg, the protection of the natives was bound to have high priority. These officials were deeply influenced on South African questions by the missionary societies, which had become a power in the land that no government could safely ignore. Unfortunately, the missionaries, whose dedication and courage had earned them a right to be heard, were inclined to assume that in any conflict between whiteman and native, the black underdog had to be right. In the opinion of the frontier settlers, the Colonial Office was unbendingly doctrinaire, and most of its mandates, conceived in ignorance, could be interpreted as anti-white.

There is no doubt that the missionaries did convey an unbalanced view of the character of the Kaffirs who were about to challenge the Boer advance into the interior. There was a tendency to paint an impressionistic picture of the brutal Dutch farmer *vis-à-vis* the primitive and harmless Bantu, who was often goaded into war by the whiteman's ruthless aggressiveness. Dr John Philip, superintendent of the London Missionary Society at Cape Town, bears not a little responsibility for initiating, involuntarily, the South African race problem by his ceaseless denigrating of the Boer frontier farmer.

Missionaries meet the Matabele, 1835.

British settlers' camp on the Great Fish River, 1837.

Moravian mission centre at Genadendal ('Vale of Grace'); lithograph after an original painting of 1817.

For some two centuries the Dutch had, like the Moslems, maintained a system of domestic slavery which was vastly different from the plantation slavery in the West Indies and in the southern United States. They were no doubt hard masters, but from all accounts less cruel to their servants than the average Jamaican or Virginian planter. Moreover, they were facing the most formidable native challenge in nineteenth-century history. Following on innumerable Kaffir wars in the eighteenth century, two serious invasions had occurred since the British occupation – in 1812 and in 1819 – and the Boer farmers, separated in scattered homesteads on the limitless veld, feared for their lives at the hands of fanatics whether at home or in Whitehall. Except under compulsion, the Bantu peoples were quite incapable of settling down anywhere in peace. It has been estimated that a million human beings were the victims of Matabele and Zulu tribal forays during the first two decades of the nineteenth century. In the words of one historian, had Lord Glenelg been 'capable of appreciating the difference between a Hottentot and a Kaffir there might have been no Great Trek and no Boer War'.

The emancipation of the slaves by an Act of the British Parliament in 1834 did much to embitter Boer relations with the colonial authorities. But a more

◀ The defile of Trekata'kou in Cape Province was 'justly dreaded by travellers' according to Latrobe, from whose journal (1818) this aquatint is taken.

drastic blow was delivered in the same year when some 12,000 Kaffirs swept over the frontier, burning, killing and driving off cattle. The governor, Sir Benjamin D'Urban, responded to the crisis by driving back the invaders and annexing the troubled area beyond the Fish River. Unfortunately, Lord Glenelg and his advisers saw not 'ruthless barbarians', as D'Urban had described the enemy, but innocent victims of systematic injustice, driven in their despair 'to extort by force that redress which they could not otherwise obtain'. The governor's frontier annexation was cancelled, and in 1837 he was recalled.

This misguided decision undoubtedly stimulated the Afrikaners' interest in the area beyond the Cape frontier, where they would be free of British control and consequently able to put into effect their own ideas of democratic self-government. There was no need for a half-baked rebellion as in the Canadas; a *trek* offered a peaceful solution not only to Anglo-Boer friction, but also to chronic frontier tensions. North of the Orange River and in Natal, many of the indigenous inhabitants seemed likely to welcome the Boers as protectors or allies; vast fertile lands would be at their disposal, and an abundance of non-white labour. Whatever the future difficulties and dangers, the vision of an independent Afrikaner state was far more attractive to the frontier farmer than emigration overseas or to the less attractive western districts of the Cape.

No one knows when the trek idea began, or who was responsible for its inception; the original organizers were bound to keep their plans secret. Suffice it to say, in 1836 began one of the great odysseys in modern history. Early in the spring, the covered wagons started moving northward into the rolling pastoral country of what ultimately became the Orange Free State, an area larger than England and Wales. They defeated the Matabele legions and drove them beyond the Vaal River. Eastward, beyond the Drakensberg Mountains, lay Natal, first penetrated in 1824 by a handful of British traders who had settled in Durban, and since ravaged by the repeated incursions of the Zulus. At Blood River in 1838 the military power of these magnificent warriors was broken, and until 1843, when the country was annexed as a British colony, Natal remained a Boer sanctuary.

The Great Trek transformed the whole character of white settlement in southern Africa and largely determined its future history. By 1840 some 6000 people had emigrated to the north and north-east of Cape Colony; within fifteen years an isolated refreshment station had expanded to include two Boer republics with access to two oceans and a vast hinterland stretching northward from the Limpopo River. The Sand River Convention of 17 January 1852 recognized the independence of the trekker community north of the Vaal River; the Bloemfontein Convention of 23 February 1854 provided for the second republic, and, for the first time, the withdrawal of Britain from a territory which she had previously annexed.

When the Boer settlers escaped into the dangerous interior in 1836, they maintained, like the French-Canadians after the Conquest in 1763, much of their eighteenth-century mode of life and thought. Like the French-Canadian habitants, they withdrew themselves as a segregated people from the main current of Western civilization. Justifying their existence on Old Testament rules of conduct, as did the seventeenth-century Puritan, they stayed obstinately aloof from worldly contacts. Upheld in their fight for survival by an unbending faith, inevitably they saw themselves as persecuted members of the elect, assured by their beliefs and tenacity of a special destiny. Safe from the temptations of Egypt's fleshpots and the aggressively humanitarian doctrines of Europe, they withdrew, not to found fortunes in gold and diamonds, but to find land, settle it, and then fight to the death, if necessary, to safeguard their peculiar society.

In most colonies of British settlement it had been assumed that possession of the coast established a claim to the immediate hinterland, and that such pre-serves were to be held by the crown in trust or sold for the benefit of the inhabi-tants. But such a doctrine was never applied in South Africa. Because all land beyond the limits of the Cape Colony was regarded as independent of the crown, the British government had refused to follow the retreating Boer voor-trekkers. Reluctantly, Natal was taken over in 1843 in the interests of firm government, but in facing up to the problem of the Boer frontier settlements British policy was hesitant and slipshod. Until nearly the end of the century, it was never clear whether the British government would recognize separate independent states that had been established beyond the borders of Cape Colony, or declare in unqualified terms that no other sovereignty would be tolerated in South Africa. This vacillation between action and passivity gave to the Afri-kaner farmers the priceless opportunity to learn the arts of administration as well as of survival, and to establish roots 'as a free and independent people', working, in the words of Andries Pretorius, 'for the glory of His Name'.

Trekkers:
a bullock wagon
crosses a
mountain.

The insatiable appetites of the great powers: Nelson and Napoleon carve up the world. A Gillray cartoon of 1805.

Chapter Seven

THE AGE OF THE EVANGELICALS

For more than two centuries, British imperial history had been dominated by strenuous competition for overseas trade and plantations, first with Spain and Portugal, then Holland, and finally France. With Waterloo, the wars for overseas dominion came to an end; the rival empires had all but disappeared and Britain's imperial position was unchallenged. Between 1793 and 1815, owing to British naval superiority rather than to any deliberate design, an empire that had, apart from India, been so largely peopled from the British Isles became one with huge areas of non-European stock. An empire whose centre of gravity once rested in the North Atlantic, had become a world-wide aggregation held together by a network of strategic bases encircling both hemispheres.

The spoils of victory might have been even bigger than they were. But both the Prime Minister, Lord Liverpool, and Lord Castlereagh, the Foreign Secretary, were far more interested in constructing a stable Europe than in extending the British Empire. History and instinct told them that a monopoly of colonial power would be unwise. None the less, at the Congress of Vienna they were careful to see that the supremacy of Britain was adequately safeguarded. On treaty matters affecting maritime rights, Castlereagh refused to compromise; he would not even discuss them. As a consequence, Britain was able to retain a unique military predominance.

Gibraltar and Malta together gave Britain tactical command of the western Mediterranean, while a protectorate over the Ionian Islands provided at least an observation post overlooking the Isthmus of Suez and the overland route to India. By taking the Cape and Ceylon from the Dutch and Mauritius from the French, she was able, with the addition of the islands of St Helena and Ascension, to 'service' the longer and most important road to the East. The Dutch East Indies were handed back, but this concession was made not only to avoid the reproach of aiming at a colonial monopoly, but to ensure the friendship of

Gibraltar under attack by Spanish forces, 1782.

Holland against a potentially hostile France. The retention of Trinidad, Tobago and St Lucia and the former Dutch Guiana colonies of Demerara and Esse⁄ quibo provided further useful bases in the Caribbean. Northward lay Bermuda, Halifax, Cape Breton and Newfoundland. Across the Pacific, New South Wales represented a foothold on a continent that Britain did not trouble to claim, far less attempt to occupy. Fortified with bases on every significant trade route and practically immune from serious competition, Britain for the first and only time in her imperial career stood in comfortable 'splendid isolation'.

As for France, most of the work of her eighteenth⁄century sailors and gover⁄ nors had been wiped out. In 1815 little remained of her old empire except Senegal, Martinique, Guadaloupe, a few isolated establishments in India – Pondicherry, Chandernagore, and Karikal on the Coromandel coast – and the small island of Bourbon, safely anchored in the shadow of conquered Mauri⁄ tius. Many years were to elapse before France could again begin to contemplate colonial expansion overseas. Yet in Britain the traditional fear of the hereditary enemy carried over far into the nineteenth century. Even when Napoleon's death on St Helena removed one acute source of anxiety, Whitehall watched with apprehension the movements of every French squadron, trader or survey⁄ ing vessel in overseas waters. Memories of Napoleonic adventures in Egypt

Port Louis, Mauritius, early nineteenth century.

Negro market in Antigua, early nineteenth century.

Sir Stamford Raffles.

lingered; even the memory of Trafalgar could not expunge the horrid vision of a French expeditionary force embarking for the final assault on India.

In fact, the most dangerous enemy of the British Empire was not France, but Russia. Because Russia possessed a Black Sea fleet, she could exert intermittent pressure on British communications with India; hence the necessity of securing the Straits, which represented India's first line of defence, and bolstering Turkey as a buffer state. Similarly, Persia's physical junction with the Russian frontier west of the Caspian Sea invited Russian aggression by land. To arrest Russian progress towards Persia and the land approaches to India's North-West frontier, became as consistent a British objective as the safety of Constantinople. Commercial rivalry was not a major consideration in producing this policy. British statesmen were more concerned with strategy and politics, although only as a means towards the supreme economic end – the security of the route to India. India was the heart of the British Empire. All eastern sea-lanes led to the sub-continent that had become in two centuries the centre of a commercial network covering the whole Indian Ocean and the South China Sea.

After Trafalgar, and especially after the capture of French Mauritius in 1810, any serious threat to Britain's eastern trade routes was remote. Consequently, faced with a deficit in its Indian budget, the East India Company was not long in abandoning Penang, the naval base on the west coast of Malaya, which, since its foundation in 1786, had watched over the Bay of Bengal. The renunciation of Penang was made easier by reason of the fact that Trincomalee, on the north-east coast of newly acquired Ceylon, had the best harbour in the eastern seas. It commanded both the Malabar and Coromandel coasts of India, offering an immediate safeguard against enemy intrusions from either east or west. By keeping Ceylon at the peace, Britain was, therefore, retaining a real, not a fanciful key of empire; its loss, in the words of the governor of the Cape of Good Hope, would 'shake to the foundation, perhaps overturn and destroy the whole fabrick of our oriental opulence and dominion'.

Further east, however, British commerce was far less secure. With the return of Java and Malacca, the Dutch were in a position to control the vital approaches to the China Sea. In contrast to the dwindling spice trade of the Indonesian Archipelago, the tea trade with China had grown by leaps and bounds, most of it channelled through the most important strategic highway in the East – the Straits of Malacca. To secure this convenient corridor to the China coast, Britain needed a naval base, and this was acquired by the impetuous Stamford Raffles, who in January 1819 hoisted the flag of the East India Company on the island of Singapore. Equidistant from the two most important commercial cities in western and eastern Asia, Calcutta and Canton, the greatest free port in the Indian Ocean emerged from the confines of dank jungle.

European factories, Canton; a painting by William Daniell (1769–1837).

Twenty years later, the conquest of Aden was to give Britain control of one more pivot of empire. In the early days of steam, Aden was to be an important fuelling station, as well as a focal point for the trade of the Middle East, but, like Singapore, its greatest value lay in its geographical position as a sentry-box on the Red Sea route to India. British overseas commerce depended on communications kept in repair and safeguarded by well-sited bases. The occupation of Hong Kong in 1842 and the island of Labuan off the coast of North Borneo in 1846 completed the chain of strategic ports running from the Red Sea to the China coast, and fulfilled Britain's commercial aspirations in the Far East.

During the greater part of the nineteenth century, however, no power was in a position to challenge Britain's supremacy at sea. The main tasks of British overseas squadrons were, therefore, to fight the slave trade on the east and west coasts of Africa, and, especially in eastern waters, to keep the peace at sea by putting down piracy. In neither of these efforts were they very successful. In many instances, operations against coastal pirate strongholds, especially in the Persian Gulf, suffered from lack of reliable charts. Inaccurate charts were a greater danger to the navigator than none at all. It was natural, therefore, in a period of peace, to employ young officers to mark the ways to pirate haunts in the Gulf and Indonesian waters, to search for a north-west passage through Arctic wastes, to map the coasts of Newfoundland and eastern Canada, or survey the ill-defined boundaries of the Indian Ocean. Beginning with Captain William Owen in the 1820s, survey work fell into the hands of an unusually competent group of sailors and amateur scientists. Thanks to their courage and endurance, by mid-century the greater part of the coasts and islands between the Cape of Good Hope and the Malayan peninsula had been reliably charted.

The wartime expansion of the Empire involved an enormous extension of imperial authority, without equivalent advances in local representative government. Apart from the West Indies, the only colonial assemblies in existence were in British North America. These, provided by the Canada Act of 1791, were new and untried, and the behaviour of Lower Canada (Quebec) was not such as to win British confidence. In the Caribbean, abuse of self-government by the white planters was eventually to lead to its abrogation.

During the war years after 1793, no other British colonies were given representative institutions, and in 1815 the British government had no intention of changing its policy. Such reluctance was partly owing to the fact that most of the new colonies were conquests, not British settlements; within conquered colonies, government was based on the laws of the conquered. Moreover, the new Empire contained French, Dutch, Spanish and Asiatic peoples, and in view of the recent war with France, it seemed the more necessary to maintain direct executive control over subjects whose loyalty could not be taken for granted.

The basic principles of the system built up after 1815 were, briefly: concentration of power in the hands of the governor; a strict control of the governor by a new department for colonies in London; and finally, the conduct of administration, as far as possible by orders-in-council under the royal prerogative, without recourse to Parliament. Even in the old settled white colonies, although representative bodies might vote taxes and even laws, they could not, until the institution of responsible government in Canada in 1840, control the executive. In other words, colonial governments, whether in conquered or acquired areas, were to be under the close direction of the British government.

The development of a distinct department for colonial affairs came about in this manner. In 1794, under pressure from Revolutionary France, a Secretary of State for War was added to the Cabinet. The Treaty of Amiens in 1801 obviously deflated this office, and in order to provide a peacetime justification for the continuance of the post it became necessary to enlarge the minister's sphere of action; hence the expansion of his title to Secretary of State for War and Colonies. As it happened, however, the renewed outbreak of hostilities in 1802 made the alliance superfluous, and the colonies soon became neglected orphans in a department absorbed in the task of defeating the French. Paradoxically, this state of affairs came to an end in 1812, at a time when in view of external dangers, colonies seemed scarcely to matter. Napoleon was proceeding to invade Russia, and the United States had declared war on the British Isles.

The change was less the doing of the new Prime Minister, Lord Liverpool, than of Lord Bathurst, the Secretary of State for War and Colonies, who was

Administration in a growing empire.

Above: Colonial Office, Downing Street, 1827.

Left: Wellington and Nelson in the Colonial Office, 1805.

Below: High Court of Justice in Kandy, Ceylon, c. 1815.

Colonial stamps in the 1850s.

to hold the post for the next fifteen years. He had none of the fiery drive of his more famous successor, Joseph Chamberlain, but he was the first real Colonial Secretary, and he was ably served by a young and conscientious Under-Secretary, Henry Goulburn, who stayed with him until he was appointed Chief Secretary for Ireland in 1821. 'Bathurst and Goulburn', wrote Helen Taft Manning, 'unquestionably created a Colonial Office where none existed before, and in so doing they performed a task which was essential if the British Empire was to survive.' Under these two men the whole balance of the dual department became gradually weighted in favour of the colonies.

When peace returned in 1814, the Treasury demanded a reduction in the establishment which, at least until 1812, had been almost wholly absorbed in war business. But Bathurst refused to dispense with more than nine or ten of his military officials, and none from the colonial section. The latter was already fully occupied with rapidly growing imperial business, and in accepting the new arrangement, the government committed itself to the maintenance of a Colonial Office as a major department in its own right.

It should be remembered, however, that the new Colonial Secretary was not the only head of a department who could give orders to British officials in the colonies. The Customs, the Treasury, the Post Office and the Ordnance each had local staffs scattered about the Empire, answerable only to their respective departments in London. Hitherto, there had been no co-ordination of these services; each had gone its own way with little or no regard for consistency or the interests of the Empire as a whole. Such a condition was intolerable to Bathurst and Goulburn, and from his bastion in the Cabinet, Bathurst was able, with resolution and some cunning, to win a general supervision over all matters affecting colonies.

In view of the growing range of commitments, he was fortunate in being able to enlist a very able staff of permanent officials. One of the most useful of the original group was James Stephen, Wilberforce's brother-in-law, a lawyer and a member of parliament. As a young man, Stephen had practised law in the West Indies, and almost inevitably his help was sought on touchy legal questions affecting slavery. His son James was also a lawyer. In 1813, aged twenty-four, he followed in the footsteps of his father, and took on the duties of adviser to the Colonial Office in addition to his private practice. Twelve years later, he gave up the Bar and was appointed full-time legal counsellor; in this capacity he dominated the department long before he was made its Permanent Under-Secretary in 1836. There he remained – the so-called Mr Mother Country – until retirement in 1847.

James Stephen Jr was an awkward man of enormous industry, damned by many of his contemporaries as an unbending doctrinaire busy-body. But

Lord Bathurst.   James Stephen Jr.

pedantry and priggishness were more than balanced by a sense of moral obligation toward alien races under the British flag, a crusading faith reflected in his
great work as a reformer. Stephen not only helped to create the modern Civil
Service, he set its enduring standards of probity and public spirit. Under him,
centralization of the apparatus of empire reached its climax. But his guiding
motive was not the crude concentration of authority over the colonies, nor selfish
exploitation on the part of the colonizing state. He was above all else the
champion of the coloured races against oppression by the whites. He became the
personification of Burke's principle of trusteeship for the under-privileged British
subjects, which thenceforward characterized so much of British colonial policy.

THE ABOLITION OF THE SLAVE TRADE AND OF SLAVERY

Nothing more clearly illustrates the closer supervision of colonial affairs than
the debate over the question of slavery. In the eighteenth century, imperial
control had been governed by material acquisitiveness. By the beginning of the
nineteenth century, the direction of British policy was to be influenced by a
weighing of moral benefits in relation to profits, a calculation which involved
the acceptance of a new valuation of human life. Those who admitted the
moral implications of the new principle renounced for ever the notion which

Branding irons: the owner's initials were marked on the slave's back.

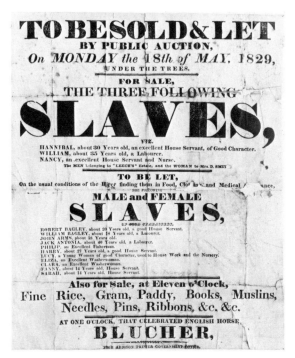

St Helena slave auction bill, 1829.

Aristotle had endorsed for Christians as well as Greeks – that 'many men are born ignorant and slavish and therefore ought to be slaves'. Inevitably they demanded an alteration in the legal status of millions of human beings hitherto regarded as chattels.

Under the Bathurst régime, the Colonial Office fell gradually under the influence of the humanitarians. Bathurst had warm links with the Clapham Sect, so called because the original members of the group (which included Wilberforce) had lived as close neighbours in Clapham. It was this group of Evangelicals, aided by the Quakers, who had been responsible in 1787 for the foundation of a Society for the Abolition of the Slave Trade, and whose philan-thropic zeal was rewarded a year later by the establishment of a settlement for refugee slaves on the West African coast, subsequently to be taken over (1791) by the Sierra Leone Company. Such men of righteous passion could be at times ill-informed and bigoted, but they were responsible for the genesis of a new spirit in the life of Britain that would have been incomprehensible to a genera-tion that applauded the War of Jenkins' Ear. Like Edmund Burke, they battled for a less barbarous policy towards the sufferings, and a more Christian attitude towards the rights, of primitive peoples, whether in India, Africa or North America; and, of portentous significance for the future of the British Empire, during the first three decades of the nineteenth century they had the ear of British governments.

Slave deck:
from a watercolour by
Lieutenant Francis Meynell
(1821–70) in his logbook.

Conditions in a slave ship, 1830.

Model of the slave ship *Brookes*,
prepared for the Wilberforce
committee.

In those years the issue of slavery overshadowed all other purely colonial questions. When Parliament abolished the British slave trade in the spring of 1807 (eight months before the United States), the promoters of the Bill had no intention of demanding the abolition of the institution of slavery. They looked forward to gradual amelioration. Self-interest, it was assumed, would drive the planters to protect their slaves, now that they could not replenish by fresh stock. Actually, the Act of 1807 did not operate as expected. The traffic was not stopped; the slaves had still to be protected against their owners.

In 1811, new amendments were added to the law (which had previously prescribed nothing more severe than heavy fines and confiscation), making slave trading a criminal offence for which the punishment was transportation. It was evident, however, that illicit importation would continue until a rigid registration, requiring a clearly identifiable description of every individual slave, put a stop to smuggling. And James Stephen Sr persuaded his friend and patron, the Prime Minister, Spencer Perceval, to try the experiment in the new colony of Trinidad. Stephen himself prepared the first draft of the order and selected the registrar to implement action on the island.

In 1815, the same system was applied to St Lucia and Mauritius without any special difficulty. It was a different matter to force it upon the older colonies; there it meant interference with long-established rights of self-government, and the Colonial Secretary was reluctant to impose registration by Act of Parliament. Meanwhile, it was agreed to enforce the law in all of the crown colonies, and to recommend it sternly to the self-governing colonies.

Unhappily, in the crown colonies the Colonial Office had to rely on local officials not only to enforce the desired measures, but also to adapt them to local conditions, which meant that there were plenty of opportunities for obstruction. In the self-governing colonies, the assemblies neither accepted nor rejected the recommendations of the Colonial Office, but adopted policies of evasion. They fiddled for time, reviewing their slave laws, making minor changes, but in general maintaining the *status quo*.

In the end, Bathurst, weary of intransigence, ordered the law officers of each colony to introduce Bills of his own making into the local legislature. With the exception of Nevis, every legislature either threw out the Bills or would not allow them to be brought in. Despairing of colonial action, which would pave the way for the gradual elimination of slavery, the anti-slavery crusaders raised the cry of immediate emancipation by Act of Parliament. By May 1832, when Wellington had failed to form a ministry and Grey had been returned to power, it was clear that the planter interests had lost the battle. Thenceforward, their effort was to get the best possible terms. On 1 August 1834, wrote G. M. Trevelyan, all slaves under the British flag were to become free. On the last night of slavery, the negroes in our West Indian Islands went up to the hill-tops to watch the sun rise, bring-ing them freedom as its first rays struck the waters. But far away in the forests of Central Africa, in the heart of darkness yet unexplored, none understood or regarded the day. Yet it was the dark continent which was most deeply affected of all. Before its exploita-tion by Europe had well begun, the most powerful of the nations who were to control its destiny had decided that slavery should not be the relation of the black man to the white.

It was a glorious start for the new reformed Parliament of 1832. Emancipation produced a kind of natural exhilaration; men felt they were at the beginning of a new age, when political action could alter the course of history. 'I often tell the young men who are coming on', remarked Gladstone in 1880, 'that we had a better time than they can have in the next half century. Take one thing only – the abolition of slavery.' Unfortunately, some of the more passionate Victorians pushed virtuous doctrine too far; not until much later did the legitimate claims of the prostrate West Indian sugar-planters, and indeed the population generally, receive sympathetic notice. Free trade had become too closely linked with the moral law.

Actually, the process of emancipation was intended to be a gradual step by step advance under a system of apprenticeship or indenture, leading to complete freedom and, it was hoped, a new-found sense of responsibility. Although the legislatures of Antigua and Bermuda did away with the system almost immediately, elsewhere apprenticeship worked reasonably well, except in Jamaica. There it was abused, and, as a result, general abandonment followed as from 1 August 1838. The final liberation of some 750,000 Caribbean Africans had been achieved.

THE SYSTEMATIC COLONIZERS: AUSTRALIA

It was well that humanitarian doctrines of trusteeship, originating with Burke, and firmly established with the abolition of the slave trade, should have retained their appeal during the period of empire-building after 1815. For the first time in her history, Britain experienced serious population pressures accompanied by growing and widespread unemployment. To Malthus and his followers, poor relief was unsound and wrong; poverty was a consequence of increasing population. In the days before birth control, one practicable solution was to encourage or force the surplus to leave the country. Since the indigent were assumed to be a socially disintegrating element, emigration would act as a national safety-valve; it would not only ease the threat to Britain's subsistence, it would be the means of reducing crime and disorder. Charles Buller, in a moment of whimsy, called the process 'shovelling out the paupers'.

133

But the 'shovelling' had to be carefully organized and directed; systematic emigration only made good sense if the receiving areas were parts of the British Empire. In 1830, advanced liberals or radical imperialists, such as Wakefield, Molesworth, Buller, Grote and Durham, formed themselves into the National Colonization Society. Their object was not simply to relieve population pressures; they hoped to give decent and ambitious labouring folk a chance to better themselves in the colonies, and at the same time strengthen the links of sentiment and interest that tied their settlements to the mother country.

In the beginning, however, it looked as though the eastern cities and western plains of the United States would divert part of the projected imperial stream. Between 1815 and 1830, thousands of British emigrants poured into the Mississippi Valley, adding to the frontier numbers that impelled the creation of five new states. But greater numbers were soon on their way to Canada, chiefly under schemes of planned emigration. On an average, probably 30,000 settlers a year embarked from the Highlands of Scotland, where the agrarian revolution was in progress, and many thousands fled from southern Ireland, especially after the famine of 1833. Most of them went to Upper Canada, where in 1824 John Galt, poet and novelist, had established his Canada Company, with over 1,000,000 acres available to immigrant farmers. The cities of Guelph, Galt and Goderich are a testimony to his perseverance and acumen. By the end of the 1840s, the population of the newly united Upper and Lower Canada was nearly 1,500,000, of which total the French-Canadian share of some 700,000 was based chiefly upon natural increase.

Unfortunately, the lure of free land continued to draw many prospective British settlers over the Canadian border and south into the Mississippi Valley. During the 1830s, only about a third of the newcomers to Upper Canada remained in that province, and the situation worsened with the coming of the railways. The Grand Trunk Railway, with its terminus at a border point on Lake Huron, became after its completion in 1853 an important traffic funnel in the development of the American north-west.

The Australian stream was thinner; but the growth of sheep-farming brought increasing numbers of free immigrants, and from 1824 onwards, land companies began to operate in tillable areas. It is worth noting that the first wholly free settlement was established in Western Australia, at Swan River near Perth in 1829. By 1833, the population of New South Wales was 60,000, of whom 40 per cent were convicts. By 1850, it was 265,000, and the percentage of convicts almost negligible.

The growth of the wool industry was, as has been noticed, the vital factor in early Australian history. Before the gold discoveries of 1851, wool-growers had dominated the country's commercial and political development, immigration and land distribution being carried out almost entirely in their interests. For fifty years, John Macarthur was the central figure. He not only introduced ploughing, but in 1796 set about a series of experiments in sheep-breeding based on merino sheep from Cape Colony. By 1794 agriculture had taken root, though it scarcely amounted to subsistence farming. In the early days famine was never far away. Indeed, agriculture deteriorated even in districts well suited to it. In 1833 only about 60,000 acres were under cultivation – about one acre per inhabitant; by 1850, the proportion was barely three-quarters of an acre per head. In 1850 seven-eighths of the total agricultural production of New South Wales was wool. Except at shearing-time, wool required less labour than wheat; wool was easily compressible and easily carried over narrow primitive roads and hill country seventy or so miles to Sydney. Similarly, cattle-breeding fell gradually behind sheep-farming. In 1821 the settlements had 100,000 cattle to 290,000 sheep; in 1850, the round numbers were 1,739,000 and 13,000,000 respectively.

John Macarthur.

Sheep-shearing in Australia, 1874.

Emigrants leave for Australia, 1869.

The Beyers and Holter-mann nugget, the largest mass of reef gold ever dis-covered, was found in New South Wales in 1872.

A hundred years later, Australians were still facing the urgent task of growing more food to supply the needs of a rapidly increasing population. The relatively high price of wool, the recurrence of droughts and the capital expenditure required for economic large-scale farming threatened to reduce further the proportionate level of beef and wheat production. In 1850, the omnipotence of King Wool had gone unchallenged. By the beginning of the twentieth century, however, scientific research was to demonstrate, as in the West Indies, how diseases and pests could be eradicated, deficiencies of soil and climate overcome, and grazing pastures improved by periodic return to crop. And a few years later, experts were to bear witness that beef cattle in the semi-arid plains of northern Australia might be increased by nearly 40 per cent, if stations were efficiently watered and fenced and adequate rail facilities provided to the fattening pastures of the south-east.

The gold-strikes scarcely altered the basis of the Australian economy, which continued to rest on sheep. Their main effect was to hoist population. In one decade, the total grew from 405,000 to well over 1,000,000, and in the colony of Victoria, separated from the parent New South Wales in 1852, from 76,000 to 540,000. The paradoxical result of this immigration was to make Australian society substantially urban. Once his fortune was made, the 'digger' preferred the bright lights of metropolitan existence, and his gold turned Sydney and Melbourne into large cities. Within a generation, Melbourne was larger than any city in the British Isles except London, Manchester, Liverpool and Glasgow, although it had yet to reach the cultural heights of colonial Philadelphia or Boston.

In other words, neither the 'miner's frontier' nor the 'sheep-grazier's frontier' was followed by settlement. Pastoral fringes took root in the hinterland, but

The Forest Creek diggings, 1852.

The growth of towns: Sydney in the late nineteenth century.

Homestead in Gulgong,
New South Wales,
one of many new
towns which sprang up
in the 1870s.

communities were rarely established. The dry, semi-deserts forced a wide dispersion of men and sheep. Station life was not village or small-town life, but one of isolated huts and homesteads. The settler looked to the coast and to a coastal city, whence came his supplies, and to which his wool was sent. The sheep-graziers had common interests as a class, but unlike Canadians they never built a true rural society.

Obviously, any plan of British emigration to Australia based on agricultural communities would amount to little in sheep-grazing areas like New South Wales. The main effort of the systematic colonizers, led by Edward Gibbon Wakefield, was made in areas further west. Wakefield was concerned with the national problem of surplus population, but more important to himself and his colleagues was the creation of new producing areas and markets overseas, which would eventually become self-governing colonies. Industrial Britain needed more cheap food and raw materials to extend her industrialization; such an expansion through colonization would augment British prosperity by creating new markets. Admittedly, the required large-scale emigration would cost a good deal of money, but Wakefield argued that, while loans from the British government would be necessary in the initial phases of settlement, eventually the scheme could be self-supporting. In the long run, total expenses would be met through the operation of his land system. The essence of the scheme was the sale of waste lands at a fixed and sufficiently high price to prevent easy purchase. Since the immigrant colonists would ordinarily not have the money to buy farms and implements on arrival, they would have to work as labourers for a few years before becoming owners. In brief, the plan promised safety for the investing capitalist and hope for the ambitious working man.

In 1833, Wakefield organized a company to sell lands in South Australia under the auspices of the National Colonization Society. No convict labour was to be used; the returns from sales were to be expended on the transport of immigrants; when 10,000 settlers had arrived, they were to be granted self-government. Unfortunately, the machinery of perpetual motion failed to function, and the anaemic colony remained insolvent until its finances were restored by a shrewd and enterprising governor, Sir George Grey. In South Australia as elsewhere, Wakefield's theories were never fully applied; only in New Zealand can he be credited with substantial success. But the main snags were always obvious: variations in the quality of the land to be auctioned, and above all, the absence of sufficient capital.

Undoubtedly, Wakefield suffered from a lack of mental balance which was bound to restrict his achievement. On the other hand, he had vision and

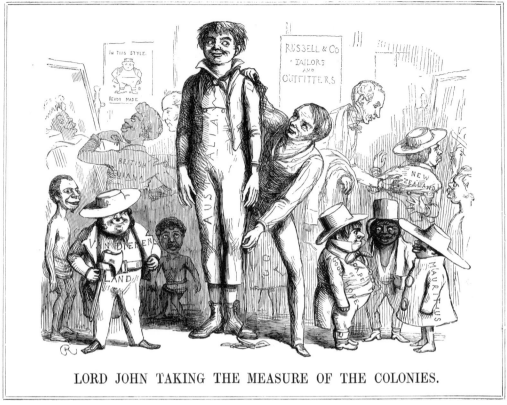

LORD JOHN TAKING THE MEASURE OF THE COLONIES.

Lord John Russell, the Prime Minister, 'taking the measure of the colonies', 1850.

enthusiasm, and was the main inspiration of the distinguished group of reformers who suspected the capacity of Whitehall's bureaucracy to deal generously with the problems of a maturing empire. It is possible that his personal influence on imperial policy has been exaggerated; yet this curious and far from attractive human being not only directed public interest to the needs and benefits of empire, he brought life to voluntary emigration organizations and energized previously indifferent or lethargic statesmen. Lord John Russell and his Colonial Secretary, the third Earl Grey, were not unaffected by his ideas. Lord Durham, despite the fervent opposition of political critics, took Wakefield with him to Canada, where he helped Charles Buller to prepare one of the most important parts of the famous Durham Report – that on land policy. But above all else, in the era of pessimism that accompanied the growth of free trade, and when the denigration of colonies had become a fashion, Wakefield and his school of radical imperialists provided sufficient fire to keep alive a connection between the older white colonies and the mother country that was beginning to grow cold.

139

The first half of the nineteenth century might well be called the Age of the Missionaries. The beginnings of the movement roughly coincided with the anti⁄slavery crusade, and both had roots in the same robust Evangelicalism. In some respects missionary work encouraged colonial expansion, and, because Evangelical sympathizers were near the heart of government, cynics have often referred to missionary efforts overseas as a form of aggressive cultural imperialism. But neither the Baptist Missionary Society (1792), the London Missionary Society (1795), the Church Missionary Society (1799), nor the British and Foreign Bible Society (1804) had or wished to have any connection with government. In 1840 John Campbell wrote: 'The soldier and the missionary were not mess⁄mates. Gun⁄powder and the gospels were not carried in the same packet. The alternative to proselytism was not the gibbet.' The church often needed official support and protection, but in aboriginal lands especially, its agents feared the consequences of secular oppression and moral pollution. 'Must we not', cried Wilberforce in 1813 (with reference to India), '. . . endeavour to raise these wretched beings out of their present miserable con⁄dition, and above all, to communicate to them those blessed truths, which would not only improve their understandings and elevate their minds, but would, in ten thousand ways, promote their temporal well⁄being, and point out to them a sure path to everlasting happiness.'

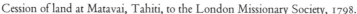

Cession of land at Matavai, Tahiti, to the London Missionary Society, 1798.

John Williams, the missionary, killed on the beach at Erromanga, New Hebrides, in 1839.

By the beginning of the nineteenth century, Western Christianity was following the flag – or occasionally preceding it – into the Pacific Ocean. With a talent for pioneer adventure comparable to that of the early Jesuits in North America, the missionaries won the confidence of barbarous chiefs or, as sometimes happened, lost their lives in the attempt. Most of them were good men, some were temperamentally unfitted for so exacting a life, a few were outstanding leaders and teachers; nearly all, as soldiers of the Cross, tended to be over-confident in their beliefs and therefore dogmatic in their approach to so-called 'inferior' religions. The benefits of Christianity could scarcely be conferred in full on peoples worshipping strange gods and clinging to grotesque customs. Denial of the validity of ancient faiths like Hinduism was an understandable, but none the less dangerous mistake.

New Zealand is probably the best example of a British colony where missionary societies and systematic colonizers met and clashed. As in South Africa, the missionaries usually took the part of the natives against the settlers and traders; and not infrequently they opposed at home as well as on the spot any disagreeable form of government interference. This antipathy to governmental intervention, once the sect or society had established a foothold, was largely based on the fear that the Maori peoples might be contaminated by too much commercial and bureaucratic attention.

The Maoris were one of the larger branches of the Polynesian tree. About a thousand years ago, they moved across the Pacific from the Society Islands and landed in New Zealand. Four hundred years later they came in substantial numbers, conquering the original inhabitants, the Moriori. Nearly five centuries later, on Christmas Day 1814, Samuel Marsden landed unopposed among a warlike but essentially religious people, and to the amazement of the heavily armed warriors on the beach, declared: 'Fear not, behold I bring you glad tidings of great joy which shall be to all people.' The missionary conquest of New Zealand had begun.

During the next few years, the country remained a picturesque but violent paradise. The missionaries had not yet tranquillized the Maoris, and Europeans were haunted by the memory of the *Boyd*, whose crew had been massacred in 1809. Whalers, sealers and traders, some of them escaped convicts from Australia, following in the train of the missionaries, sought pleasure and profits. Bullying, wheedling and offering their women, local chieftains competed for British manufactures, suffering rude disillusionment when trinkets rather than muskets proved sole payment for the much-sought preserved heads.

In 1836 Wakefield described New Zealand as the fittest country in the world for colonization.

Adventurers go from New South Wales and Van Diemen's land . . . We are, I think, going to colonize New Zealand, but are doing so in a most slovenly and disgraceful manner.

In 1837 Wakefield, Durham, Molesworth and Francis Baring founded the New Zealand Association for the purpose of settling New Zealand systematically and economically. Under the scheme, the Maoris were assured of government protection. The crown was to appoint an Inspector of Natives, and a tenth of all land purchased was to be set aside as an inalienable native reserve. Wakefield was willing to co-operate with the missionaries, but the Church Missionary Society opposed the project tooth and nail. The missionaries wanted to keep the islands as a native sanctuary:

Only let New Zealand be spared from colonization and the Mission have its free and unrestricted course for half a century or more, and the great political and moral problem will be solved – of a people passing from a barbarous to a civilized state, through the agency of Europeans, with the complete preservation of the Aboriginal race, and of their national independence and sovereignty.

The Church Missionary Society had powerful allies in government circles; both Lord Glenelg, the Colonial Secretary, and James Stephen were members of the council. Consequently, the efforts of the New Zealand Association were

London Published by Alexr Hogg at the Kings Arms Nᵒ 16 Paternoster Row.

A curiously ARCHED ROCK *on the Coast of New Zealand.*

A New Zealand Chief, whose head is ingeniously TATAWED, *and a Subaltern Warrior of the same Country.*

New Zealand and the Maoris; from a late eighteenth-century engraving.

William Hobson.

temporarily halted. In 1839, however, the Association decided to go ahead and colonize New Zealand without the sanction of the Colonial Office. It was this action, at a time when the French were strongly suspected of harbouring designs on the islands, that forced the hand of the British government. In January 1840 the annexation of New Zealand to the crown was reluctantly proclaimed.

Captain William Hobson was sent from Sydney to effect the transfer, and to act as Lieutenant-Governor under the administration of New South Wales. With the help of the missionaries, he assembled a congress of Maori chiefs and concluded the Treaty of Waitangi, whereby the chiefs, in surrendering rights of sovereignty, were guaranteed full possession of their lands. The crown possessed an 'exclusive right of pre-emption', but only over such lands that the proprietors were willing to sell at prices agreed between themselves and government agents.

Inevitably, the processes of settlement became complicated. On the one hand, there were the emigrants who wanted to colonize and who were only too willing to ride over the tangled Maori rules of land tenure. In fact, New Zealand Association agents went ahead, and concluded contracts on highly dubious evidence of title before the government had time to investigate; moreover, they often paid for the land with blankets, gunpowder and cheap jewellery. On the other hand, there were the sensitive and bellicose Maoris, who rapidly learned to exploit the complications of English law and Maori custom, and whose general attitude to colonization tended, like that of the missionaries, to be

Baptism of the Maori chief Te Puni in Otahi church, New Zealand, 1853.

Auckland in 1857.

dog-in-the-manger. To make matters worse, there was a serious lack of capital. Success in colonization depended, as Wakefield had said, on an adequate supply of land, labour and capital. The crown's right of pre-emption under the Treaty of Waitangi was obviously not affected by a shortage of land, but the local government could not afford to buy on a large scale, and with small sales to settlers there was little money available for emigration. The little that had accrued was swallowed up by civil administration. Consequently, immigration declined; indeed, for a time it practically came to a stop.

Happily for the islands, Sir George Grey was called from South Australia in 1854, and he proved himself, in very tricky circumstances, to be a firm and fair governor. He was able, by purchase, to obtain large areas from local chiefs, mainly in unoccupied regions, and these were transferred to the Association for settlement. By 1850, troubles had been smoothed over, and a precarious peace endured until renewed crises over land led, after 1860, to ten years of intermittent war.

Meanwhile, the Free Church of Scotland settled Otago near the borders of Antarctica, while the Society for the Propagation of the Gospel took a hand in developing Canterbury province. By 1852, when the New Zealand Company resigned its charter, there were 30,000 settlers living in six distinct settlements, Auckland, Taranaki and Wellington on the North Island, Nelson,

Canterbury and Otago on the South. Geographically, these two islands were closer together than the settlements along the far-flung Australian coastline, where colonial life was focused in the principal seaports, which were also the capitals. Yet, for nearly twenty-five years after the grant of responsible government (1852), they were administered as a loose federation. Not until 1876, after a prolonged struggle between provincialists and centralists, were the six provincial councils abolished to make New Zealand a unitary rather than a federal state.

During this time little or no official interest was taken in the myriad island clusters of the neighbouring Pacific. So long as other powers did not compete for settlement, Whitehall was content to base a policy of non-intervention on the ascendancy of the Royal Navy, plus the fact that distance, the ferocity of many of the inhabitants and limited resources offered few inducements to British trade. Eventually, of course, the policy of non-intervention broke down. There were just enough natural products in the islands and in south Pacific waters to attract specialized commercial interests from Great Britain and New South Wales, and resulting contacts between European whalers and traders and the native peoples were bound sooner or later to raise important administrative problems. Moreover, when missionaries demanded protection in the islands they were seeking to christianize, or complained that traders and whalers were committing crimes with impunity, British governments were forced to take notice.

Missionary and his wife, a mid nineteenth-century wood-carving from the Queen Charlotte Islands, off British Columbia.

As early as 1836, the London Missionary Society sent thirty missionaries to Tahiti and Tonga; other missionary bodies, including French Roman Catholics (who came out after the French annexation of Tahiti in 1843), followed during the next few years. In 1849, the Church Missionary Society undertook the hazardous task of proselytizing the unfriendly inhabitants of Melanesia. Sure in their faith and conscious of their destiny as pioneers of the Cross, the chosen few faced a life of self-imposed exile, persistent discomfort and frequent peril, for rewards which were not always visible in terms of genuine conversions. Unlike their New Zealand confrères, most of them favoured annexation as a means of shielding the natives from the barbarities of the traders. In the long run, however, it was the need not only to protect the natives, but to protect the traders against foreign competition, that was respon-sible for a *minimum* British intervention in the Pacific. It was a policy founded on cautious self-restraint that was to end finally with the abandonment of any form of 'limited liability'.

By the end of the fifties, marketing conditions had improved, and with increased competition from European rivals, the process of removing the brakes on imperial expansion was bound to be examined. Commercial safeguards such as extra-consular jurisdiction, and the formation of local island governments, were at first frowned upon. Not until the late sixties, after Australia became involved in the black Kanaka labour trade (at the worst, scarcely more humane than the African slave trade), and when British, Australian and New Zealand interests began to invest heavily in island export projects, did the British government begin to reconsider their attitude towards the *status quo* in the Pacific, and prepare to take legislative action.

The problem came to a head in 1871, when Bishop Patteson was murdered on one of the islands in the Santa Cruz group. For a moment, the tragedy concentrated public attention on island conditions bordering on anarchy in the Pacific, and it was responsible for the Act of Parliament of 1872 condemning kidnapping, requiring licences for the conscription and transport of native labour, and defining procedures for the trial of offenders. A second Act appointed a High Commissioner for the Western Pacific, who was given authority over all British subjects, with power to hold local courts and enforce regulations. The culmination of this volte-face came in 1874 with the annexation of Fiji, which became the headquarters of the High Commissioner, who had jurisdiction over all the islands of Polynesia and Melanesia not already annexed by other powers. Since most of them had not been occupied by rival Europeans or Americans, in effect they came under British supervision, a form of protectorate that broadened twenty years later into the Western Pacific High Commission.

Under an order-in-council of 1893, the High Commission's authority was extended to embrace Tonga, Samoa, the Union, Phoenix, Ellice and Gilbert Islands, the Marshalls, the Carolines, the Solomons, Santa Cruz, Rotuma, New Guinea (east of 143° E), New Britain, New Ireland, and the Louisiade Archipelago, provided they were not already within the jurisdiction of a civilized power. Any other islands in the western Pacific not within the limits of Fiji, Queensland or New South Wales, 'and not being within the jurisdiction of any civilized power', were also included in the Commission's domain. Throughout this vast and fluctuating area, a centralizing agency of government and law could now attempt the almost impossible task of administering all British islands, with the exception of Fiji and those under the jurisdiction of the Australian colonies. Legislative power was left in the hands of the High Commissioner, who could make laws in the form of queen's regulations, except on matters where his authority was specifically restricted.

The substantial result of the order-in-council of 1893 was the establishment of a framework of colonial jurisdiction over territories hitherto regarded as no-man's-land. British policy had, in fact, gone into reverse. After a century of determined resistance to political responsibilities in the Pacific, Britain, under the challenge of foreign competition, had renounced her cherished principle of *laissez-faire* and organized what amounted to a new colony of Southern Oceania.

The diverse appeal of two civilizations.
Gothic architecture comes to India: Victoria Railway Terminus, Bombay; from a watercolour of 1878.
India fires the imagination of England: the Royal Pavilion, Brighton, completed in 1821.

Chapter Eight

THE AGE OF DISILLUSIONMENT

Trade remained the mainspring of the British Empire. As J.L. Morison put it: 'Commerce as soon as it leaves the domestic sphere becomes really a branch of government; what we call empire is as much the expansion of national trade, as it is the overseas settlement of British subjects.' Trade demanded the rule of law and order, and often against the wishes of the home authorities, this meant territorial extensions for the sake of peaceful frontiers. In India, between the régimes of Lord Wellesley and Dalhousie, a sub-continent was brought under British rule; a handful governed hundreds of millions.

Expansion produced successive problems in the art of governing alien populations and revealed the tremendous gap between civilizations. In matters of government involving racial cleavages it was extremely important to pick the right man. Britain stood fairly high in administrative talent, but time and time again brilliant achievement was marred by folly – a slip in common courtesy, a touch that offended – or blind stupidity. In the history of empire, good manners proved to be as important to enduring imperial stability as ideas or administrative ability; and good manners assumed an essential imagination and sympathy. In India, as Annie Besant once remarked, the problem was fundamentally one of India's pride and Britain's arrogance, an assertion which if sound would amply justify the aphorism, that self-government is always to be preferred to good government.

The problem of race or nationality was to complicate the whole process of evolving empire after 1815. The conquered peoples, even those of highly civilized origins, such as the Hindus or the French, were ignorant of the arts of self-government. Yet, they had become part of a union called the British Empire, wherein homogeneity of race, religion or culture was not demanded. In tropical colonies inhabited usually by large and illiterate native populations, it was clear early in the nineteenth century that even limited self-government as practised in the former American colonies could mean oppressive control by a white minority; under the compulsions of the new humanitarianism, supported by missionary effort, a radical change in traditional policy was imperative, and, as we have seen, it took the form of a crown colony system, whereby the governor and his council were responsible not to a popular assembly but to the Secretary of State for War and Colonies, and through him to the British Parliament.

At first glance, the new colonial policy might appear retrogressive; but whatever the blunders committed by the Colonial Office, the ideal of trusteeship was henceforward basic to imperial conduct. Volumes of parliamentary papers testify to the probing activities of committees, which over the next half-century scrutinized conditions in under-developed communities. The growth of a sense of moral responsibility for the underdog was gradual, at home as overseas, but the work of the reformers did pave the way for a twentieth-century doctrine, namely, that the claims of imperial advantage must take second place to those of colonial economic and social betterment.

But the older colonies of settlement were hardly likely to be content for long with a system which provided for tighter rather than more relaxed political and economic controls from London. Almost inevitably, after the passage of the Constitutional Act of 1791, the first serious agitations to break from the bonds of centralized administration occurred in the two Canadas, where executive authority had been most carefully guarded against the hazards of popular intervention, partly because of the presence of a French population in the Lower province, and partly owing to the proximity of the acquisitive American republic, that was soon to declare its Manifest Destiny.

Although it was mixed up with racial unrest and bitterness, political consciousness was growing apace in the Canadas. The problem was essentially one of reconciling self-government with imperial supremacy, and while many of the grievances were economic, there existed, as in Britain, an abounding trust in political effort. The popular assumption was: 'Give us the power, and we can change the system.' In English Upper Canada it was assumed that grievances connected with land development, clergy reserves, tariffs and the monopolistic authority of a few entrenched families could be solved by giving political control to the assembly. Hence the cry for responsible government and the demand that the executive be made responsible to the representatives of the people, as in Britain.

In contrast to the Upper province, the popular movement in Lower Canada, as we have seen, was more racial than political in its aims. Race consciousness was stronger than the love of liberty for its own sake, and when

The spread of British administration in Canada: the Governor of Assiniboia in Saskatchewan and leaders of the Chippewa tribe in council at Fort Douglas, 1823.

the War of 1812 was over, the cry for constitutional reform became merely cover for the demands of race nationalism. Both provinces shared real grievances; the assemblies of both fought against a bigoted governing group and a privileged social class who used the power of patronage for their own ends; both sought enlarged powers for their elected representatives. The real gulf lay not between differing constitutional objectives, but in political honesty.

The rising of 1837 did not deserve to be called a rebellion; only small sections of the population participated. It was never dangerous, although civil conflict of any sort might have encouraged invasion from the United States. The rebellion, so called, was chiefly the work of a few extremists. In Lower Canada it did not represent militant French-Canadian nationalism; the Roman Catholic Church refused to back it. Indeed, the Bishop of Montreal spoke about 'the sin of rebellion', a dictum which made certain its speedy collapse. In Upper Canada it was planned more elaborately, but doomed to greater failure. The inept and eccentric Lieutenant-Governor, Sir Francis Bond Head, purposely tempted the rebels to action in order to destroy them. Firm and resolute authority in the beginning could have prevented bloodshed and retribution.

News of the rebellion reached England about Christmas-time, 1837. On the assembling of Parliament in January 1838, Lord John Russell introduced a Bill making temporary provision for the government of Lower Canada; its constitution was suspended until November 1842. Meanwhile, Lord Durham was appointed head of a mission of investigation. As governor-in-chief of five provinces, this Curzon-like potentate regarded himself as a sort of Indian viceroy. Durham had brains and imagination, but he was not politically adroit. His staff appointments drew particular criticism. Charles Buller, a student of Carlyle, was made Chief Secretary, specializing in land reform; Thomas Turton, the legal adviser, had gained some notoriety in the divorce court, something which Victorian England remembered; Edward Gibbon Wakefield, the expert on colonial immigration, had run off with an heiress under the age of consent; her enraged parents had pursued him and he had been clapped in jail. Despite his peculiar genius, that episode was not forgotten.

Durham reached Quebec at the end of May 1838; he sailed for home on the first day of November. His famous report was completed in the following February, scarcely a year before his death. It was an inauspicious time to talk about the mother country's obligations to her colonies. While amateur econo-mists prepared balance sheets showing the staggering costs of administering ungrateful colonies, nervous politicians were beginning to talk about the pecuniary advantages of easing them out of the Empire.

On the basis of a first-rate piece of research which was, in its final com-position, the work of one man, Durham challenged his countrymen to face their responsibilities and accept the fact that certain maturing colonies were qualified to run their concerns more effectively than an imperial power some 3000 miles away. The concession of self-government might conceivably lead to an eventual break-up of the Empire, but was there any promising alternative apart from a second American Revolution? This unambiguous advice did not embody a highly original solution, but as an exposition of the principles of local self-government, it was far ahead of any other British statesman's conception of the ends of imperial evolution. The Durham Report recommended simply that the Cabinet be made responsible to the majority in the assembly on issues of colonial concern, and it insisted on the compatibility of this notion with the imperial connection.

There is a natural inclination to think of the past in terms of the present, to assume that what has happened was bound to happen – that a colony was bound to be a dominion, and that an empire was bound to turn into a commonwealth. No approach to the evolution of the British Empire could be more unreal, more unhistorical. Indeed, the concept of colonial self-government which was precipitated by the study of a minor Canadian rebellion in 1837

Canadian rebels at Beauharnois, Quebec, 1837.   First Earl of Durham.

was only barely grasped by the man who officially proposed it – the first Earl of Durham.

Today it is not difficult to recognize that the Durham Report of 1839 was a great, if not the greatest landmark in the history of the British Empire. It presented the alternative to revolution – namely, evolution towards dominion status through the grant of internal self-government. But at the time there was no such assumption of inevitable progress towards a final destiny. There were substantial reservations laid down by Lord Durham himself, which left, for example, the regulation of trade and foreign affairs in the hands of the mother country; likewise, the form of government, the disposal of public lands and the determination of immigration policy. Most of these imperial reservations were short-lived, a circumstance which might suggest that they represented the last tired efforts of retreating vested interests. In fact, they were deliberate limitations of local autonomy, approved, if not taken for granted at the time, in Canada as well as in Britain.

It was many years before politicians on either side of the ocean realized the full implications of the Durham Report. Until well into the second decade of

153

the twentieth century, problems of foreign policy, despite the angry controversies that they aroused, were not regarded as being strictly colonial concerns; and it was assumed in the middle of the nineteenth century that, if empire meant anything, a colony should *not* have complete control over its domestic trade regulations. As late as 1849, the Canadian Minister of Finance, Francis Hincks, argued that to set up a protective tariff in Canada would be equivalent to a declaration of independence. What inducement, he said, would England have to maintain any connection with Canada if she were barred from the colony's market?

Durham's second major recommendation – union of Upper and Lower Canada under a single government with one legislature – was the most vulnerable part of his report. He wanted not only a union of parliaments, but an amalgamation of peoples. Indeed, he advised the gradual adoption of English as the one officially recognized language, and he advocated parliamentary 'representation by population', since he believed that the British inhabitants of the colony would soon outnumber their neighbours on the Lower St Lawrence. In short, Durham wanted to swamp the French and submerge their nationality. Like the elder Pitt, he wanted an empire for the Anglo-Saxon: 'God has given the North American continent as the ample appanage of the British race.' Fragments of other nationalities had no place in that ideal. For such presumptuous counsel, French Canada has never forgiven him. But entirely apart from its lack of sensitivity, Durham's recommendation was entirely impracticable. He failed to appreciate how deep and tenacious were the roots of French Canada; he underestimated the resistant quality of French-Canadian nationality, and, it should be added, the fertility of a race whose crusading slogan soon became: 'La revanche des berceaux' – more babies.

Meanwhile, there were outcries by the ruling élite in Upper Canada and by French nationalists in Lower Canada. There was bitter opposition by the Tories in England and fear on the part of all, whether Tory or Whig. To whom, said Lord John Russell, should the government be responsible – to the crown or to the Canadians? If to the colonial ministers, the result is an independent country, and the Empire is ruined! The years that followed were to reveal the frightened efforts of British statesmen to try and reconcile that painful anomaly – colonial self-government and imperial unity.

The final settlement did not come until 1848, when the governor, Lord Elgin, accepted an Anglo-French alliance – the Baldwin-La Fontaine administration – dependent for its existence on the favour of the newly amalgamated assembly. It meant the end of the struggle for responsible government, a struggle which had provoked just as many battles against conservative Canadians who feared certain unhealthy aspects of American democracy, as against the bureaucrats of an over-cautious mother country. Indeed, it is fair to say that self-government in Canada was achieved and the way opened towards independent nationhood without a revolution, because Canadian leaders, disdaining republican models, turned towards British parliamentary procedures.

Meanwhile, 'responsible government' faced its first, and what proved to be its final test. In 1849 the new government submitted for approval of the assembly the Rebellion Losses Bill, a measure which authorized payment of claims to those who had suffered injury during the troubles in the French-speaking Lower province. In all probability, many of the applicants were rebels; but the Bill was passed, and Lord Elgin signed it. As a consequence, he was rotten-egged, and the mob burned the Houses of Parliament in Montreal. But the essential issue, self-government, even if it meant a piece of dubious legislation, had triumphed. By 1855, the practice had been accepted and applied in Australia and New Zealand, and was to find its way in the future to other dominions of the British Empire.

Burning of the Houses of Parliament in Montreal, 1849.

The Industrial Revolution is the conspicuous watershed in modern British history. Coal, iron and steam, ships and railways, transformed the whole structure of the economy, reshaped the social order, and laid the foundations of an empire that was to become a world-wide business concern. By the time of Waterloo, the first phase of a revolution which put local industry a generation ahead of continental rivals was nearing completion. The consequent movement in favour of freer trade was influenced by the exigencies of war after 1793, but the chief impetus came as the result of the creation of a new class in British society. The adoption of machinery for cotton-spinning, the use of steam as motive power, and the rapid development of coal-mining, iron-smelting and engineering – all these technical advances were proceeding under the guidance of self-confident manufacturers and ambitious merchants.

Men who were dominated by the new wealth and opportunities of the factory age were unable to respect the sacrosanct traditions of the past which still influenced the majority of the old governing classes. Bitterly critical of all institutions or laws which might stand in the way of their personal advancement, they demanded a free field for the instruments and products of the Industrial Revolution. The manufacturers had no need to fear competition in foreign markets; the world was their oyster to open and exploit, and they wanted to get their raw materials and food on the cheapest possible terms. It was obvious to astute observers in Westminster, as they watched the chimneys in the Midlands belching more and more smoke, that sooner or later radical adjustments would have to be made in the commercial as well as in the political sphere. Indeed, the subsequent paring away of the ancient trade and navigation system and the reduction of British political supremacy in the colonial field were part and parcel of the same process. The final steps in the establishment of free trade were to follow quickly the achievement of colonial self-government.

During the reigns of William and Anne, Tory political thinkers had advocated policies of freer trade, but under the Whigs, who began a long period of power after the Treaty of Utrecht, faith in mercantilist principles of high protection and exclusive colonial exploitation was renewed. Not until after the middle of the eighteenth century were these common European doctrines challenged; in France a group of intellectuals known as 'physiocrats' were responsible for inventing the phrase *laissez-faire*, which was to become a colloquialism in nineteenth-century Britain. Their teachings were familiar to a Glasgow professor called Adam Smith, whose *Theory of Moral Sentiments* had given him a considerable reputation as a scholar. Smith met the physiocrats and the equally iconoclastic encyclopaedists during a brief sojourn in France. On his return to

Adam Smith.

The new wealth: *Dividend Day at the Bank*, 1859.

Scotland in 1766, he settled down to pursue his exhaustive study of commercial policy, which was published in 1776 as an *Inquiry into the Nature and Causes of the Wealth of Nations*. It is possible, according to C.R. Fay, to anticipate in *The Wealth of Nations* the whole story of free trade from the American Revolution to the end of the nineteenth century.

Smith's examination of the Navigation Acts and other instruments and agencies of the Old Colonial System aimed at demonstrating that traditional notions about the balance of trade were fallacious, that the wealth derived from overseas trade was the result of an exchange of goods and had nothing to do with territorial possession. In short, age-old attempts to achieve imperial self-sufficiency impeded the natural flow of trade and handicapped rather than safeguarded the growth of national strength.

In questioning the value of overseas possessions, Smith did not, however, deny the importance of coastal trading posts or factories. Nor did he doubt the advantages of an exclusive colonial trade in certain indispensable overseas products. Such articles enumerated under the Navigation Acts could be obtained, under the British monopoly, more cheaply than by rival states, which often had to import them from Britain. None the less, argued Smith, such an advantage was obtained only at the cost of rejecting a higher absolute advantage.

157

If other European nations could trade freely with British colonies, colonial exports generally would be available at lower prices. In the broadest sense, by excluding other nations from any share in colonial commerce, Britain was submitting to a relative disadvantage in almost every other branch of trade.

Adam Smith's critical appraisal of the trade and navigation laws was widely acclaimed, but even if widely read, its incisive message could scarcely have had any immediate effect on a venerable system whose strongest appeal was to the emotions. Deep-seated prejudices are always difficult to uproot, even when their unsoundness can be scientifically demonstrated. So long as a monopoly of the colonial carrying trade was regarded as a source of wealth and the foundation of national security, all arguments in favour of a freer commerce were bound to beat against that doctrine in vain. The reformers could only attempt to shake traditional faith in the navigation laws by demonstrating that the old protective system handicapped the increase of national wealth without safeguarding Britain's supremacy at sea. They had to prove that Britain owed her present carrying trade to the superiority of her manufactures rather than to any legislative restriction, and that expanding profits did not necessarily mean loss of security.

As it happened, evidence was forthcoming that the nation need not be weakened by a breaching of the traditional security code. During the Napoleonic Wars, concessions to neutral shipping had followed one after another; such relaxations in the interests of survival had in no way jeopardized British supremacy at sea; nor, when peace came, did they appear to have affected British commerce adversely. Although the modifications were the result of accident rather than design, declared the President of the Board of Trade in 1822, who would say 'that the interests of either commerce or navigation have suffered; or rather who will deny that they have materially benefited by the freedom which they have thus enjoyed'. Because there was no alternative in time of war, people were learning to accept change and even becoming reconciled to it.

William Huskisson.

Outside events following the war hastened the process of gradual revolution. The trade of South America, so long reserved for the mother country by Spain, was opened to the world. After 1811, Brazil and San Domingo offered to unlock their ports on a reciprocal basis and prepared to apply punitive tariffs against British vessels if equal treatment was not granted them. In the circumstances, the traditional commercial monopoly seemed certain to damage Britain's own interests as well as those of her remaining colonies. Not until the twenties did the House of Commons provide a partial solution to the painful dilemma. The legislation that was presented to Parliament was principally the work of a first-rate businessman, William Huskisson, President of the Board

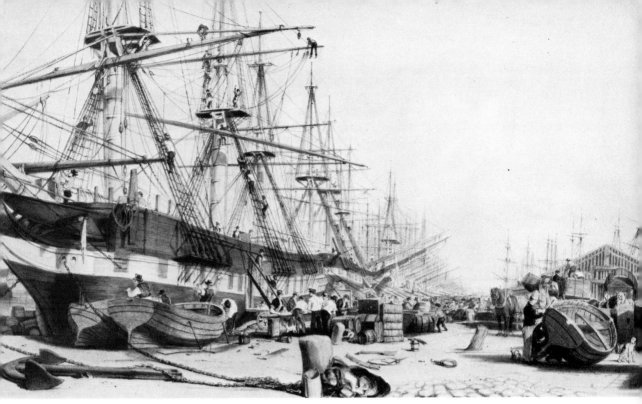

West India docks in the 1840s.

of Trade between 1823 and 1827, whom posterity remembers chiefly as the first man in history to be killed by a railway engine – the occasion being the opening of the Manchester and Liverpool line in 1830.

Huskisson's policy rested on the belief that the Old Colonial System had failed to meet the needs of a nation that had experienced an industrial revolution. Ireland and America provided ample proof that a policy of subordinating the economic interests of the dependency to those of the mother country had been disastrous. Only the abolition of hampering trade restrictions and the concession of freer trade could save Britain's second Empire from the fate which had befallen the first. The reform of the navigation laws, in Huskisson's opinion, was simply an act of constructive imperialism that would in the long run strengthen colonial attachments to the mother country. In place of monopoly he would establish a form of imperial preference.

In 1825, his great Bill was passed. All foreign countries were to be allowed direct trade with the British colonies, subject only to the reservation that the cargo must be the product of the country to which the ship belonged. In keeping with this principle, trade between the mother country and her colonies was confined to British ships. Inter-colonial trade and that, say, between England

159

and the West Indies, was to be treated as if it were a coasting trade between London and Newcastle. Admittedly, this stipulation ensured a monopoly, but Huskisson insisted on the reservation as a means of maintaining the now shrunken 'nursery for seamen', so long regarded as a colonial training school for the Royal Navy.

In retrospect, the actual changes seem very moderate, but they reversed a policy of 200 years or more, and they made further changes inevitable. The Act of 1825 struck a balance between free trade and monopoly by permitting international reciprocity, limited only by certain imperial preferences. Thanks to this legislation, British colonies were able to assume some responsibility for their own economic development. They could now enter the field of world, instead of merely imperial trade. Their produce could be brought to European ports directly in either foreign or British vessels, without touching, as formerly, at British ports. Britain safeguarded herself only by certain duties on the import of foreign goods – sufficiently high to provide preferences on similar kinds of colonial goods.

The foundations of the old trading empire had been shaken beyond repair; yet the old system, at least to some of the free-trade zealots, seemed to be a long time dying. 'Free trade' was still in the academic stage of politics, and even after Huskisson's reforms, faith in the merits of the navigation laws had by no means vanished from Downing Street and Westminster. The power of tradition and the propaganda of vested interests were still strong enough to repulse the arguments of the more radical intellectuals and theorists. Even pressures from the United States were insufficient to demolish the stout relics of what Lord Brougham once called, 'that obstinate perverse system that refused to vary with the alteration of circumstances, and clings superstitiously to what is now inapplicable'.

Nevertheless, by the beginning of the 1840s, the movement towards complete free trade had obtained enormous momentum, and there ensued a bitter campaign which saw its grand climax in the abolition of duties on foreign grain. This spectacular struggle over the so-called Corn Laws was essentially a struggle for the right to buy food staples in the cheapest market, whether colonial or foreign, and it involved the same principle as freedom to transport colonial or any other goods at the lowest available freight rates, whatever the nationality of the ships. Following on the radical budget of 1842, the repeal of the Corn Laws four years later practically destroyed the colonial preferential tariff. Obviously the British government could not insist on maintaining British preferences in the colonies when colonial preferences were being abolished in Britain. The colonial as well as the Englishman must, in all fairness, be allowed to buy in the cheapest market. Late in 1846 a Bill, applying to the British

PAPA COBDEN TAKING MASTER ROBERT A FREE TRADE WALK.

PAPA COBDEN.—" Come along, MASTER ROBERT, do step out."
MASTER ROBERT.—" That's all very well, but you know I cannot go so fast as you do."

Robert Peel, Prime Minister
during the crucial years
in the 1840s, did not
move as quickly towards
free trade as its advocates,
like Richard Cobden,
would have liked.

colonies in North America and to Mauritius (these were the only colonies to
which the parliamentary duties extended; the others were subject to executive
order-in-council), empowered the queen to give assent to the acts of colonial
legislatures reducing or repealing protective tariffs imposed upon their imports
from foreign countries by the Imperial Parliament.

The Bill did not, however, confer full commercial autonomy upon the
colonies. It enabled them to repeal or reduce existing imperial duties, but it
gave them no authority to impose a protective tariff upon any British goods, or
even new protective duties upon foreign goods. It did not, as the Colonial
Secretary, Earl Grey, pointed out, mean the abandonment of 'the right and
authority which Parliament always possessed of regulating the general trade of
the colonies and the mother country in the manner most conducive to the
welfare and prosperity of the Empire'. Indeed, for several years after 1846, the
governors of colonies possessing representative legislatures were instructed to
withold assent to Bills imposing differential duties.

Henry, third Earl Grey.

In 1847, the Canadian legislature passed a new provincial tariff, repealing all imperial duties in Canada and abolishing the distinction in taxation between British and foreign goods. Similar action was taken by the legislatures of the other colonies. Within a few years, British preference was a thing of the past. In 1849, as a logical sequence to the repeal of the Corn Laws, the Navigation Acts were abolished. And with the collapse of this centuries-old system, all that remained of protection, as Disraeli remarked, was 'rags and tatters'. The British tariff Acts of 1853 and 1860 disposed even of these remnants, the most important item being timber.

At the end of it all, when the torrent of legislation had slackened, it was perhaps logical for moderate men to ask what good were colonies in a world of free trade. Once they had gained full control of their own governments, they would inevitably drop off of their own accord – in fact the sensible thing would be to assist them on their way out; they had become merely expensive adjuncts of national prestige. 'Those wretched colonies will all be independent in a few years,' declared Disraeli in 1852, 'and are a millstone round our necks.' Less capricious statesmen, such as Lord John Russell, looked to the day, albeit reluctantly, when the ties which they had once hoped to make 'easy and mutually advantageous' would be finally severed.

Not all members of the famous Manchester School were agreed on the need to encourage separation on grounds of economy. Indeed, most political thinkers, influenced no doubt by Richard Cobden's campaign prediction that free trade would gradually erode the connection, took the middle ground of pessimism. But no political group or party can be fitted into a watertight compartment. The Tories were responsible for some very liberal measures, and the Liberals, especially in the seventies and thereafter, were to show themselves to be markedly conservative. One can only say that probably more Liberals than Tories believed that the ultimate departure of the colonies was certain; but both parties were in general agreement that no effort should be made to hold them within the Empire by compulsion.

The so-called Radicals are even more difficult to place under one rubric. They included Tory radicals, militant ex-Chartists, visionaries, rationalists and obstinate and obtuse humanitarians like Joseph Hume. Many of them were 'reformers' sympathetic to Wakefield and his colonial ideas; all of them were incorrigible individualists. Most of them inclined to see the Empire in economic and political terms as a heavy burden. But this negative attitude expressed their distaste for the Old Colonial System rather than any abhorrence with the idea of empire *per se*.

Edward Gibbon Wakefield.

The Wakefield school of Colonial reformers (whose members have been referred to previously as supporters of immigration schemes), was a small coterie of younger men, sometimes brilliant in their concepts, sometimes merely glib. They believed that the Empire could be preserved by granting self-government to the more mature parts. Most of them were free traders and opponents of imperial preferences. Many of them believed that prosperous colonies should bear a proportionate share of the financial costs of empire. Some of them favoured an expansionist imperialism, and all were opposed to a lethargic policy of the *status quo*.

The Manchester School took a predominantly economic line: free trade and peace. They wanted to relieve the mother country from the burdens of imperial government, including defence. The process might expedite the dissolution of the Empire, but such a fate they were prepared to accept in the interests of good business and world tranquillity. Like the Radicals, most of them would have approved of a British Empire without restrictive political ties and tariffs. As the economist J. R. McCulloch wrote in 1840:

We hope it will not be supposed, from anything now started, that we consider the foundation of colonial establishments as, generally speaking, inexpedient . . . It is not the establishment of colonies . . . but to the trammels that have been laid upon their industry, and the interference exercised by the mother country that we object.

Indian stand at the Great Exhibition of 1851.

Even John Stuart Mill thought there was nothing to be gained by separation. He was a Radical, and was sometimes called a Little Englander; yet he believed that the Empire might survive permanently, for he wrote in *Considerations on Representative Government* (1861):

But though Great Britain could do perfectly well without her colonies, and though on every principle of morality and justice she ought to consent to their separation, should the time come when, after full trial of the best form of union, they deliberately desire to be dissevered; there are strong reasons for maintaining the present slight bond of connection, so long as not disagreeable to the feelings of either party. It is a step, as far as it goes, towards universal peace and generally friendly co-operation among nations. It renders war impossible among a large number of otherwise independent communities. . . . It at least keeps the markets of the different countries open to one another. . . . And in the case of the British possessions it has the advantage, specially valuable at the present time, of adding to the moral influence and weight in the councils of the world, of the Power which, of all in existence, best understands liberty. . . .

This temperate and optimistic statement reveals that common ground existed for aggressive Radicals, benign Liberals and the bulk of Colonial Reformers such as Wakefield and Molesworth. But again one cannot be precise; beliefs, policies and hopes were blurred even within the minds of individuals. Even Gladstone had his moments of doubt. In his *Diary* for 2 March 1872, Lord Kimberley recorded:

Gladstone, Lowe and Cardwell make no secret of their opinion that we should be well rid of the colonies, and Cardwell evidently thinks the Australian demand for power to establish an Australian intercolonial tariff, a good opportunity for bringing matters to a head.

But every diary ever written registers some private occasion of despair. In general, Gladstone and his Liberal colleagues did not favour hasty action on the part of the mother country. Provided the costs of government were not too great, provided the colonists shared them, they were only too willing to recognize the importance of bonds such as sentiment and the possession of a common heritage – language, law and custom.

In other words, the public debate on the colonial problem around mid-century was not concerned fundamentally with the question of separation versus preservation of empire, but with the character of a reorganized empire in terms of government, defence and commerce. The Radicals' cry for the abolition of tariff preferences and the ruthless cutting of defence and administrative costs represented a demand for separation only if the existing system should prove inelastic or unchangeable.

Burma in the 1820s, a lithograph from Moore's *Rangoon Views* ▶

Meanwhile, the Empire had continued to grow. Much of it was the result of inland expansion from coastal points and strips that had been previously in British possession; and in view of Britain's unchallenged command of the seas and the absence of foreign rivalry, such extensions were without risk, and accepted as a matter of course. Sometimes, as in India, territory was increased by the action of officials 'on the spot', bent on pacifying a frontier or occupying lawless and unstable kingdoms. Between 1843 and 1856, Sind, the Punjab, Kashmir, Nagpur (the greatest of the surviving Maratha dominions) and Oudh were annexed, the culmination of expansionist processes which consolidated the British Raj. In 1853, following the Second Burmese War, strategic control over the whole eastern coast of Bengal was secured as a result of the annexation of Lower Burma.

In South Africa, colonists poured forth across makeshift frontiers, often forcing a British military advance, either to protect the natives or the settlers. Fear of French designs was not the only reason for the annexation of New Zealand in 1840, but it was probably one factor. Sometimes, as in the Gold Coast, territory was acquired for strictly humanitarian reasons – the suppression of the slave trade. After Napoleon had been insulated in St Helena, Tristan da Cunha and Ascension were occupied to prevent a repetition of the flight from Elba, and, as has been noticed in a previous chapter, Singapore, Aden, Hong Kong and the island of Labuan off the Borneo coast were taken as bases to safeguard British trade routes to the East.

Hence, the initiation of Great Britain's free-trade policy and the abolition of the last remnants of the Old Colonial System did not necessarily mean getting rid of the Empire, as has sometimes been alleged. The die-hard Little Englanders – those who rejected empire under any circumstances – were extremely few. Certainly, a policy of 'scuttling' was never seriously considered by any British government. 'Little Englandism' was merely a label, temporarily attached to a small and vocal section of English politicians whose objectives were ambiguously expressed, and whose message never penetrated very deeply into the English consciousness. To the vast majority, careful accounting and voluntary membership in a self-governing empire were compatible objectives. Indeed, the abolition of the preference system and the navigation laws, and (with increasing colonial self-government) a diminution in the financial burden of empire through the withdrawal of imperial troops, undermined and finally extinguished the principal arguments of the outright separationists.

In retrospect, it could be argued that policies or attitudes of separatism and/or indifference to colonies carried less weight among policy-makers than the imponderable forces which made overseas expansion possible, if not inevitable. The advance of imperial free trade went hand in hand with the steady extension of naval bases, coaling stations and dockyards, simply because no other power had sufficiently developed its industrial resources to offer serious competition, and thus slow the process by means of protective tariffs or military threats. After the middle of the nineteenth century, British ascendancy in the fields of industry, finance, commerce and shipping was complete. Iron, coal and other basic materials were available within the British Isles and British manpower was sufficient to exploit them. Master of all she surveyed, Britain was in a unique position to scrap traditional doctrines of national advantage and establish a new form of international monopoly under the umbrella of free trade.

◀ Hong Kong was ceded to Britain at the Treaty of Nanking, signed on HMS *Cornwallis* in 1842.

Britain's industrial might. Above: the *Great Eastern* under construction in the naval dockyards at Millwall, 1857. Left: *Iron and Coal*, a mural painting of 1861.

The era of self-confidence: Queen Victoria's son, Prince Albert, receives an exultant welcome in Cape Town, 1860.

And because there were no strong rivals to challenge this project of monopoly, British policies of free trade were generally acceptable. At least in the colonial world, there was no active attempt to reduce or eliminate the special advantages which Britain derived from her naval supremacy.

Hence, in promoting policies of free trade, British statesmen were endangering neither commerce nor national security. During these mid-Victorian years, there was more talk about wealth, and less about power than in the eighteenth century, but this was simply owing to the fact that Britain felt confident in the possession of all the power she might on occasion feel called upon to use. The so-called *Pax Britannica* was not the simple consequence of naval power wielded with restraint by the self-appointed policeman of the world. The fact that the United Kingdom market, together with most of the markets of a huge empire, were open to the products of other states not only stimulated general economic activity, it contributed to the relaxation of tensions within the entire trading world. If maritime power was beyond the reach of other nations, this was not true of wealth. By introducing a kind of international sharing of economic benefits, free trade encouraged acquiescence in the British hegemony.

THE ROAD TO CANADIAN FEDERATION

The crescendo of anti-colonialism which accompanied the free-trade movement, during the first quarter of the nineteenth century, reached its peak in the 1860s. This antipathy to empire, as we have noted, was never absolute. In fact,

India and most of the British territories occupied chiefly by non-European peoples were rarely mentioned as millstones for discard, even by thorough-going Radicals like John Bright. Nevertheless, a flood of parliamentary eloquence, pamphleteering and historical or pseudo-historical writing had, by the sixties, given the anti-colonial movement a sort of philosophy of parsimony. As the commercial and industrial classes increased their influence at Westminster, the annual budget became the supreme example of careful national housekeeping.

In this climate of opinion, colonies, like everything else, had to pay their way; indeed, it seemed preposterous to both Gladstone and Disraeli that the British taxpayer should have to provide for the administration and the defence of healthy self-governing colonies. Between 1825 and 1832, for example, the British government had spent more than £7,000,000 on the fortification of Quebec; in 1843, the military expenditure in British North America was about $3,500,000. With free trade on the world's horizon, industrial Britain could see little sense in spending further sums on the upkeep of colonies which would ultimately control their own destinies, or in the case of Canada, be absorbed by the United States. Indeed, the pervading ethos of mid nineteenth-century Britain seemed to justify the view that recourse to military force as the fashioner and guardian of empire was no longer natural.

In 1846, the first garrisons were withdrawn from British North America; thenceforward, military support from the mother country would be conditioned, so it was intended, by the extent to which the colonies were prepared to assume responsibilities on their own account. By 1870, all troops were withdrawn from Canada with the exception of a small garrison at Halifax. In April of that year, the Canadian Prime Minister, Sir John A. Macdonald, remarked with gentle irony: 'We may perhaps be obliged to appeal from the Government to the people of England.'

A similar retreat from New Zealand seemed to confirm a policy of 'scuttle'. Gradual withdrawal had been practised for some years, but in 1868, at a moment when hostilities between the colonists and the Maoris threatened to desolate the country, the Colonial Secretary, the Duke of Buckingham, tactlessly announced the final removal of all British forces. Even after the massacre of some thirty colonials in the neighbourhood of Cook's landfall at Poverty Bay, the Colonial Office declined to cancel the order, and Lord Granville, on taking office, was equally cold-blooded in promising to adhere to his predecessor's policy. At the same time, the government refused to loan the necessary sums to cover the costs of the campaign, an act of ostentatious parsimony that aroused much bitterness and anger. In Australia, the recall of imperial troops was not an immediate problem, since the country had no substantial native population with which to contend. None the less, the belief was widespread that Britain

Sir John A. Macdonald.

was contemplating, or at least prepared to accept, the final dissolution of the Empire. In Cape Colony, where harbour fortifications had been steadily deteriorating despite brave efforts in the forties to stop the rot, military observers looked fearfully to the time when the impelling *Zeitgeist* would leave Britain's chief fortress on the route to India ungunned, untenanted and available to rival powers.

Various circumstances and events coalesced to make possible the Confedera/ tion of Canada in 1867, but the explanation of the precipitate decision on the part of the British government to hasten the union of the British North American colonies lies not so much in local political and economic embarrassments, as in the fear of aggressive action by the northern United States. To confront the threat of American power along an indefensible land frontier, the colony could call on scarcely more than 4000 trained troops. In the event of war with the North, which seemed likely following British recognition of the South as belligerents, the British colonies seemed ripe for the picking.

It was clear to many members of the House of Commons that Canada had no chance of surviving the pressures of a mighty and bellicose neighbour under the existing mixed government which Durham had provided. The union of French and English 'within the bosom of a single state' produced so much friction that stable administration had become impossible. On the other hand, there was no strong feeling in favour of joining the republic, little disposition to exchange King Log for King Eagle at Washington. And on a hundred platforms, Canadian politicians like D'Arcy McGee argued that only through a federal union of the Maritime provinces with Canada, and the extension of that union to include the Hudson's Bay Company prairies, could the colonies perpetuate their connection with the mother country, and save themselves as a potential nation.

British statesmen rose to the occasion. At a time when confidence in empire was waning, and when leaders of opinion like Gladstone and John Bright were tempted by the thought that the cession of Canada to the United States might be worth the price of peace, the British government in 1864 suddenly threw its weight in favour of a wide federal union. Here was a dignified way of creating a state that, on paper at least, was big enough to assume responsibility for its own existence. Colonial loyalty merited at least a decent start in life – an opportu/ nity for the colonies to survive through their own joint efforts. To leave them to their own separate resources would mean, almost inevitably, piecemeal con/ sumption by the United States, with a consequent accession of American territory and power. One large and united colony would be less likely to invite armed attack and far more able to resist hostile economic pressures.

In other words, fear of American designs proved to be the decisive catalyst; the foundations for a dominion 'stretching from sea to sea' were laid by Great Britain primarily as a measure of defence against the possible aggressions of the republic to the south. There was no other practical way of restraining or counterbalancing the republic's advance towards continental hegemony. The Royal Navy might, in the event of war, harass American shipping and possibly pillage coastal cities, but British armies could not invade and subdue the United States, and despite the hundreds of thousands of pounds spent on inland fortifications, they were incapable of defending Canada.

By March 1867, the British North America Act had been completed and passed by the Imperial Parliament. It went through, according to Macdonald, who viewed the proceedings sardonically from the gallery, like 'a private bill uniting two or three English parishes'. On 1 July its provisions were put into force. Expanded to include the Hudson's Bay Company territories in 1870, British Columbia in 1871 and Prince Edward Island in 1873, the blueprint of a transcontinental nation had been made. Eventually, what tough bargaining failed to achieve in 1864 and 1895 was accomplished by generosity and cunning in 1949, when Newfoundland, the oldest British colony, became the tenth province of the Dominion.

Parliament buildings, Ottawa, in the 1870s.

THE "IRREPRESSIBLE" TOURIST.

B-SM-RCK. "H'M!—HA!—WHERE SHALL I GO NEXT?"

Chapter Nine

THE AGE OF COMPETITIVE EXPANSION

In the years after 1713, when France and Britain fought for colonial possessions, the European framework of the balance of power had widened to include the whole world. After 1815, the fields of force contracted, as Britain along with other powers considered the problem of lessening, not adding to colonial burdens. What was the use of maintaining colonies whose commerce could be more cheaply exploited by treaty arrangement than by possession? During the 1860s, Britain renounced her protectorate over the Ionian Islands; and the federation of the Canadian provinces seemed likely to be the first step towards friendly separation; given time the Australian colonies would no doubt follow suit. France had withdrawn from her Mexican adventure with serious loss of prestige, and Russia had sold her American possessions to the United States. In a world apparently succumbing to Cobdenite doctrines of peace and free trade, there seemed little to be said in favour of acquiring colonial empires.

Following the Franco-Prussian War of 1870, France had recuperated with characteristic vigour, but whatever the demands of *la gloire* – and in Africa they were to be considerable – French public opinion panicked at any considerable diversion of troops from the border with Germany. Indeed, long after the 'scramble' for colonies started, both in Germany and in France, European issues continued to predominate. Bismarck was determined not to waste vital German strength in the pursuit of overseas will-o'-the-wisps. When Hamburg merchants pleaded for the acquisition of French Cochin-China, Saigon, Martinique, Réunion, St Pierre and Miquelon, he preferred to take Alsace-Lorraine and a milliard francs of tribute. 'I will positively have no [overseas] colonies', he declared in February 1871. 'They offer no advantage except as refreshment stations. Colonies are of no more use to us than a sable fur to a Polish nobleman who has no shirt.' Not until 1881 did France occupy Tunis, chiefly as a prestige gesture. Not until 1884 did Germany lay claim to territories

◀ The 'scramble' for colonies: Bismarck ponders on what colony to acquire next.

By buying the khedive's shares
in the Suez Canal Company,
Disraeli insured British influence
over the key Suez route to India.

on the south-west coast of Africa and in New Guinea, political masterstrokes
that might bolster Bismarck's majority at the next election.

Yet during this curious age of antipathy to colonial effort, when the spirit of
'Little England' seemed likely to reproduce itself in 'Little Europe', there
slowly dawned a new and frightening period in modern history – the so-called
'Age of Imperialism'. France, Germany, Belgium, Italy and finally the United
States, began to compete for the remaining spoils of the world. As a result, the
balance of power in Europe was no longer the main preoccupation of European
statesmen. Once again, as in the eighteenth century, the framework of the
balance had expanded to include the world.

One explanation of this volte-face is plausible. The Industrial Revolution
had spread beyond the boundaries of the United Kingdom, and, by the beginning of the seventies, was transforming western Europe. Advancing industrial
techniques represented by machine equipment, steel, railways and mass production generally, were promoting a thriving interest in tropical and semi-
tropical countries, whose unsophisticated and teeming populations would
eventually become large-scale buyers of manufactures as well as suppliers of
useful raw commodities. To guard their economies against the competition
of their neighbours, the newly industrialized nations of Europe began to close
their markets by tariff barriers, and to seek, under pressure of overproduction,
additional world outlets for their surplus goods. In this period of extending
political rivalries, the protection of home industry and the acquisition of pro-
ductive overseas colonies offered the prospect of greater self-sufficiency and
power. By the end of the seventies, the general abandonment on the Continent
of free-trade principles under pressure of industrial growth had opened the way
to new and aggressive policies of colonial expansion.

No single explanation is sufficient to account for the swelling tide of competition on which the European powers were about to embark. It is fair to say, however, that nothing makes men put so high a value on possessions as the knowledge that they may be coveted by their neighbours; and British governments were forced to recognize that unclaimed and unoccupied territories would sooner or later fall to other European powers, either to satisfy prestige demands or political and economic need. Hence, the object of British policy, however tardily initiated, became one of 'keeping the other fellow out', whether in Fiji (1874), Cyprus (1878) or eventually along the African coasts. Such a 'dog-in-the-manger' attitude was often reinforced by the strategic argument. British fears and suspicions continued to be aroused by any power whose actions, real or imagined, seemed to threaten the route to India. Disraelian 'imperialism' was primarily anti-Russian and not infected by any jingo lust for colonial expansion. Both Liberal and Conservative governments were determined to avoid new commitments, especially in tropical Africa.

Probably the greatest single event in the promotion of the 'new colonialism' was the opening of the Suez Canal by Napoleon III in November 1869. Until the genius and persistence of Ferdinand de Lesseps suddenly altered the world's geography, East and West were separated by some ninety miles of sand. Once this barrier had been removed, continuous sea carriage was available from Portsmouth to Bombay. But even before, the Isthmus itself offered a time-saving portage to the East. 'Of all our scattered possessions,' a political observer had written in 1851, 'the mightiest in importance as well as extent is incontestably

The spread of modern communications beyond Europe: the opening of the Cape Town and Wellington Railway, 1864.

our Indian Empire. . . . And yet, but for one circumstance she [Britain] would have had half the circuit of the globe to make, to communicate with it. That one circumstance is the Transit across Egypt.' In 1839, Aden had been occupied chiefly to secure the Red Sea passage to the Isthmus. In 1842, when the Peninsular and Oriental Steam Navigation Company began their monthly mail service to Bombay via Alexandria, Egypt became the most important military, political and commercial gateway in the whole British Empire. In a pinch, Britain was prepared to fight both France and Russia to keep her overland route to India intact.

The first effect of cutting the Isthmus was an urgent quickening of British interest in the eastern Mediterranean and the Middle East. Within the next few years, all the main policy decisions made in respect of the Ottoman Empire were influenced by fears that Egypt and the Levant might fall into hostile hands, an occupation that might bar the canal linking Britain with India.

In the beginning, however, Britain had taken no direct share in the work of construction; indeed, Palmerston had for a time done his best to obstruct the French project. Consequently, Britain came close to losing the almost exclusive advantage she had hitherto managed to maintain, and was only saved from an embarrassing predicament by the insolvency of the Khedive of Egypt, Ismail Pasha, who had become viceroy in 1863, under the nominal suzerainty of the Sultan of Turkey. In the late autumn of 1875, the khedive let it be known that he needed £4,000,000 immediately to pay interest on various loans contracted with international bankers and less respectable vultures who battened on the

176

Disraeli offers his queen
an imperial crown.
Victoria became Empress
of India in 1876.

Opening of the Suez Canal, 1869.

country and its careless ruler. Disraeli acting 'off his own bat' persuaded Roths-childs to find the money on the British government's behalf. By this daring masterstroke, he was able to acquire the khedive's shares in the Suez Canal Company. It was a minority stake, amounting to a little less than half the total capital. On the strength of these shares alone, the Company was not in White-hall's pocket, but Britain had, nevertheless, become a major partner in the Canal enterprise, and had done so, on the recommendation of the Prime Minister, not as a financial investment or a commercial speculation, but as 'a political trans-action . . . calculated to strengthen the Empire'.

Disraeli's *coup* illuminated, as did the new diadem of his empress, Victoria, the imminent shift in nineteenth-century British imperial thinking and practice. He had no wish to occupy Egypt, and had coldly ignored Bismarck's hints in 1876 and 1877 that he should take it. None the less, after keeping clear of Egypt's internal affairs for nearly three-quarters of a century, Britain suddenly found herself drawn into African territorial commitments. Largely at the expense of French aspirations, both Egypt and the Sudan were shortly to become enmeshed in Britain's imperial defence system.

Ismail Pasha,
a photograph taken
in the Crimea
where he was
in command of
the Egyptian army.

The drama opened in 1876 when Ismail Pasha finally declared himself bankrupt. In consequence, the United Kingdom and the other principal stockholder, France, made arrangements to set up a joint control board to regulate the country's economy, and thus reassure future investors. Unfortunately, the situation worsened, and both countries appealed to the sultan, urging him to depose his Egyptian feudatory. On 26 June 1879, Ismail was informed of his deposition by a cryptic telegram, addressed to 'the ex-Khedive, Ismail Pasha'. His son, Tewfik, became the new Khedive of Egypt.

The many economies forced on the puppet ruler included a severe reduction of the army and the dismissal without pay of many officers. Ultimately, this form of interference precipitated bitter discontent, leading to a military revolt headed by an astute Egyptian called Arabi. This remarkable man organized what became, in modern political terms, a national movement, directed primarily not at European financial control, but at the Turkish clique which was believed to surround and guide the khedive. In other words, the revolt was by no means an hysterical anti-European crusade, unless, as interpreted by British ministers, the slogan 'Egypt for the Egyptians' could be so construed. It was much more national than military; it had, of course, an anti-European bearing, but above all else, it was anti-Turk.

Between 1881 and 1882, spreading turmoil soon brought Britain and France actively on the scene. Britain looked to the sultan to restore order, but France was opposed to Turkish intervention, and British public opinion, even before it felt the weight of Gladstonian oratory, was antagonistic to the sultan. In the end, France and Britain came to the joint decision to uphold the khedive's rule and Turkish suzerainty. Meanwhile, an assembly of Egyptian notables under Arabi had begun to draft a constitution. They admitted their readiness to concede to European advisers the administration of that part of the budget allotted to the payment of the debt, but the remainder, they insisted, should be left in their hands. This modest concession, the creditor powers refused to accept.

The sultan refused to co-operate by sending troops, and in the end, France was prevailed upon to join Britain in a fleet demonstration before Alexandria.

The British fleet demonstration before Alexandria, 1882.

General Gordon.

The immediate consequence was an effervescence of anti-foreign feeling. Some fifty Europeans were murdered, with the result that British guns bombarded the harbour forts. France abstained on the ground that such an operation would be an act of war. Fearful of Bismarckian intrigue behind the scenes, she refused to risk embroilment outside Europe. An invitation to Italy was also rejected. Britain was, therefore, left to restore order alone. On 13 September 1882, General Sir Garnet Wolseley (with the indispensable help of General Sir Gerald Graham) defeated Arabi at Tel-el-Kebir. Hitherto opposed to any form of armed intervention without French co-operation, Great Britain suddenly found herself in single occupation of Egypt. Yet the Cabinet were unanimously opposed to anything like a permanent occupation. Once order had been restored, it was assumed that British troops would withdraw. In fact, the Foreign Secretary, Lord Granville, declared that Britain would leave the country in 1888.

Meanwhile, the rise of the Pan-Islam movement in the Sudan, and the cry for war against the infidel, threatened to spread beyond the desert borders into Egypt. Early in 1884, General Gordon hastened southward to quench the uprising. Ignoring orders to evacuate the area as soon as possible, he found himself, between March 1884 and January 1885, besieged in Khartoum, which fell to the Mahdi's crusading forces two days before Wolseley's relief expedition reached it. For the next ten years, the Sudan remained a fevered and restless land in the hands of its brave and fanatical tribesmen.

For Gladstone, the death of Gordon seemed the last straw; everything had gone wrong – the humiliation of Majuba Hill, Ireland, now Khartoum (and two months later, in March, a war with Russia in central Asia seemed imminent, following the Russian defeat of Afghan forces at Penjdeh). The Prime Minister had failed completely to understand the shattering effect of Gordon's death on public opinion. He was not altogether wrong in viewing Gordon as a kind of Bible-thumping buccaneer, a supreme egotist whose histrionics had hampered and diverted the policy of Her Majesty's government. But he failed to appreciate the extent to which Christian knight-errantry, in an age of good shopkeeping and scrupulous accounting, could appeal to the romantic and religious feelings of the masses. In days to come, the image of the imperial servant, ready to die at his post, was to be impressed indelibly on the national conscience. And a new generation of politicians in Whitehall did not forget the public reaction against a ministry whose carelessness and neglect had been held responsible for the martyrdom of Khartoum.

Battle of Tel-el-Kebir, 1882.

Gladstone had opposed the permanent British occupation of Egypt:

We are against it on the ground of our duty to Egypt; we are against it on the ground of the specific and solemn pledges . . . pledges which have earned for us the confidence of Europe during the course of difficult and delicate operations, and which, if one pledge can be more solemn and sacred than another, special sacredness in this case, bids us to observe.

Statesmen in power tend to change when confronted by the circumstances of the moment and the special influences pervading government offices. In office, as Ernest Bevin once observed, facts are more easily recognized. Gladstone had won the election of 1880 with speeches jammed full of idealism and international morality. He was known as a man of peace and a lover of liberty. Yet within three years of his taking office, the Egyptians were crushed and England's relations with France further embittered by a policy of expansion in the Nile Valley.

In the meantime, while Egypt was subject to reorganization by Lord Cromer and General Kitchener, the Sudan remained a prey to anarchy. The Mahdi was poisoned in 1885, but under his successor the tyranny and conflict continued. The longer the British occupation lasted, the more urgent and querulous became the demands of Turkey and France for its termination. On 22 May 1887, a convention was arranged providing for evacuation in three years. Two years after the British forces were withdrawn, British supervision of the army was to cease, and Egypt would thereafter enjoy territorial immunity – an indefinite status which the sultan preferred to neutralization. On ratification, the powers were to be invited to recognize and guarantee the inviolability of Egyptian territory, with the proviso that Turkey and Britain were to have the right of re-entry. Unhappily, owing to pressures and threats from France and Russia, the sultan refused to accept the arrangement. Later on, when he tried to continue the negotiations, Lord Salisbury, then Foreign Secretary, annoyed as much by Turkey's cowardice as by French intrigue, refused. Anxious to oust Great Britain from Egypt, France had merely strengthened and made more permanent Britain's unwanted occupation.

Although the Sudan had been nominally abandoned from the beginning of 1885, Egyptian sovereignty had not been renounced, and the hope of eventual reoccupation by the khedive had never been relinquished. Under British guidance the Egyptian army was completely reorganized and in 1896 the government of the khedive determined to reconquer the turbulent Sudan. In command of the Nile expedition, General Kitchener slowly and surely advanced towards Khartoum. On 2 September 1898, the power of the Mahdi was broken at Omdurman; two days later, British and Egyptian flags rose above Khartoum, and where Gordon had died a funeral service was held.

French statesmen of the time, and even writers of a later date, have argued that the abandonment and reconquest of the Sudan were part of a calculated plot for re-establishing British supremacy on the Upper Nile, but it is difficult to recognize so farsighted a project in the fumbling actions of reluctant British Cabinets. Admittedly, British action in the Upper Nile was powerfully influenced by developments taking place beyond the limits of Britain's traditional sphere of influence. The extension of British dominion in central Africa both directly and through Chartered Company enterprises had led to the completion, between 1890 and 1894, of agreements with Germany, Italy and the Congo Free State, by which 'spheres of influence' of all four states were defined. The object was to exclude the possibility of an invasion of the Upper Nile Valley. A central African arrangement with France was attempted in 1890, but it was a limited agreement. France preferred to keep a free hand. For example, when neighbours anticipated her in Africa, she was able on occasion to cut in at the rear, occupy hinterland, and, in the case of the Upper Nile, gain control of rivers upon which the prosperity of the lower territories depended. Indeed, by the 1890s, French territory stretched in a solid block from the Mediterranean to the Congo. It now remained for France to extend eastward through the Sudan and Abyssinia to the Gulf of Aden where she already possessed a strip. This ambitious project brought her to the brink of war with Great Britain.

First charge of the dervishes at Omdurman, 1898.

Captain Marchand's expedition, consisting of half a dozen French and a hundred Senegalese, left Brazzaville in March 1897, dived into the forests of central Africa and suddenly emerged at Fashoda, 300 miles south of Khartoum, on 10 July 1898. Marchand hoisted the French flag. Kitchener at Khartoum, hearing of the arrival of six white men at Fashoda, hastened southward to satisfy his curiosity and reached the spot on 8 September. It was a delicate situation, but there was no angry wrangling or pulling down of flags. Kitchener complimented Marchand on his amazing journey, but pointed out that Fashoda belonged jointly to the British and Egyptian governments. He then handed him a written protest against any occupation of any part of the Nile Valley by France.

The parting at Fashoda was amicable, but in France there was furore. In the end Marchand was recalled, and in March 1899 France concluded with Britain a comprehensive agreement whereby the rights of Great Britain over the whole Nile Basin from source to mouth were acknowledged. France was confirmed in possession of her West African empire, but the whole of the Egyptian Sudan was recognized as subject to the government of Cairo. Henceforward, Anglo-French relations slowly improved. In 1904, with the initiation of the entente cordiale, France agreed to give Britain, for thirty years, a free hand in Egypt. Paradoxically, as it may appear, the very variety of the antipathies, based on disputes ranging from Newfoundland to the Nile, compelled a settlement. Conflicting so directly and so constantly in so many areas of the world, the grounds for negotiation and compromise were available. Unhappily, this was not the case with Germany.

Anglo-French negotiations over the confrontation at Fashoda in 1898.

At the beginning of the last quarter of the nineteenth century, the Empire grew mile by mile under the spasmodic impulses of reluctant governments. That Egypt should be vacated as soon as possible was a dogma of Gladstone's as well as of his Cabinet; until 1887 it was a principle of Salisbury's, and it was the accepted opinion of the country generally. After the Gordon disaster, Edward Dicey, the publicist, who continued to seek support for an Egyptian protec-torate, found himself almost alone. When New Guinea and Zululand were discussed by the Cabinet in 1883–84, Lord Derby's remark that 'England has already black subjects enough' seemed good common-sense. It was clearly up to the British government to maintain order and stability in areas like Zululand whose rulers had been broken by British arms; a protectorate was the only means of giving effect to that responsibility. Yet Gladstone was not ready for such a step, and his government was allowed by public opinion to stick to irresolute policies of expansion for several years.

The builders of the new African empire, Company directors like Goldie, Mackinnon, Harry Johnston and Rhodes, did their early work without en-couragement from home. Indeed, Rhodes, who was eager to get Afrikaner support for his northward advance, was anxious to avoid any popular support from Britain which might publicize his imperial dream. In this he was probably too successful, for many men suspected Rhodes of seeking to build for himself a huge South African kingdom.

On the whole, the Press in the 1880s did not favour painting the so-called primitive areas of the world in red. There was little propaganda about extending the Empire, and when, in 1886, the Prince of Wales suggested the establishment of an Imperial Institute to advertise the moral and material importance of empire, the response was lukewarm. The men who pointed the way to the exotic glamour of the Diamond Jubilee were not yet on the national stage.

As early as 1870, however, various literary authorities had shown an interest in the Empire. John Ruskin at Oxford declared that Britain, besides cherishing the old, must found new colonies – or perish. James Anthony Froude, at the price of some inaccuracies, was doing for English history what Treitschke was doing for Germany: England had a world mission on water and overseas. He made Henry VIII a 'blood and iron' man like Bismarck; *Oceana, or England and her Colonies* came from his pen in 1885. Thomas Carlyle also contemplated the expansion of the Anglo-Saxons over as much as possible of the habitable globe. Charles Dilke, writer, traveller, politician and the centre of a *cause célèbre*, contributed the famous statement: 'The world will rapidly become English.' J. R. Seeley's classic, *The Expansion of England* (1881–82), gave background and significance to the British Empire.

J. R. Seeley.

'A young man . . . walking slowly
at the head of his flocks,
while at his knee
ran small naked Cupids.'
From *The Kipling Reader*, 1908.

But the poets were first to point the way. As far back as Crimean days, Tennyson had written *Maud*; now in the new era of expansion he urged, 'Hands all Around, God the Traitor's Hope Confound', and with Kipling and Henley in support, 'One Flag, One Fleet, One Throne' became the core of a philosophy of empire. The influence of these people, which was probably considerable, was chiefly with the Empire as then existing. Not many of them asked for a bigger empire; on the other hand, they too helped to explode the notion that colonies, once they reached maturity, were bound to go. By condemning apathy and nourishing imperial pride, they influenced the mode of national thinking.

The gradual revolution in British thought and purpose was also stimulated by the immense improvements in communications, which tended to counteract the divisive effects of distance. By 1870, steam navigation was almost universal; telegraph communication across the Atlantic began in 1866; the Suez Canal brought India, Australia and New Zealand closer than ever to the mother country. A revival of interest in emigration helped to strengthen the links. Towards the end of the 1860s, a period of prosperity had been followed by a frightening depression in British trade and industry, accompanied by a marked increase of unemployment and pauperism. In one year, 1868–69, emigration rose from 58,000 to 95,000.

Queen Victoria opens the Imperial Institute in 1893.

Queen Victoria, a nineteenth-century wood-carving from Sierra Leone.

But perhaps the main incentive to expand into new areas of the world came from Africa – the last of the continents to succumb to the European explorer, missionary, trader and soldier. Within some forty years after the accession of Queen Victoria, its darkest mysteries were dispelled and vast tropical regions lay open to the acquisitive attentions of European powers. For centuries Europeans and Arabs had felt their way along African coasts, and trading posts had sprung up at various focal points. Yet little was known about the interior until after the middle of the nineteenth century. Admittedly, the lower reaches of the Nile beyond Khartoum were familiar; Mungo Park, Clapperton and Lander had explored the Niger to its source; the Sahara had been crossed and venturesome missionaries from South Africa had reached the Limpopo. But apart from such sporadic efforts, little had been done to break inland from traditional trading settlements by the estuaries of great rivers. This invaders' task was left chiefly to intrepid travellers from Germany, France, Portugal and Britain.

The greatest and most dedicated of the British explorers was David Livingstone, who had been sent by the London Missionary Society in 1840 to their northernmost station, in Bechuanaland. In 1849 he pushed northward, past Lake Ngami, to the Zambezi River. Four years later he was following that river to its source, reaching westward to Loanda on the Atlantic coast of Angola, and then, on the return journey, eastward along the Zambezi to its mouth in the Indian Ocean. In 1866 he set out on his last and most strenuous expedition.

The 'mode of travelling' in Africa, an aquatint of 1821.

Livingstone's steam-launch, the *Ma-Robert*, encounters elephants in the shallows of the River Shire, Nyasaland, 1859.

Before he died in 1873, he had mapped a substantial part of east central Africa. Livingstone's work was completed by Lieutenant Verney Cameron, who had been sent out by the Royal Geographical Society in 1872 to assist him, and who explored with infinite care and resource the upper waters of the Congo Basin. His effort to annex the area was hastily repudiated by the Disraeli government. Meanwhile, in 1858, Burton and Speke had discovered lakes Tanganyika and Victoria, and between 1860 and 1864, Speke and J. A. Grant traced the main stream of the Nile from Lake Victoria to Khartoum. Such feats of studied enterprise, incredible endurance and courage contributed to the new ethos of imperial expansion.

David Livingstone.

In West Africa, British processes of expansion were in the beginning leisurely, if not sluggish, confirming a genuine government reluctance to undertake new responsibilities. Had the unprofitable coastal stations at the mouth of the Gambia River, in Sierra Leone and along the Gold Coast not provided useful bases for the campaign against the slave trade, they might well have been abandoned. In 1850 the Danish and in 1871 the Dutch governments cut their losses by selling their Gold Coast forts to Britain, leaving the British government in control of the entire coast, as well as a hinterland some forty miles in depth. As it happened, the mere fact of possession, along with the growth of trade, combined to force policies of action. In 1873–74, Sir Garnet Wolseley broke the power of the Ashanti and cleared the routes to the interior. To the east of the Gold Coast, the island of Lagos had been occupied in 1861 as a base for combating the slave trade. It proved to be a useful commercial port and gateway to the rich palm-oil region of the Lower Niger.

Almost unconsciously, Britain had become the dominant power on the west coast of Africa. France was her only serious trade rival. For some years French explorers had been feeling their way up-river to the Sudan, that vast area south of the great desert, stretching from Cape Verde to Abyssinia. Contemplating the fertile Upper Valley of the Niger, French merchants and politicians dreamed of a huge tropical empire that would cut off the British and other rival advances from the coast. Beginning in the eighties, they began the penetration of the interior, marking the advance by a series of treaties with native chiefs, which subsequently embraced accessions around Timbuktu and Lake Chad.

Already fearful for their trade on the Lower Niger, in 1879 an amalgamation of small British trading firms known as the United Africa Company, under the direction of Sir George Taubman Goldie, took the initiative in confirming and extending their footholds. By 1885 the existence of the Oil Rivers Protectorate was a recognition of the fact that British influence was now firmly entrenched along the coast and within the immediate hinterland. In January 1886, Lagos itself became a separate British colony.

Trading station on the River Ankobra in the Gold Coast, 1868.

The Gold Coast in the 1870s: a croquet party at Cape Coast Castle.

Ten years earlier, Leopold of Belgium had founded his International Association for the Exploration and Civilization of Central Africa, with the object of opening up Africa on a partnership basis and at the same time eliminating the slave trade. The Berlin-Congo Conference of 1885 recognized the Association as ruler of the Congo Basin, and the Congo Free State became in practice a Belgian enterprise, over which Leopold assumed personal sovereignty. In addition, Portugal was pushing claims to transcontinental dominion that embraced decrepit settlements on both the Atlantic and Indian Oceans. In Germany, Bismarck had become a convert to empire, and British traders and missionaries watched with suspicion as great stretches of African coasts and of New Guinea were snatched from under their noses and enclosed within a German tariff ring.

Bismarck started in 1884 by taking over the claims of Adolf Lüderitz, a merchant who had arranged a treaty with local natives at Angra Pequena (present-day Lüderitz) on the desert coast of south-west Africa, some 260 miles south of Walvis Bay; later in the same year, Gustav Nachtigal proclaimed German protectorates over the coasts of Togoland and the Cameroons. Already busy in Indo-China as well as the Pacific, France had moved on Tunis in 1881.

The age of indifference was over, and statesmen of the Western industrial nations, as ruthless in their ambitions as their predecessors of the eighteenth century, prepared to win their shares of new wealth and colonial prestige.

Yet British imperialism, as has been noticed, was not, in the beginning at least, crudely expansionist in an aggressive or territorial sense. British governments were fearful of entanglements that might lead to war. None the less, they were determined to maintain existing trading facilities and remained suspicious of any foreign efforts to seize coastal areas that might threaten the route to India. That they showed more hostility to the French than the Germans was chiefly because French colonial policy was more active, and therefore more provocative, and the French colonial system more rigidly protectionist. The Berlin Conference in 1885 did something to regularize the process of occupation in Africa; but it could not stop competition. On the contrary, it opened the continent to the European invaders, merely seeking to ensure that competitors should stake their claims without using their Maxims against each other. But even under stress of growing competition, Britain continued to show a marked distaste for the responsibility and expense involved in direct annexations. She preferred the old and established method of the chartered company. In 1886, the United Africa Company was reorganized as the Royal Niger Company, with Taubman Goldie as president. This was followed by the granting of a charter to the Imperial British East Africa Company in 1888, and the British South Africa Company in 1889.

Lord Lugard.

Not until 1899 were the territories of the Royal Niger Company taken over by the crown and organized as the protectorates of Northern and Southern Nigeria, and nearly four years were to elapse before the High Commissioner, Colonel Frederick Lugard, was able to pacify the Hausa states of the Moslem north, and introduce, under the supervision of British residents, the system of indirect rule by local emirs or their equivalents.

This system, based on the maintenance of native law and custom, was similarly applied in Ashanti, which was annexed in 1901 following four campaigns, and placed as a separate colony under the governor of the Gold Coast. At the same time, the hinterlands of both Sierra Leone and Ashanti were finally demarcated. Not until 1914 was Northern Nigeria united to the southern region as the colony and protectorate of Nigeria, with Sir Frederick (from 1928, Lord) Lugard as Governor-General. With the pacification and the delimitation of frontiers, commerce slowly expanded from the coastal and river entrepôts deep into the interior. The reduction in freight rates, partly the result of competition between rival shipping companies, now enabled the trader to undertake the exhausting and costly journey to inland markets with less risk of loss. With the coming of railways, increasing quantities of ground-nuts,

Malay House in the 1880s.

cocoa, minerals, palm kernels and hides found their way to the coast. The great era of West African development had begun.

The competition of the European powers was not limited to Africa. On the Malay Peninsula, by successive treaties, Britain added to her Singapore stronghold various crown colonies which included Penang, Province Wellesley and Malacca, known as the Straits Settlements. By 1896 the Malay states of Perak, Selangor, Negri Sembilan and Pahang were federated under British suzerainty; some years later (1910) treaties were concluded with Kelantan, Trengganu and Kedah, which remained like Johore unfederated states under British protection. Meanwhile, in 1841 that incredible adventurer, James Brooke, had become Rajah of Sarawak on the north-east coast of Borneo. Although maintaining its independence, Brooke's kingdom, like that of his neighbour, the Sultan of Brunei, was eventually accepted as a British protectorate. Further north, the flag followed trade. By 1881, as a result of the efforts of the British North Borneo Company, the whole of the north-east coast of the island had passed under British control, and continued to be administered by the Company, even after the establishment of a protectorate in 1888.

As the dependent empire grew in size and value during the last quarter of the nineteenth century, the ties of sentiment and interest which bound the

Sir James Brooke.

self-governing Dominions to the mother country continued to show signs of strain. Separatism scarcely counted as an active element in either British or colonial political life. Indifference was the infection that threatened the health of the Empire, and in the view of the more resolute imperialists this could only be eradicated by some process of constitutional reconstruction. From the seventies onwards, their more provocative proposals were concerned with means of strengthening the framework through some form of imperial federation.

In 1884 the Imperial Federation League was founded, and for a decade it carried on a campaign for the constitutional as well as the commercial and military integration of the self-governing Dominions and the mother country. Although the doctrine of imperial unity was under fire from the start, there was no denying the existence of serious tendencies in the Dominions and mother country favouring disintegration. Composed in its origins of 'the best' in society and politics, the movement was a carefully organized protest against the carelessness with which the imperial connection had been handled in the past. Unhappily, its colonial supporters, while united in aspiration, were divided on methods of realizing the ideal. Despite the League's expressed declaration that a united empire would not interfere with local liberties, responsible Canadians and Australians viewed any attempt at centralization as a threat to colonial self-government. Regional nationalism proved even stronger than imperial loyalty, and after 1892 the movement withered away, leaving to successor organizations the task of publicizing the advantages of preferential tariffs and the need for common imperial defence.

NEW NATIONS: AUSTRALIA AND NEW ZEALAND

The failure of the Imperial Federation movement in no way betokened a weakening of imperial attachments or the end of imperial unity. The depth of interest and sentiment was revealed not only in festivities accompanying Queen Victoria's Diamond Jubilee, but in small trade preferences, the gift of battle-ships, the contributions of men and supplies to the Sudan campaign and more significantly in support of Britain's South African War. In New Zealand and Australia, as in Canada, progress towards dominion status was clearly associated with the growth of something like a national spirit.

Unlike the Canadian provinces, the Australian had not yet, by the 1860s, reached a stage when anything like a federation could be successfully attempted. In many respects, the southern continent was still an empty land; the Wakefield system of subsidized settlement had been abandoned in the forties, and only Queensland (created in 1859) profited by assisted emigration. It was after the discovery of gold in New South Wales and in Victoria (which had hived-off from New South Wales in 1852) that the population began to leap ahead.

The opening up of Australia: workers and officials of the Overland Telegraph in the Northern Territory, August 1872.

The rush of the 'diggers' stimulated both agriculture and manufactures, and it also encouraged a lawlessness, best expressed in the enterprise of the 'bush-ranger' whose buccaneering adventures, comparable to those of Jesse James in the American Wild West, continued until the sixties.

The unknown continent gradually unfolded its desert mysteries. Burke and Wills had died in the attempt to cross the centre from south to north in 1860–61; a year later, John Stuart succeeded. In the seventies, Forrest and Giles mapped the scarcely less cruel wastes of Western Australia. As in Canada, private enterprise could not alone provide the means to build the roads and railways that linked the back country with the capital cities on the sea coast. The state governments undertook the task, despite serious financial crises that pressed some of them to the edge of bankruptcy. None the less, by the nineties all six were prosperous – even Western Australia, whose rich gold-fields were already competing in lavish production with those of her more prosperous neighbours.

Although wide range was given to the individual capitalist, especially for the projects of economic development, free enterprise played a less conspicuous

Bank of New South Wales in the booming gold town of Gulgong in the 1870s.

part than in Canada, where a distrust of too much state action retarded the development of a strong labour movement and delayed the growth of social services. Admittedly, the frontier sheep-grazier or the gold-miner preferred to make his fortune with as little governmental interference as possible. On the other hand, he could not break with his inheritance. The early years of dictatorial government had set a precedent for state initiative in the development of the community; bureaucracy assumed positive authority over enterprises which in North America would have been undertaken by private corporations.

The majority of freed settlers – many of them from Ireland, and bearing with them the traditional hatred of British authority – wanted to be rid of the feudal shackles of the Old World. Consequently, proletarian pressures were stronger than elsewhere in the Empire, even more dominant than in New Zealand. The environment fostered radical or collectivist ideals, but not many of the later nineteenth-century Australians could be called either Philosophic Radicals or Socialists. Bigoted, recalcitrant and often violently racialist in attitude, they were, none the less, responsible for establishing concepts of social democracy which could be applied within the British parliamentary system. Despite the myth of rugged individualism, the tradition of government paternalism has never entirely disappeared.

Although the population was free of fundamental racial divergencies, the task of providing unity for a continent of semi-isolated colonies demanded the conquest of regional rivalries and immense distances. Long separated from one another by vast spaces, Queensland and the four colonies once contained within the boundaries of New South Wales were too engrossed in their own affairs to concern themselves with a union that might bring them material loss rather than gain. Federation was a possible project for the future; at that moment, no broad national sentiment existed sufficient to fire the imagination of politicians, busily striving to work the unfamiliar machinery of responsible government within their own domain. There were local problems of far greater urgency than that of welding a constitution for a confederation of mutually antagonistic states.

Already, by mid-century, each colony had developed a regional consciousness and a truculent patriotism that made any suggestion of closer association something distasteful to the astute politician. The Australian colonists thought of themselves first as citizens of Victoria, South Australia, Tasmania or New South Wales. Economic and social differences, especially after the gold discoveries, created jealousies that increased tensions. Since each levied its own

By the 1860s, Australia had left her convict origins far behind and had begun to develop a sense of national pride.

PUNCH, OR THE LONDON CHARIVARI.—October 29, 1864.

COLONISTS AND CONVICTS.

[Australian Colonist. "NOW, MR. BULL! DON'T SHOOT, ANY MORE OF YOUR *RUBBISH* HERE, OR YOU AND I SHALL QUARREL."

customs duties, they conflicted, often bitterly, on matters of tariff policy. Internal free trade was impossible without a uniform tariff system and repeated efforts to stop the eternal inter-colonial wrangling failed; but not simply owing to lack of legal authority to conclude an agreement: each one feared that its financial position and general welfare might be altered for the worse if a federal parliament was given control of general economic policy.

In the fifties, it had been assumed that the British North American colonies were too far apart to make a central government workable and British Columbia had remained obdurate in opposition to a federation until promised railway connections with the eastern provinces. Before the end of the century, such bonds of steel embraced the Australian continent, but unfortunately the various systems created by individual state enterprise could not be joined because of differing gauges. Yet even uniform gauges would have been insufficient to bridge conflicting interests. What was needed was the compulsion born of some common interests and especially a common problem such as security. Just as a sense of Canadian nationality was fostered by the challenge of an aggressive republic to the south, so the urge to Australian unity was stimulated by the competition of imperial powers in the Pacific Ocean.

The international scramble beginning in the eighties reminded the most parochial observer that a continent which had offered serene existence to six prosperous colonies under the protection of the Royal Navy might not always be immune from invasion by sea. While France and Germany garnered islands in the adjoining ocean, and while Japan transformed herself into an industrial power, anxiety over the exposed position of the Australian continent gave enormous impetus towards the achievement of a federal union under one government.

The need for security provided the most debated and the strongest argument; yet federation, when it came, was the result of a slow gathering of forces. There was no one issue so immediately persuasive as that which had, almost precipitately, moved the British government to support the cause of Canadian federation; there was no urgent crisis, such as the American Civil War produced, to demonstrate both to Britons and Canadians the need for solidarity.

The first proponent of federation was Lord Grey, the Secretary of State for Colonies, who sought to establish such an association during the period of the gold-rushes, or, in the last resort, to provide the means for self-motivating action, should the colonies see fit. But his proposals were greeted without enthusiasm in Australia and equally strong disapproval at home was sufficient to bring repudiation in the House of Lords. By 1855 federation by Westminster decree was a lost cause; the British government, declared Lord John Russell in July of that year, would take no further action to federate the Australian colonies until they themselves jointly requested it, and had framed a suitable scheme of union.

More than a quarter of a century was to elapse before such a scheme became practical politics. Not until 1890 did a conference consisting of the representatives of all six colonies and New Zealand unanimously request a national convention to draw up a federal constitution. The draft of 1891, which was submitted individually for local approval, seemed for a time likely to drop by the wayside. New Zealand withdrew and only economic depression helped to force the hands of the wealthy and 'free-trading' New South Wales. Between 1897 and 1898, a second national convention completed the final labours of constitution-making, broadly on the lines laid down in 1891. By the end of July 1900, Western Australia, the last of the colonies to achieve responsible government (1890), had followed Queensland into the federal enclosure.

On 1 January 1901 the Australian Commonwealth was born of a compromise. Modelled more closely on the loosely federated American structure

The Australian states stand by Britain; from *Punch*, 1896.

BRAVO, YOUNG 'UNS!
Young Cubs. "Well done, Dad! We'll stick to you!"
British Lion. "Thank you, my Boys! I never doubted it!"

199

than on the Canadian, a high measure of independence was retained by the individual states. Moreover, unlike the Canadian constitution, which could only be changed by reference to Westminster, the Australian could be altered by a vote of Parliament confirmed by a majority of states and a majority of the total electorate. But, in contrast to American practice, the Cabinet system of government was adopted, with the executive responsible to the legislature. Indeed, this principle of Cabinet responsibility was to be common to all the self-governing dominions, including South Africa, whose closer union was to be celebrated nine years later.

A Victorian view of the dramatic effect of Christianity on a village in the Cook Islands; from engravings of the 1870s.

Attack on a Maori pah during the Maori Wars.

In 1876, New Zealand, having outgrown regional and political segmentation, had abolished her provincial legislatures to become a closely integrated union, with the capital, Wellington, more or less mid-way between the two main islands. Once the long-drawn Maori Wars (1860–71) were over, this essentially pastoral and agricultural dominion moved nervously ahead to the alternating prosperity and depressions which marked a maturing economy. At the same time, with a boldness and swagger comparable to Australia, she embarked upon experiments in social legislation far in advance of anything hitherto attempted elsewhere in the world. With a near classless society of almost purely British stock (a purity which both political parties were determined to maintain by tight immigration laws), and unimpeded by the trammels of tradition or the pressures of vested interests, she was able, paradoxically, to combine a feudal devotion to the mother country of kings and castles with radical policies of socialization.

By means of taxation, the government encouraged the break-up of large estates and consequently the proliferation of small farms; it promoted the introduction of conciliation boards and arbitration courts, established old-age pensions, nationalized coal-mines and even engaged in the business of insurance. Within sixty years of the Treaty of Waitangi, New Zealand had a population of 750,000, a sophisticated and highly individual political existence and a relatively high standard of living. Largely as a result of the introduction of refrigeration in 1882, the main trading connections shifted from Australia to the United Kingdom, with the result that New Zealand became a highly specialized exporter of dairy produce, meat and wool, to meet the demands of an almost monopolistic British market. For ten years after the end of the Second World War, some 88 per cent of the country's exports went to, and up to 60 per cent of the imports were drawn from Great Britain.

In terms of social habits, political institutions and intellectual roots, a similar commitment existed. At the beginning of the twentieth century, New Zealand was in fact a miniature replica of the mother country, a condition that some, times approached a point of unhealthy submissiveness. The author of *The Long White Cloud*, William Pember Reeves, expressed in verse the nostalgic ob, session of the settler for his homeland. Standing in his garden, the colonial expatriate reads a letter from a friend, who challenges him to return to 'England, life and art'.

Write not that you content can be,
Pent by that drear and shipless sea
Round lonely islands rolled,
Isles nigh as empty as their deep,
Where men but talk of gold and sheep
And think of sheep and gold.

('A Colonist in His Garden', *New Zealand Verse*, 1906.)

Unfortunately, just as the professional 'brains' from Canada continued to be tempted to the United States, so did many of the most eminent New Zealanders in arts and sciences emigrate to Britain. Yet, literary quarterlies and periodicals, based largely on private enterprise, have flourished. As in Canada, the search for 'intellectual maturity' as well as national identity goes on, but already the country's achievements in prose and verse suggest, as Keith Sinclair put it, that a civilization 'based on grass and equality' may yet foster a distinguished national literature. Contemplating the span of Scottish history between the extremes of cannibal savagery and civilized life, Edward Gibbon (who must have been writing a very few years after Cook's discovery of the islands) was encouraged to hope, 'that New Zealand may produce, in some future age, the Hume of the Southern Hemisphere'.

Isolated at the southern extremity of the world, New Zealand depended on the Royal Navy and this bred a loyalty to the mother country, which, in contrast to the other Dominions, retarded the growth of a political nationalism. As late as 1911, Joseph Ward could lecture the Imperial Conference of that year on the need for a federal structure of empire. Twenty years later, the tem, porary refusal to accept dominion status under the Statute of Westminster was the consequence of a tenacious tradition of 'imperial partnership' within an undivided empire. In 1939, the New Zealand Prime Minister did not hesitate to range his country 'in gratitude' and 'without fear' beside Great Britain. 'Where she goes we go and where she stands we stand.'

The outbreak of war in 1939 meant the end of an era. The sudden onslaught of Japan in 1942 was to shatter the customary intimate dependence. Having failed in her lone effort to enforce collective security under the League of Nations, and increasingly conscious after 1945 of her geographical isolation in the Pacific, New Zealand was, like Australia, forced to take shelter under the umbrella of American sea power. The old cultural ties with Britain remained; indeed, the emotional commitment could at moments transcend strategical considerations and trade. None the less, for a new generation who wrote and talked about a distinctive national culture, the age of British guardianship was over.

Lacking numbers and great riches, New Zealand has compensated by seeking and exercising influence through world agencies like the United Nations and the Commonwealth. Such a role, as in the case of Canada, offers not only an enhanced international status but the opportunity for honest missionary effort in under-developed countries. It is scarcely likely, however, that today's New Zealander will find, within the Commonwealth association, the same outlet for moral and romantic fervour once provided by his long-cherished mother country.

Commemorative medallion
produced for George V's
Silver Jubilee in 1935.

Chapter Ten

THE PHENOMENON OF IMPERIALISM

MAKERS OF IMPERIALISM: ROSEBERY, CHAMBERLAIN, RHODES

Although Britain, in the 1880s, had demonstrated a restored imperial purpose, a powerful generation was coming on the scene, whose leaders expounded a more confident and more attractive faith than had their predecessors. Curiously enough, the most significant figure in the initial work of arousing the country to the new imperial ideal was not Joseph Chamberlain or Cecil Rhodes, but Lord Rosebery. In a sense, Rosebery fathered Liberal imperialism, because he drew a large section of the younger Liberals, like Asquith and Haldane, away from Whiggish Cobdenism to fresh fields that promised robust action. As Rosebery saw it, Liberalism should cease to be primarily the instrument of sections and minorities; rather, it should expound comprehensive views on policies that would appeal to the whole nation. The idealism and civilizing zeal which had always been dynamic elements within true Liberalism should be harnessed to the imperial idea and given direction and purpose. He told the Colonial Institute on 1 March 1893:

Lord Rosebery.

It is said that our empire is already large enough, and does not need extension. That would be true enough if the world were elastic, but unfortunately, it is not elastic, and we are engaged at the present moment in the language of mining in 'pegging out claims' for the future. We have to consider what countries must be developed either by ourselves or some other nation, and we have to remember that it is part of our heritage to take care that the world as far as it can be moulded by us, shall receive an English-speaking complexion, and not that of other nations. . . . We have to look forward beyond the chatter of platforms and the passion of party to the future of the race of which we are at present the trustees, and we should in my opinion, grossly fail in the task that has been laid upon us did we shrink from responsibilities and decline to take our share in a partition of the world, which we have not forced on, but which has been forced on us.

His sentimental pride in empire is perhaps difficult for this generation to

Sons of the blood, a lithograph dating from the late nineteenth century ▶

understand, yet he was completely honest. In the course of his Glasgow Rectorial address in November 1900, he said:

How marvellous it all is. Built not by saints and angels, but the work of men's hands; cemented with men's honest blood and with a world of tears, welded by the best brains of centuries past; not without taint and reproach incidental to all human work, but constructed on the whole with pure and splendid purpose. Human and yet not wholly human, for the most heedless and the most cynical must see the finger of the divine. Growing as trees while others slept; fed by the faults of others as well as by the character of our fathers; reaching with the ripple of a resistless tide over tracts and islands and continents, until our little Britain woke up to find herself the foster-mother of nations and the source of united empires.

Rosebery was not a very successful Foreign Minister; but he helped to initiate a new age, and for a brief but crucial spell in English history his influence within the country was enormous. On the matter of Irish Home Rule, he probably followed Gladstone out of respect, but in 1892 he forced him to abandon the idea of evacuating Egypt. Two years later, despite the nagging opposition of Sir William Harcourt, Rosebery was responsible for making Uganda a protectorate. The decision to keep Uganda marked a turning-point in British policy. To the dismay of hoary party survivors, a policy of empire-building had now become as acceptable to Liberals as to Disraelian Tories. In the view of cynics, Liberal imperialism was the only form of contemporary Liberalism that was visible either on the public platform or in the halls of Westminster.

Yet, to Rosebery and his disciples, the popular identification of Tory or Unionist principles with imperialism was an illogical and unnatural state of affairs. After all, the main Tory driving-force within the expanding field of empire development was coming from ex-Liberals like Joseph Chamberlain, who had left the fold in 1886 when Gladstone's conversion to Irish Home Rule had almost shattered the party by threatening the destruction of the old British Empire. If Home Rule could be gently dropped, a good many dissenters would return to the party, and under the banner of Liberal imperialism, leadership of the nation might again be assured. The new faith would be broad and yet sufficiently precise and ordered to appeal to both the idealist and the earthy. It would offer an imperial creed, according to one exponent, which would dignify and intensify 'every detail of the politics of the home, the school, the factory and the field'. Liberalism would become 'elevated into an all-pervading faith'.

If Rosebery might be called the aloof and learned instructor, Joseph Chamberlain was the *enfant terrible*, and subsequently the hero, of the im-

In this cartoon of 1886, Queen Victoria declares her affection for Ireland: 'With all thy faults I love thee still.'

perialists. Educated in Birmingham as a businessman, he was, despite a strong imaginative streak in his nature, a compound of energy rather than of intellect. The sharply chiselled facial contours, so tempting to the caricaturist, rightly suggested an aggressive will that brooked no ordinary opposition. In pursuit of ends deemed worthy of achievement, he fought with boisterous zest and reckless courage.

Like Rosebery, Chamberlain was a Liberal, but he was never a Radical except in the social sense, in the same way as the Tory Randolph Churchill. He finally parted company with Gladstone over the first Irish Home Rule Bill of 1886, but the man who was to become the arch-imperial federationist was never an anti-colonial nationalist. As early as 1887, he had declared that 'True Democracy' did not mean the dismemberment and disintegration of the Empire. He welcomed the 'coming of age' of Australia and Canada, and under his tutelage (after he became Colonial Secretary in the Salisbury Ministry of 1895) a sense of kinship gradually began to supplant the old possessive attitude of Downing Street. Indeed, colonial delegates and commissioners were to receive during his brief years of hope and glory a respect and a sympathy that sometimes reached the point of unctuousness. His cherished project for the maturing white nations was a formal scheme of imperial partnership, with an elaborate assortment of fiscal preferences and a centrally controlled imperial defence system.

Joseph Chamberlain.

Because he was trained as a businessman, he wanted a business-like organization of empire. Although he continued to preach the doctrine of imperial federation fervently until the fall of the Conservative government in 1905, Chamberlain never ceased to think along commercial lines, nor tired of reiterating his favourite slogan that 'empire is commerce'. New estates had to be exploited and new markets secured, if the mother country were to be saved from decline and ultimate starvation. 'History teaches us that no nation has ever achieved real greatness without the aid of commerce, and the greatness of no nation has survived the decay of its trade.'

Such mundane statements might suggest that Chamberlain's ideal of empire was, in the words of a critic, 'nothing better than a partnership agreement in a trade of pepper and coffee, calico and tobacco, or some other such low concern'. Undoubtedly, the rich potentialities of a world-wide organization appealed to the man whose object was to put it 'on a business footing'. On the other hand, the Empire also appealed to him as a great civilizing force, embracing with compassion as well as profit, the long-neglected 'lesser breeds'. Like Kipling, he contemplated the 'White Man's burden' romantically, but without pretence. 'You cannot', he said, 'make omelettes without breaking eggs; you cannot destroy the practices of barbarism, of slavery, of superstition . . . without the use of force.' But then he added: 'We feel that our rule over these territories can only be justified if we can show that it adds to the happiness and prosperity of the people, and I maintain that our rule does, and has, brought security and peace and comparative prosperity to countries that never knew these blessings before.'

Canada, Australia and New Zealand went their ways unobserved, on the whole, by the masses. The man on the London street was more interested in Africa, and especially the South Africa of Cecil Rhodes. 'Darkest Africa' was showing more and more bright patches of red on giant sketch-maps that successively decorated shop windows in the Strand. Exciting native wars were followed closely by the British popular press. Great powers shouldered each other to claim kingdoms; unknown adventurers made private fortunes overnight. The drama of imperial success was even carried into the theatre, where the drop-scene might reveal the closing prices of Rand securities.

To generalize very simply, four European powers wanted to establish empires across the African continent. Britain alone hoped to drive a corridor of occupation not east and west, but north and south. One man who attempted to make this dream a reality was Cecil Rhodes, who aimed at building a Cape to Cairo railway. By 1886, the termini had been secured; it only remained to fill in the gap of a few thousand miles. To do this meant wiping out the claims of Portugal and more difficult, the claims, and especially the opposition, of Germany and France.

By the time of Rhodes's appointment as deputy commissioner of Bechuana-land in 1884, Britain's rivals were closing in from both flanks. Germany, at last free from the contagious free-trade doctrines of the Manchester School, had established herself on the west coast, north of the Orange River, from whence she began to press inland. The Transvaal Boers had already begun to expand over the Cape to Cairo line. In the circumstances, Rhodes needed the home government's consent to break the restraining barrier. The British South Africa Chartered Company, founded in 1889, gave him practically a free hand to advance his 'South to North' project; Rhodesia was added amid Matabele wars. Meanwhile, the British East Africa Company (1888) had struck in from the east coast towards the centre. Here the competition was between German and English companies. Arrangements were made to divide or define spheres of influence and action in various areas, some of which had been under the nominal suzerainty of the Sultan of Zanzibar. Italy was given a fragment in the north, and, as a *pourboire*, the sultan received a strip ten miles broad along the mainland coast, which the British Company was subsequently to lease (1887). The recognition of Zanzibar as a British protectorate in June 1890, followed by the protectorate over Uganda (1894), were aimed at safeguarding the approach to the head-waters of the Nile. The final step could only be made by severing the east and west routes of France, Portugal and Germany. Portugal,

209

with little power of resistance, had to submit to the designers of the 'Cape to Cairo'. But Germany proved to be a tougher proposition. A strip of territory which linked Rhodesia and Uganda was finally begged from King Leopold's Congo State in 1890; but, for reasons of a deeper diplomatic significance (because she felt Britain was not sufficiently backing her claims in Africa against France), Germany joined the French in opposition, and the dream of a through route from Cape to Cairo had perforce to be abandoned until 1918.

The son of a country clergyman, Rhodes went to South Africa at the age of seventeen in the hope of repairing his health. Outwardly robust, a towering giant of a man, without fear of man or beast, he never regained full physical strength; indeed on his second visit to Africa he was given six months to live. The prediction was unfulfilled, and on the newly discovered diamond-fields close to the western borders of the Orange Free State, the man who had been granted an unexpected lease on life found a fortune.

In so many respects Rhodes provides the model Kipling or Rider Haggard hero, the strong, silent man, who might not be always scrupulous in his personal conduct, but who 'played the game'. And the British public backed him as they backed Palmerston, as they so frequently back the eccentric leader of driving energy and adventurous folly. 'What were you doing, since last I saw you Mr Rhodes,' said Queen Victoria in her best Elizabethan manner; 'I have added two provinces to Your Majesty's Dominions' was the perfect courtly answer. In the manner of Oliver Cromwell, he may well have believed himself the chosen instrument for furthering British expansion.

Rhodes liked money and amassed stupendous wealth. He organized the scattered mining companies; amalgamations meant efficiency in gold production, especially with low-grade reefs. Money was power, but like Lord Beaverbrook he subordinated it to an idea: 'building an empire'. He had no use for yachts or parties or racehorses, or even women. Undoubtedly, he could be a bully, but he won the respect and sometimes the admiration of many great men. The shrewdest of Afrikaners preferred the ambitious autocrat of public spirit to the money-grubbing speculator. The Jameson Raid, as we shall see, was a blow to his prestige. Yet, stripped of all his powers, he continued to be the greatest single force in South Africa. Chamberlain dreamed in terms of colonies, Rhodes, of whole continents.

Although authoritarian in outlook, impatient and not always punctilious in his official behaviour, like Chamberlain he grasped the meaning of liberty in so far as the white component nations of the Empire were concerned. But unlike Chamberlain, he became a strong supporter of Irish nationalism, insisting only that the grant of Home Rule should be accompanied by continued

representation at Westminster. His ideal for South Africa was one nation,

Rhodes's favourite photograph
of himself.

Briton and Boer living in equal partnership within its borders under the British crown. Determined to promote friendly relations between Dutch and English, he cultivated an alliance with Jan Hofmeyr, leader of the Afrikaner Bond, and during six years as Prime Minister of Cape Colony he had the confidence and support of both white races. Had Rhodes been given time and patience, he might have foreseen the inevitable departure of the ageing and obstinate President Paul Kruger, a more tractable Transvaal within the customs union (which the Orange Free State had joined), and the stage set for a true federation. But he was haunted by a sense of his own impending death, and in hastening the fall of Kruger by helping to organize what proved to be the disastrous fiasco of the Jameson Raid (2 January 1896), he ruined his career and discredited his country in the eyes of the world as well as the Cape Dutch. The greatest man in the history of modern South Africa had tragically destroyed his own cause, restored Kruger's fading prestige, and unwittingly laid the way to bitter war.

211

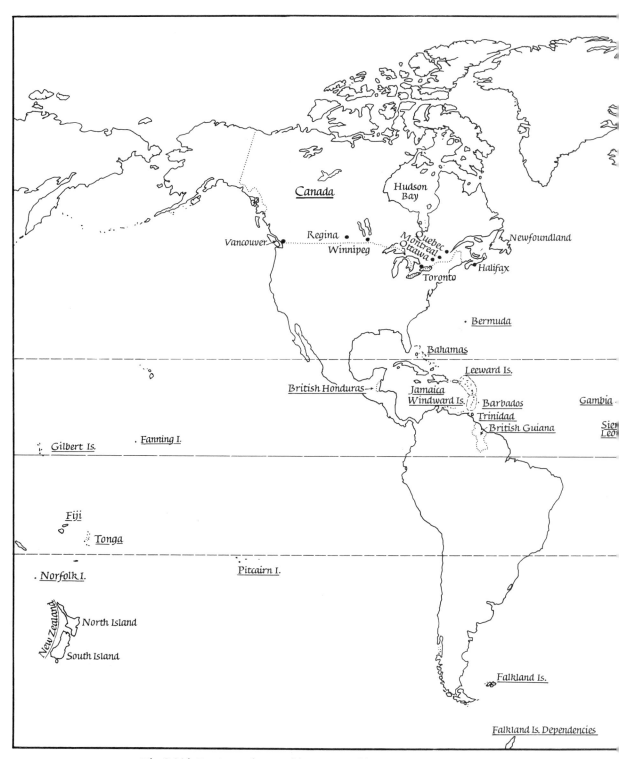

The British Empire on the eve of the First World War.

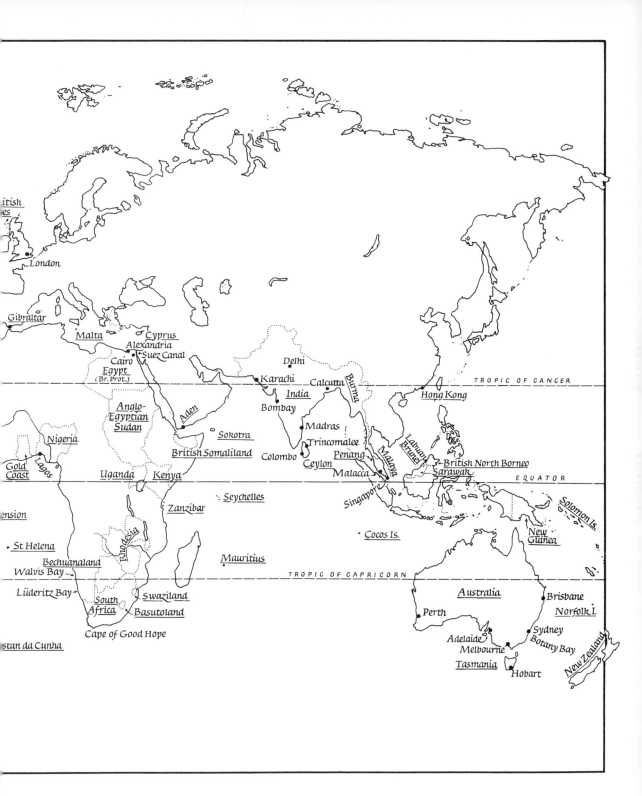

British
es

London

Gibraltar

Malta
Cyprus
Alexandria
Suez Canal
Cairo
Egypt
(Br. Prot.)

Anglo-
Egyptian
Sudan

Aden

Sokotra

Nigeria

British Somaliland

Gold
Coast

Lagos

Uganda
Kenya

ension

Zanzibar

Seychelles

St Helena

Rhodesia

Cocos Is.

Mauritius

Bechuanaland
Walvis Bay

Lüderitz Bay

South
Africa

Swaziland
Basutoland

Cape of Good Hope

stan da Cunha

Delhi

Karachi
India
Bombay

Calcutta

Burma

TROPIC OF CANCER

Hong Kong

Madras
Trincomalee
Penang
Colombo
Ceylon
Malacca

Malaya

Labuan
Brunei

British North Borneo
Sarawak

EQUATOR

Singapore

Solomon Is.

New
Guinea

Australia

Brisbane

Norfolk I.

Perth

Sydney
Botany Bay

Adelaide
Melbourne
Tasmania

New Zealand

Hobart

TROPIC OF CAPRICORN

Colombo harbour in 1882.

THE CLIMAX OF IMPERIALISM

By the end of the nineteenth century, the western European powers had reached exhaustion point in their race for undeveloped parts of the earth. In West Africa, Britain had added the huge colony and protectorate of Nigeria and considerable extensions had been made to Sierra Leone and the Gold Coast. In south central Africa, she now possessed Nyasaland and the rich lands of Rhodesia, of which the southern part was climatically favourable for European occupation; on the eastern side, British East Africa (later to become Kenya), the protectorate of Uganda and the coastal strip of Somaliland. Moreover, the whole Valley of the Nile from source to mouth was under effective British control. It seemed clear that the masters of the khedive and the Suez Canal would not retreat from Egypt within measurable time. In eastern seas, the Empire had been rounded off with the Malay Peninsula, Burma and Baluchistan. Diagonally across the Indian Ocean, a large section of New Guinea, and a hundred or more islands in the Pacific Ocean were under British direct rule or supervision. Within less than twenty years, she had managed to acquire the lion's share of the spoils – at a rough estimate some 3,500,000 square miles.

In the last resort, the spur of competition was decisive; none the less, it was obvious that British governments had entered the mad scramble with considerable distaste. Not only in Egypt and the Sudan, but in Africa and Polynesia, they had been more often pushed than lured by circumstances. Positive aversion

Britannia, assured of the support of her colonies, feels she can ignore the other European powers; a *Punch* cartoon of 1901.

Reluctantly, John Bull decides to take in one more 'black baby' found on his doorstep. Uganda was annexed at the time of this *Punch* cartoon in 1894.

Reception at the British residency in Zanzibar, *c.* 1910. Zanzibar became a British protectorate in 1890.

A treaty made with the Kikuyu tribe in Kenya, August 1889.

Missionaries in Tanganyika in the 1880s.

Europeans surrounded by warriors and musicians in Borneo; a late nineteenth-century photograph.

lay in the fact that the bulk of the new acquisitions were not, like Canada and Australia, 'whiteman's country'. The Canada of 1763, with its tiny population of Europeans, had meant trouble enough; most of the newly occupied areas were the homes of primitive or backward peoples barely connected with Western civilization, and quite unlikely to fade away in the manner of American Indians or Australian aborigines.

Indeed, substantial parts of these new territories had been taken at the pressing insistence of self-governing colonials. Against heavy Whitehall opposition, Queensland won direct control over a large section of New Guinea; and the boisterous demands of Australians and New Zealanders for distant south Pacific islands horrified both Lord Salisbury and Mr Gladstone. At the Colonial Conference of 1887, Salisbury was coldly disdainful of Australian grumbles regarding French intrusions in the New Hebrides.

Lord Salisbury (Prime Minister from June 1885 to January 1886, July 1886 to 1892 and 1895 to 1902) resented being pulled into a race for spoils in Africa or anywhere else, and he suspected Chamberlain of enjoying the process of making omelettes by breaking eggs. To Chamberlain the possession of power meant opportunity; to Salisbury it was a sad fact of life arising from original sin. As a cautious statesman of the old school, with a contempt for the vulgar catchwords of imperial expansion, his main concern in the international field was the security of India. Although instinctively opposed to extended commit ments, he was never an isolationist. Slowly and sombrely he followed behind the vanguard of cut-throat contestants for empire, responding reluctantly to his country's clamours for added magnificence.

As events after 1885 had shown, the masses with the new vote wanted vigo rous action. Power and dominion proved to have a greater appeal than peace, freedom and independence. Rosebery once remarked that as larger and larger numbers of Englishmen were admitted to the suffrage, each of them had come to feel that his personal honour and name were implicated in the honour and name of the Empire. This was demonstrated beyond dispute at the great Dia mond Jubilee celebration of 1897, a display of pomp and power that brought home the splendour of Britannia's heritage.

The emergence of a popular press designed to appeal to the common man served further to quicken the public pulse. Alfred Harmsworth, later Lord Northcliffe, got control of the *Daily Mail* in 1896 and sold it at a halfpenny. He dropped the old-fashioned news and 'threw his pebble in the pond' each day; this meant selecting a talking-point and, with striking headlines, exciting opinion on one thing at a time. During the first year, the *Mail* had an average sale of 200,000 copies. By 1901, it had reached a million. First and foremost, said Harmsworth, 'the *Daily Mail* stands for the power, supremacy and great ness of the British Empire . . . The *Daily Mail* is the embodiment and mouth piece of the imperial idea.'

The same might be said of popular poets and novelists who were adding to their fame in the eighties and nineties: not only Henley and Kipling, but Stevenson with *Treasure Island* and Rider Haggard with *King Solomon's Mines*. But it was Kipling who best interpreted and reflected the diverse elements that composed imperialism. Gunga Din, Mandalay and a host of colourful Eastern tales and poems brought the idea of empire to the man on the street. Tommy, the private soldier, was made into a hero; his very toughness and his commonness were glorified; *Barrack Room Ballads* appealed to a pugnacious pride.

It was a self-satisfied age – arrogant, smug and slightly hysterical. As Henry James strolled about the Common beside the Royal Artillery Barracks at Woolwich, his imagination quickened in the presence of 'this nursery of British valour'. Any glimpse of the imperial machinery always stirred his emotions to the point of jingoism. 'I know not what to call this sentiment,' he wrote, 'unless it be simply an admiration for the greatness of England.' He thought of 'the great part that England had played in human affairs, the great space she has occupied, her tremendous might, her far-stretching rule', and he found himself wondering whether the imperial epoch was 'completely closed'.

The Diamond Jubilee celebration of 1897: New South Wales Lancers in procession in London ▶

James's cerebral vibrations, but not his doubts, were shared by the masses, even in what he called 'the slums and purlieus of this duskiest of modern Babylons'. The new democracy which sang 'Soldiers of the Queen' felt, as did the builders of the Crystal Palace in 1851, that theirs was 'the greatest show on earth'. To the upper classes, people on the Continent were interesting because they were exotic, and useful in that they provided a select clientele with barbers, bakers and music-hall ladies. Apart from a veneer of Western civilization on the Atlantic coast of the United States, Americans did not count. In its optimism and triumphant pride it was a dazzling age of achievement. The year 1897 saw the Empire at its zenith. With the ships, the colonies, the men and the money, Britain could confidently face the whole world from the heights of 'splendid isolation'. Despite the tremors which occasionally agitated the earth's crust, there was an atmosphere of permanence. In her old age Queen Victoria appeared as the enduring symbol of the *status quo*; and the veterans who embodied the nineteenth-century ethos – Gladstone, Salisbury, Chamberlain and Harcourt – had not yet given way to younger men like Winston Churchill, Edward Grey and Richard Haldane.

Such assurances of enduring stamina did little, however, to improve the demeanour or the status of the peregrinating English tourist. The strongest and richest nation in the world was disliked abroad in much the same manner as the United States inspires certain jealousies and resentments among weaker nations today. But unlike the Americans, the British rarely concerned themselves about other peoples' opinions. The middle and the lower classes made no bones about their contempt for the outsider: 'He's a blinkin' foreigner; 'eave 'arf a brick at 'im.' Years before the Diamond Jubilee, Charles Dickens had thus epitomized the national genius for 'making friends and influencing people'.

On the other hand, British imperialism, in retrospect, strikes one as far less militaristic in tone than continental. Despite the brassy bravado of the time, few people were willing to contemplate a big war with any relish. Little colonial wars, such as the Sudan campaign, Indian frontier adventures or battles with the colourful Zulus were a different matter; they were exercises in character-building and often provided heroes as well as martyrs. Moreover, *fin de siècle* was not approached without some general apprehension. Although British commercial and financial supremacy was still a fact, the contest for world leadership was becoming increasingly exacting. Already there was public controversy over the rapid progress of American and German trade, and the adaptability of the Americans and the aggressiveness of the Germans was compared with the conservatism and lethargy of the British.

But it was the Boer War which finally shattered the concept of invulnerability, and thus pin-pointed *fin de siècle* as a turning-point in British history.

Queen Victoria, symbol of the British Empire at its zenith ▶

Except for variable American support, Britain stood friendless and alone. Not only her military power but her trading wealth seemed to be receding with new tides that were slowly undermining the sandy foundations of her magnificence. Not without foreboding, despondent observers recalled Rudyard Kipling's warning of 1897:

Far call'd our Navies melt away
On dune and headland sinks the fire
Lo, all our pomp of yesterday
Is one with Nineveh and Tyre!

The new and fashionable biologists and embryonic sociologists were little affected by such ominous warnings. While Benjamin Kidd taught the importance of war in the evolution of human society, J. A. Cramb, in his lectures *The Origins and Destiny of Imperial Britain* (1900), saw universal peace less as a dream than a nightmare, to be realized 'when the ice has crept to the heart of the sun, and the stars left black and trackless, start from their orbits'. This pseudo-Darwinian glorification of a struggle encouraged the growth of the notion that divine destiny invited and impelled progress and expansion by the strongest. According to the accepted social evolution theory, the world would belong to the three or four fittest nations. Certainly, Joseph Chamberlain seems to have been influenced by this idea. 'The day of small empires with their petty jealousies is past. The future is with the great empires, and there is no greater empire than the British Empire.'

Such doctrines or hypotheses were not incompatible with an honest core of religious zeal, which as H. D. Traill pointed out, made some Englishmen believe they had a sort of roving commission from on high to carry the blessings of good government to those races of the earth who were either too underdeveloped or too effete to provide it for themselves. Any interference by rivals was resented, 'not only on personal and self-interested grounds but as a perverse attempt to obstruct the manifest designs of Providence'. Every Englishman, according to Bernard Shaw in *The Man of Destiny* (1898), is born with a certain miraculous power that makes him master of the world.

When he wants a thing, he never tells himself that he wants it. He waits patiently until there comes into his mind, no one knows how, a burning conviction that it is his moral and religious duty to conquer those who have got the thing he wants. Then he becomes irresistible. . . . He is never at a loss for an effective moral attitude. As the great champion of freedom and national independence, he conquers and annexes half the world and calls it Colonization. When he wants a new market for his adulterated Manchester goods, he sends a missionary to teach the natives the Gospel of Peace. The natives kill

P&O

EGYPT INDIA CEYLON
STRAITS CHINA JAPAN
AUSTRALASIA

OCEAN CRUISES - WORLD TOURS
P&O TOURS 14. COCKSPUR STREET SWI

A world cruise was almost
equivalent to a sightseeing
tour of the British Empire,
as this P & O poster indicates.

the missionary: he flies to arms in defence of Christianity; fights for it: conquers for it; and takes the market as a reward from heaven.

Some years ago, it was widely assumed that the imperial conundrum was answerable by economic argument, namely that colonization and empire-building were essentially economic acts undertaken for economic reasons. 'The savage no sooner becomes ashamed of his nakedness', observed Sydney Smith with glib irony, 'than the loom is ready to clothe him.' But was imperialism a mask for industrialists who deluded the mob by appealing to their worst appetites of race and nationalism? If keeping capital at home lowered prices, obviously there would be a constant need to find markets on which surplus capital could be expended, which in time would bring in more new capital. According to influential Liberal publicists like J. A. Hobson, whose book *Imperialism* appeared in 1902, the export of capital to economically under-developed colonial areas was the necessary safety-valve of capitalism. Conspicuous expenditure at home might absorb some of the surplus, but the purchasing power of the masses could never keep pace with increasing domestic production. The surplus had to be exported; capitalism had to expand, or, along with the whole economic-social system, 'die of congestion'. Adherents of the Marxist-Leninist theory of imperialism carried this accumulation of capital theory further by arguing that imperialist expansion represented the last stages in the development of capitalism. The parts of the earth still open to exploiting imperial powers were limited and the time was bound to come when the safety-valve would be closed. The resulting crisis accompanying the death pangs of capitalism would produce revolution, assuming, of course, it did not come earlier as a result of war between rival imperialisms fighting for the diminishing markets of the world.

This 'accumulation theory' is, to a certain extent, plausible. Since the middle of the nineteenth century, Britain, France and Germany had exported large amounts of capital, and the financial returns from these investments in many instances came to overshadow completely the income derived from foreign trade. Indeed, British capital abroad increased from £700,000,000 in 1860 to £9,300,000,000 in 1896. In fact, however, the export of capital seems to have had little direct connection with territorial expansion; it did not stop at political boundaries. In 1913, Great Britain had more money invested in the United States than in any colony or in any other foreign country. Less than half of her total export of capital had gone to the Empire. The United States sent more capital into Canada than did Britain, and when after the First World War, the United States became a creditor nation, 43 per cent of her investment was placed in Latin America, 27 per cent in Canada and Newfoundland, and 22 per cent in Europe. When France added one by one to her colonies, she did not feed them capital. By far the larger part of her exported funds, according to W. L. Langer, went to Russia, Rumania, Spain, Portugal, Egypt and Turkey. In 1902, only about two billion francs, out of a total foreign investment of some thirty billion, went to overseas colonies.

In short, colonies solved neither the question of surplus capital nor the trade problem. The white Dominions in particular were not prevented even by tariff restrictions from following their own economic interests. Indeed, very few colonies conducted as much as half their trade with the mother country, and a good many, less. All told, colonial commerce in the nineteenth century was relatively unimportant in comparison with the total foreign commerce of the imperial power.

No economic motive is sufficient, therefore, to explain the growth of imperialism in the late nineteenth century. The Marxists, and neo-Marxists in particular, paid too little attention to imponderables like prestige, which had already become associated with nationalism. Nation and empire were concepts which were both capable of generating popular emotions and, if need be, driving ordinary individuals to sacrifice their lives. Nor can the 'moneyed interests' of the emerging bourgeoisie be held responsible for breeding expansionists and jingoes. As Jacob Viner has pointed out, when 'dangerous foreign policies', or 'dangerous wars' were in question, the historical role of the businessman has been more often that of the appeaser than the warmonger. In the British Parliament, it was the spokesmen for the emerging middle classes of the northern manufacturing towns and for the City bankers in London who were the appeasers and compromisers from the Napoleonic Wars to the time of Hitler.

This newspaper cartoon of 1910 blames the export of capital on the British policy of free trade in a world of protection.

MONTHLY.

NOVEMBER 1900.

Vol I ॰ Part I.

PRICE 1/- NET.

C.P. 3778 ga.

THE IMPERIAL & COLONIAL MAGAZINE & REVIEW

ILLUSTRATED

EDITED BY

"CELT" AND E. F. BENSON.

Publishers:

LONDON:
HURST & BLACKETT, LD.,
13, Great Marlborough St., W.

Canada & America:
The International News Co.

Australasia,
South Africa, &c.:
Messrs. Gordon & Gotch.

India, East Indies & Ceylon:
Messrs. Thacker, Spink & Co.
    „   Thacker & Co., Ltd.,
    „   A. H. Wheeler & Co.

China, Japan, &c.:

Title-page of *The Imperial & Colonial Magazine & Review*, November 1900.

Chapter Eleven

THE NEW NATIONALISMS

By 1897, the year of the Diamond Jubilee, more than forty years had elapsed since Britain had fought any war on the European continent. On the whole, the age of *Pax Britannica* had been one of unique material progress, and most Britons were ready to pay tribute to a sacrosanct economic system that had enabled their country to enjoy the world's abundance at the least cost. Under free trade, a merchant marine totalling more than half the tonnage of the world had been built to carry from abroad the food-supplies and raw materials for consumption in the vast island labyrinth of factories and workshops. It was generally acknowledged that free trade had given the United Kingdom its industrial supremacy over other nations.

The power and glory had not yet waned. In 1896 Lord Rosebery had told an Edinburgh audience that within twelve years 2,600,000 square miles had been added to the Empire, chiefly in Africa. Yet there was no disputing the fact that within the markets of the Empire, British trade was losing ground. Between 1881 and 1900, British possessions had increased their purchases by 17 per cent; but British exports to those same colonies had revealed an actual decrease of 1 per cent. In other words, the trade between the mother country and her colonies was not increasing at the same rate as the total trade of those colonies. A limit seemed to have been reached not only in the territorial extension of the Empire, but in the development of imperial markets. Moreover, the emancipated foreigner was now beginning to carry his own manufactures in his own ships. Where, then, could new markets and new incentives be found, if British industry and commerce was not to lose still further ground?

To the devotees of a new school of imperialism the answer seemed to lie in the closer economic union of the existing Empire. The United Kingdom as a

single economic unit was losing ground, but could not the consolidation of the Empire – the substitution of empire for nation – help to offset the waning supremacy of the mother country? Already the expansion of banking and joint-stock investment techniques was stimulating the flow of capital for overseas railways and public works, and encouraging large-scale specialization in such commodities as Canadian wheat, Australian wool, African cotton and Malayan tin.

For the first time in history, tropical areas were becoming important fields of industrial enterprise. Improvements in communications alone were transform-ing the economic pattern. The older, white colonies had long shared the services of the engineer and financier; now similar agencies were at work in the tropical dependencies. West Africa was shortly to move into the forefront as a laboratory of industrial experiment, and even stagnant backwaters like British East Africa, or bankrupt colonies like the West Indies, were to respond to the mechanical and capitalistic impulses of the new age. Cocoa, ground-nuts, sisal, cotton, coffee, sugar, palm oil and minerals were to flow in increasing abundance from the agricultural perimeter to the metropolis of Empire. If the far-flung and hitherto neglected British colonies and dependencies could be bound together as a commercial whole, Britain was assured a safe market for her manufactures in the fast-developing regions of the earth, and the colonies in turn a protected market for their raw materials in Britain. Such in essence was the idea that gradually matured in the mind of Joseph Chamberlain, who had entered the Colonial Office in 1895 determined to subordinate the 'annals of a kingdom' to

The development of Africa.

Loading a train
in Uganda, *c.* 1890.

◀ Indian railway carriage;
from an engraving in
the *Illustrated London
News*, March 1864.

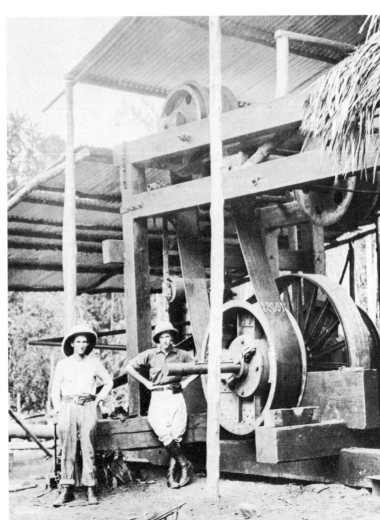

Drilling in the Niger
Delta by the British
Colonial Petroleum
Corporation, *c.* 1910.

the 'history of an Empire'. Whatever the political and administrative failures, as a wholesale business partnership the British Empire was to experience its most creative phase during the Chamberlain era.

But running a family business meant sacrifice as well as profit. The new trusteeship conception of empire involved responsibilities that embraced moral as well as economic, universal as well as imperial considerations. Colonial policy would naturally still be directed to the advantage of the imperial power, but self-interest in the age of Chamberlain was beginning to be linked with the material welfare of millions of coloured peoples. Hitherto, British governments had been content to justify their benevolent rule in terms of political education, law and order; British theories of colonial government in the nineteenth century had been largely a reflection of their own domestic *laissez-faire* ideas. Parliament had steadily refused to vote sums demanded by enlightened governors to deal effectively with pressing social problems, and colonial revenues had been inadequate to meet even the minimum needs.

The change came almost dramatically in 1897 with the appointment of a Royal Commission to inquire into the conditions and prospects of the British West Indies. The pledge contained in its report was to be repeated in 1910 when a similar Royal Commission investigated prospects of trade with Canada: 'We have placed the labouring population where it is, and created for it the conditions, moral and material, under which it exists, and we cannot divest ourselves of responsibility for its future.'

At the end of the nineteenth century, the British West India islands seemed destined to remain, in Lloyd George's words, a 'slum of Empire'. Less than one-tenth of Britain's sugar imports came from her own islands; in the face of beet-sugar competition, the cane-sugar industry stood in danger of extinction. In 1898, the British Parliament voted more than £160,000 for the immediate relief of the West Indies. In view of the injuries wrought by *laissez-faire* and free trade the contribution was trifling, but it laid the foundations for a long series of colonial development schemes. One of the first and most important was the establishment of an imperial department of agriculture, with Barbados as headquarters. Over an area stretching some 800 miles from north to south, and 1000 miles from east to west, the department strove to revive stricken communities. Its responsibilities included experiments not only in cane and plant culture, but in animal breeding and soil fertility, and in the destruction of insect and fungoid pests, as well as education in field cultivation and marketing. Sea Island cotton was introduced into St Vincent, Barbados and the Leeward Islands, the cultivation of limes was accelerated in Dominica, and rice in British Guiana, while the banana, so vulnerable to hurricanes and 'Panama disease', became the symbol of precarious salvation in Jamaica.

In all British tropical possessions, advances in medical, agricultural, chemical and entomological science cleansed the Empire of some of its worst physical blemishes. The discovery in 1897 of the association between the mosquito and malaria marked the beginnings of a new era in tropical medicine as well as a revolution in tropical labour conditions. In India, Ceylon, Malaya, and in West and East Africa botanical gardens grew into, or were linked with, research stations. Kew, which had become after 1900 the centre of botanical economy for the whole Empire, contributed in knowledge and personnel to these developments.

The last quarter of the nineteenth century had seen the opening of vast colonial wildernesses; the first quarter of the twentieth was to witness an intensive imperial effort to understand these hitherto obscure environments and subdue their worst perils. Such projects required the spending of a good deal of money, often with no immediate prospect of a return; but a new generation of British people, increasingly subject to the pangs of self-reproach, were to gain that salve of conscience which in later years helped to reconcile them to even sharper attacks on their purse.

In an age when science was also annihilating distance, the problem of merging the interests of Great Britain in the interest of the colonies seemed to be simplified. Faster and cheaper facilities for communication, whether by submarine cables or steamships, inevitably brought all parts of the Empire into closer correspondence, and encouraged Chamberlain in his plans for the development of a single grand entity. Imperial unity would mean added commercial strength, and vice versa. Closer commercial relationships based on a preferential tariff system would encourage intra-imperial trade and at the same time prevent foreign rivals from dumping their cheap surplus goods in imperial markets. Increased prosperity, shared by all partners, would check separative tendencies and consequent weakness. Good economics was good politics. Given a form of commercial union based on the imposition of small duties on various foreign raw materials and foods, political centralization might follow as a matter of course.

Unhappily for Chamberlain's plans, most British people, either by conviction or tradition, were 'free traders'. For this reason, the Colonial Secretary was careful to insist in the beginning that his grand conception meant no radical deviation from economic orthodoxy. In theory, he was himself, he declared, a convinced free trader, but he had 'not such a pedantic admiration for it that, if sufficient advantage were offered to me, I would not consider a deviation from the strict doctrine'.

But would the self-governing colonies provide the 'sufficient advantage'? Since the middle of the century, economic conditions within the Empire had

One of Britain's foreign competitors thanks John Bull for encouraging her goods to come into the country by his free trade policy; from a Tariff Reform League pamphlet of 1903.

changed radically. With the granting of self-government, anything like a common fiscal policy for the Empire was out of the question. Differences of revenue requirements, differences of attitude and practice made the adoption among the varying colonies of a common policy almost impossible to achieve. Canada, for example, would probably be unwilling to contemplate anything like a central customs authority, which suggested a diminution of national self-government. At bottom, the question of an imperial tariff system was bound to turn on constitutional as well as economic issues.

Indeed, the desire for political autonomy asserted itself in a growing un-willingness to open markets wide to British manufactures. Behind newly erected tariff barriers local manufacturing industries had developed, and even the Liberal Prime Minister of Canada, Sir Wilfred Laurier, who took office in 1896, had learned the political wisdom of his predecessor's 'National Policy' and was already dexterously extricating himself from the meshes of free trade. Imperial preference in the form of differential duties favouring the mother country and Empire was one thing, but an enclosed domain of empire with no internal tariff barriers, fenced against the outside world, was a different matter. Few self-governing colonies were likely to risk the sacrifice of national revenue and pride for the benefit of the Empire as a whole.

Within Britain, it was evident after 1897 that free trade lay under a threat. The disciplines of Cobden were on the defensive; politicians and pamphle-teers were assailing their doctrines more assiduously than had been the case for half a century. Furthermore, the Boer War created currents of sentiment in the self-governing colonies which seemed to run stronger than ever in imperial channels. In January 1901, Australia became a federal Commonwealth, and along with Canada and New Zealand, she furnished contingents of troops for service in South Africa. Such loyal assistance in itself seemed likely to predispose British opinion in favour of fiscal alterations benefiting colonial allies.

Early in 1902 Hicks Beach, the Chancellor of the Exchequer, innocently introduced in his budget a shilling a quarter tax on corn and flour; it was an emergency attempt to raise some £2,500,000 to meet war expenditure. For Chamberlain the time had come to speak out, and the first shot in the struggle which was to convulse the Conservative and Unionist party was fired at Birmingham on 16 May 1902. In answer to Campbell-Bannerman's horrified description of the tax as 'the thin edge of the wedge', he made reproachful reference to Liberal Party bigots who would abolish the duty rather than make it an instrument of imperial union:

What? Closer relations between the mother country and the Colonies! Cobden, Cobden whom he professes to follow, the great free-trader, made a reciprocity treaty with France, but the idea of a reciprocity treaty with our own children – that fills the mind of Sir Henry Campbell-Bannerman with disgust which he is only able ineffec-

Trading ships in the Hooghly, Calcutta, during the 1890s.

tively to express; and in this he shows once more that lack of foresight, which distinguished the little Englander and the little Scotchman. We are not going to adopt his fears.

All through the late winter and spring of 1903, Chamberlain fought a defensive battle behind the scenes, until on 15 May at Birmingham, rejecting all compromise, he cleared his conscience by declaring that food taxes, preferences and the power of tariff retaliation against foreigners were essential to the consolidation and maintenance of the Empire. The battle for imperial preference was on. In September, he resigned from the Cabinet to lead his crusade unhampered by official disciplines and loyalties. His departure split the Conservative Party and contributed to its collapse in the general election of 1906.

Although the election of 1906 meant the end of the Chamberlain crusade for imperial unity, within the Empire considerable progress had been made in developing preferential systems. Canada was negotiating tariff agreements with Australia, New Zealand, the South African colonies and the West Indies; Australia and New Zealand were similarly engaged with South Africa. In Australia and South Africa preference was granted by means of a reduction in the ordinary rate of duty, while in New Zealand more or less the same result was obtained by a surtax on certain classes of foreign manufactured goods. In Canada (excluding the surtax) there was a three-tier system which provided for a British, an intermediate and a general tariff. Not only self-governing colonies were included; the arrangement was open to India and Ceylon, the Straits Settlements and the West Indies. Moreover, a preferential tariff could be extended to any British colony or possession by order-in-council, without recourse to Parliament. To many of the more optimistic reformers a great system of inter-colonial commercial treaties seemed to be on the way to establishing itself.

When the fifth Colonial Conference (now, in deference to Dominions' sentiment, called Imperial Conference) assembled in London in April 1907, the Australian delegates pressed strongly for the adoption of a mutually preferential system which would include the United Kingdom. Still a burning issue in British domestic politics, tariffs were equally combustible material in the conference chamber, and for several days in May, Asquith, Churchill and Lloyd George were clearly on the defensive before the assaults of Australasia and the Cape. But no armoury of statistics could blunt the immovable defences of the British government, nor diminish the reluctance of Sir Wilfred Laurier to support any steps that might, by implying interference with Britain's domestic affairs, set a precedent for any meddling with Canadian autonomy. Not until the Ottawa Imperial Economic Conference of 1932 was a new generation of Dominions' statesmen able to exorcize, by a process of callous bargaining, what Dr Starr Jameson had called 'the fetish of free trade'.

234

Joseph Chamberlain, portrayed as a footman, turns away those in need at home and abroad while his master is pre-occupied with the Boer War.

The great trek of the Boer farmers northwards from the Cape served to extend rather than diminish Britain's dilemma. The original policy of keeping Cape Town as a naval base and avoiding the hinterland was impossible to maintain. Considerable numbers of British settlers had emigrated and Natal had been taken over as a crown colony. Moreover, Kaffir invasions threatened the existence of Boer and Briton alike, compelling military advances which led to the annexation of Boer-occupied territory between the Orange and the Vaal rivers in 1848. But the reaction against any forward policy had already started, and two years after the Transvaal had been declared an independent state in 1852, the Orange Free State was similarly recognized. As though to emphasize the two different conceptions of race relations between republic and colony, in 1852 the Cape received representative institutions: under the Act, equal political rights were available to black and white, provided a minor property qualification was satisfied. Twenty years later full responsible government was established.

In retrospect, a cleavage based on weak British policies, bitter Boer memories and antagonistic racial theories and practices could not endure forever. In Canada the federal arrangement of 1867 seemed to have solved the problem of

235

The rebel chief
Langalibalele and his sons
after their capture in 1879.

race; in 1858 Governor Sir George Grey had put forward a similar scheme for
South Africa. The Orange Free State was willing and in the face of Zulu
military power the Transvaal might well have been pressed into acceptance.
But the Colonial Office, still reluctant to add to its responsibilities, took fright,
and a project that might in years to come have saved much money and bloodshed was allowed to drop out of sight. When Disraeli's ministry came to power
in 1874, Grey's plan of federation was revived, but it was too late. Shaken by the
imminent prospect of a Zulu onslaught led by the distinguished Cetewayo, and
fearful that the fire would spread, the British government, against Boer protests,
annexed the Transvaal in 1877, promising full self-government under the
crown.

But forty years of conflict had generated too much national individualism
and animosity. In December 1880, the Transvaal declared itself an independent republic, and after a series of British defeats, which included the disaster
of Majuba Hill, its quasi-independence was recognized under the Pretoria
Convention of 1881, subject to the suzerainty of the queen. In other words, the
independence that had been taken away in 1877, was given back in a qualified
and ambiguous form. Three years later, after further appeals, the Transvaal
was once again declared a republic, wherein white foreigners had full liberty
to reside, to trade and to be subject to no higher taxes than those exacted from
citizens of the republic. This implied independence subject to qualification.

Dr Jameson sets out on his famous raid in 1895; from a contemporary engraving.

Sir Alfred Milner.

President Kruger.

Henceforward, British-Boer relations were largely governed by this London Convention of 1884 with its curious limitations on full sovereignty, which President Paul Kruger was reluctant to admit. The large Uitlander population was undoubtedly enriching the country with gold; but Britons were denied the elementary rights of citizenship, and against the treaty provisions, were heavily taxed to provide Kruger with munitions of war. Doubtless Kruger dreamed of Dutch hegemony in South Africa and he was not without some support in the Cape. In the circumstances, Sir Alfred Milner, who subsequently became the British High Commissioner (and who dreamed of a British hegemony) was bound to fail in his efforts to reduce the issue of British rights in the Transvaal to a diplomatic dialogue.

Matters came to a head, when, on the evening of 29 December 1895, a force of about 500 men under Dr Jameson, the administrator of Rhodesia, set off from Pitsani, on the border of the Bechuanaland Protectorate, to support an uprising of the underprivileged Uitlanders in Johannesburg. This incredible piece of filibustering ended with the surrender of the force four days later and caused irreparable damage to Anglo-Boer relations. Despite Chamberlain's instant denunciation of the participants and disavowal of foreknowledge, the Boer government suspected that the imperial authorities and various financial adventurers were implicated. The organized concentration of a large police force on the Transvaal border suggested a deep-laid plot to overthrow the republic, and suspicions were by no means dispelled by the conduct of an apparently staged inquiry in 1897.

Although the area of dispute is narrowing, the problem of Chamberlain's complicity is still being debated. J. L. Garvin examined the charges in an official *Life* and came to the conclusion that Chamberlain was innocent. 'He had not a shadow of complicity.' But even granted that neither Chamberlain nor Rhodes were directly involved in this particular fiasco, the crucial question remains: did Chamberlain know that the force recruited by the British South Africa Company and stationed on the border of the republic, was intended to energize and eventually support the Johannesburg Uitlanders, without whose armed help the insurrection would fail? If this allegation could have been substantiated, the government of the South African Republic might justly have accused the British government – as did Wilhelm II of Germany – of interfering in its internal affairs contrary to the London Convention of 1884. Kruger might then have denounced that agreement, ridding himself of its irksome restrictions.

Chamberlain always denied any connection with the plot, but it is reasonable to believe that he had a fair idea of what was afoot. According to his purported confession to Lady Flora Lugard:

I did not want to know too much. Of course, I knew of the precautions, the preparations, if you like, in view of the expected trouble in Johannesburg, but I never could have imagined that Jameson would take the bit between his teeth.

Chamberlain was not directly involved in the actual raid, but he was certainly committed to the general scheme for a rising in Johannesburg, supported, if possible, from the outside.

In 1886, gold had been discovered in the Transvaal. As it happened, the exploitation of the Witwatersrand reefs by powerful financial and commercial interests eventually brought to fruition the crisis which gradually crystallized after the Jameson Raid. Any attempt to secure concessions from the Transvaal government or any remedy of Uitlander grievances made the British govern- ment in Boer eyes simply the agent of the mining magnates.

But capitalist pressure alone was not responsible for the ultimate catastrophe. The Boer War was also the culmination of a long and vacillating search for a united South Africa; it represented a violent effort to end nearly a century of muddled official thinking. Milner himself (who took over as High Commis- sioner shortly after the Jameson Raid) believed that the whole of South Africa would benefit by being a colony of the British Empire wherein Boers and Bri- tons would learn to live together in peace, both sharing in the benefits of a benevolent British imperialism which would safeguard South Africa's future. It is, of course, difficult to prove conclusively that Milner preferred war to peace; yet, he appears to have been willing to push matters to a show-down. In a pinch, he may have preferred war to a peaceful settlement that might postpone some form of federal integration for ever. In any event, by demanding, one by one, so many concessions from the Transvaal, he made war in the end almost inevitable.

On the other hand, there were feelings and forces on the Boer side possibly even more perverse. With a kind of cat-and-mouse cunning, Kruger played with his enemies, offering concessions and then withdrawing them. His repeated failure to give the promised franchise to the Uitlanders is one illustration. If Kruger had fully realized that a crisis was approaching – that Chamberlain and Milner might even be considering war – it is conceivable that he would have drawn in his horns and sought a compromise on the question of equal rights for Boer and Briton. Certainly, up to the last few weeks before the out- break of war, each side expected the other to concede points. Faced by the casuistry and obstinacy of Kruger, and spurred on by the fervent imperialism of Milner, Chamberlain could see no alternative to the use of force.

Early in 1899, the Johannesburg Uitlanders petitioned the British crown for support; the acceptance of this petition practically committed Britain to action. 'The case for intervention', wrote Chamberlain on 10 May, 'is overwhelming.'

Lord Roberts planning the advance on Pretoria, 1900.

Lord Kitchener and General Pole-Carew at Pretoria railway station, 1901.

Christmas mail for the British forces.

De Wet's crack Boer commando crosses the Orange River.

Three generations of Boers
in the war, aged from
fifteen to sixty-five
in 1900.

The only attempted answer is that things will right themselves if left alone. But in fact the policy of leaving things alone has been tried for years, and it has led to their going from bad to worse. It is not true that this is owing to the Raid. They were going from bad to worse before the Raid. The effect of the Raid has been to give the policy of leaving things alone, a new lease of life, and with the old consequences. . . . The spectacle of thousands of British subjects kept permanently in the position of helots, constantly chafing under undoubted grievances, and calling vainly to her Majesty's government for redress does steadily undermine the influence and reputation of Great Britain and the respect for the British government within its own dominions. . . . The best proof of its power and its justice would be to obtain for the Uitlanders of the Transvaal a fair share in the government of a country which owes everything to their exertions.

The Orange Free State and the Transvaal continued to arm and to argue about suzerainty. Kruger was uncompromising in his demand for the withdrawal of the London Convention of 1884, which he saw as injurious to a sovereign people. Britain refused to waive her quasi-sovereign and supervisory rights. On 9 October 1899, negotiations were broken off, when Kruger, contemptuous of British power after the fiasco of Majuba Hill, and counting on the support of other powers, delivered his ultimatum.

Milner had not underestimated the military power of the Boers, but like almost every other observer, he had over-estimated the competence of the British army. The war lasted for thirty-one months and in the course of it Britain put into the field 458,000 men against two states whose combined population, in Lloyd George's phrase, 'did not exceed that of Flintshire and Denbighshire'. These forces were used in operations with little regard for the after-effect on civilian relationships. Roberts and Kitchener demanded and received almost full freedom to decide on what measures were 'demanded by military necessity'. In consequence, almost the whole of the Orange Free State, and large parts of the Transvaal, were made uninhabitable; women and children were transported to 'camps of refuge' where they died in appalling numbers from epidemic disease. The indiscriminate burning of farms, the lack of hygienic precautions in the 'concentration camps', the arming of natives, the severities of martial law – all these things produced bitterness and hatred in the minds of the Afrikaners throughout South Africa, and fed the belief that the British were seeking not merely to smash a rebellion but to exterminate a race. 'The memory of the war, sedulously fostered,' wrote C. F. Goodfellow, 'did more to unite Afrikaners than Kruger had ever accomplished. The war gave to the Boers and their colonial kinsmen common victims to remember and injuries to brood upon, a common cause in the restoration of republicanism and, in the figure of Kruger dying in exile, a martyr around whom they could weave a myth.'

This German cartoon satirizes the failure of a succession of British generals in the Boer War.
The occasion was the arrival of yet more troops under Lord Roberts in March 1900.

Celebrations in Fleet Street after the relief of Ladysmith, 1900.

In the end, 'unconditional surrender' was abandoned because Britain could not defeat the Boers in the field, and the British public were weary of an expensive, distracting and humiliating war. Peace was made by negotiation and embodied in an instrument which was a treaty in all but name. On 31 May 1902, the terms of surrender were confirmed at the village of Vereeniging, about thirty miles south of Johannesburg, and they included one concession critically important for the future. *Article VIII* read: 'The question of granting the franchise to natives will not be decided until after the introduction of self-government.'

The prolonged resistance had transformed the structure of authority among the Boers. The Krugerites had disappeared as a political force and their place had been taken by younger and more adaptable men. In the old republic – a species of Calvinist Tammany Hall – the possession of power had depended upon age, aggressiveness and particular prejudices; in the fighting commandos it was obtained by youth, courage and ability. In 1902, Smuts was thirty-two, Hertzog thirty-six and Botha thirty-nine.

The Peace of Vereeniging was the first step on the road to imperial abdication. No assurances were given by the Boers in regard to the treatment of the Bantu. Thenceforward, the Colonial Office tacitly assumed that South Africans would themselves decide the pace and shape of their future association. On this matter there was no conspicuous difference between the two British parties. Both Liberals and Conservatives agreed that eventually there must be a union of British and Boer communities under a free constitution. Disagreement arose over the method of achievement and particularly on the time required for the transition. Chamberlain had accepted Milner's recommendation that South African unity must be delayed until British hegemony was beyond question. Under Campbell-Bannerman, the Liberal Prime Minister who came to power in December 1905, responsible government leading to federation was to be promoted as quickly as possible under the aegis of South Africans. Milner had aimed at a South Africa dominated by a British-controlled Transvaal. He had planned for an influx of British farmers, hoping in the manner of Lord Durham that they would ultimately submerge the rival white race. The Liberals envisaged self-government for a future dominion whose leaders, even if Afrikaners, would be bound to the Empire by gratitude.

General Botha (seated, second left) and Lord Kitchener (seated, second right) meet to discuss peace terms, 1902.

Four years after the end of the war, self-government was given to the Transvaal, and in 1907 to the Orange River colony. It was a precipitate political move, which Campbell-Bannerman's biographer has described as 'an act of faith', but one that was roundly condemned by the Conservative opposition. It has been argued that this hasty step forward should have been delayed until the British government was quite certain of the policy that would be adopted by the two conquered colonies towards their native African subjects, but on this particular matter both parties remained silent. Magnanimity usually exacts a price, but as Professor Mansergh has remarked, 'it is not always those who act magnanimously who pay it'. In being magnanimous to the defeated Boers, the Liberal government salved its own conscience and that of the British electorate, but they did so at the expense of the native and non-European peoples living within the frontiers of what was to be the Union of South Africa.

Meanwhile, spurred by economic necessity – the inter-colonial customs and tariff agreements which Milner had arranged were about to expire – the movement for some form of integration grew rapidly. Four separate parliaments, with separate ministers, governors and staffs, four tariffs and four different legal systems produced a situation too complicated, too troublesome and too costly to endure. The main question concerned the kind of union that should be established – a fairly loose federation or a closer legislative union. Federalism had been the fashionable solution for half a century in Europe, North America and Australia. The grant of Irish Home Rule would mean federalism within the British Isles. Small states like Natal would obviously prefer a less centralized constitution.

In the end, union and not federation was the result, and chiefly because the leaders, both Boer and Briton, agreed that the first need was white unity. A federation project presented too many economic difficulties; South Africa, for the sake of efficiency, had to be one economic unit. Moreover, the Canadian precedent had convinced the most influential Afrikaners that a loose federation must be avoided at all costs. Chief Justice De Villiers of the Cape had visited Canada for the Quebec tercentenary, and he did not like what he saw. 'The result [of Canadian federalism] has been to establish a distinctly French province without any prospect of its being merged ever into a Canadian as distinguished from a purely French nation.' He was determined to prevent such a misfortune in his own country.

On 12 October 1908, nine years to the day after the war had begun, the National Convention met. As it happened, federalism scarcely came into consideration. Only Natal was prepared to fight for a federal union, and Natal carried little political weight. The big dilemma was produced by the franchise question. Under the terms of the surrender of 1902, the question of granting the

The first Cabinet of the Union of South Africa, 1910. Seated members include three South African Prime Ministers, Botha (centre), Smuts (far left) and Hertzog (second right).

franchise to natives was, as we have seen, not to be decided until after the intro- duction of self-government. Self-government had been granted to the white population, and information received by the British government from the Com- missioner of Native Affairs suggested that there had been a wholesome change in South African public opinion on native questions. To insist on special safe- guards in the constitution might check the growth of sympathy.

However suspiciously this prognosis may have been regarded, there was no eagerness in Westminster to impede the process of union by raising embarras- sing questions about safeguards and native rights. Believing that the future of the country depended upon the speedy union of Britons and Boers, both British parties were content to rely upon what Churchill had called 'the spirit of charity that will be kindled by union'. 'If I had known as well as I know now', said Lord Milner with reference to the peace treaty, 'the extravagance of the prejudice on the part of almost all the Europeans, and not the Boers alone, I should never have agreed to so absolute an exclusion.' Until the Jameson Raid and the cruel war that followed, Afrikaner nationalism had been the vague and romantic creed of a frontier people who had survived the assaults of the Zulu impis, and the even more threatening advances of British 'big business'. The raid and the war had left a heritage of bitterness that men like Milner had utterly failed to estimate. Despite the goodwill of such Boer leaders as Botha, Smuts and Hofmeyer, the healing 'spirit of charity' which Campbell-Bannerman and young Winston Churchill had counted on, did not flower because it did not exist.

On 4 November 1908, the National Convention agreed that membership in the Union parliament should be limited to Europeans, but that the Cape franchise permitting natives and Coloured alike to acquire the vote should remain unaltered unless a two-thirds majority of both houses sitting together saw fit. Twenty-four clauses dealt with the future of Basutoland, Bechuanaland and Swaziland. Here there was no question of policy; the safeguarding of the welfare of these native enclaves, pending their ultimate transfer to the Union, was recognized as a matter of honour, and until the moment for take-over came, they were to be administered by a commission.

The Bantu, therefore, had not been disregarded, but their prospects within an evolving empire whose members showed increasing tendencies to run their own affairs in the manner of sovereign states, were not bright. With European survival and security guaranteed by statute, an Afrikaner ideology had, with the blessing of the erstwhile conquerors, re-established itself. Indeed, one confronts the tragic paradox that British statesmen, not unnoted since Lord Durham's day for speculative 'acts of faith', helped to lay the foundations of a united South Africa wherein the British community virtually surrendered all political power. The history of South Africa since 1908, wrote Arthur Keppel-Jones, 'may be regarded as the peaceful conquest of the sub-continent by the Transvaal, before which the Cape Province with its liberal tradition has gone down in defeat.'

Compared with Canada and Australia, the liberal spirit of compromise is lacking in the modern South African story; better if there had been severe and challenging tensions before the Union of 1910, instead of British blessings and wishful thinking which suggested that conciliation was sufficient cement for the foundations of a new nation. In the past few years, the conflict, then tacitly and graciously ignored, has been reopened. It involves two views of the relationship between the white race and the older native population, Bantu, Indian and Coloured. It began in the nineteenth century – a conflict to determine which of the two white races should impose its social and political outlook on the southern expanse of the continent. It remains today essentially an internal Afrikaner problem which outside interference can only exacerbate; yet on the achievement of a solution the ultimate fate of South Africa depends.

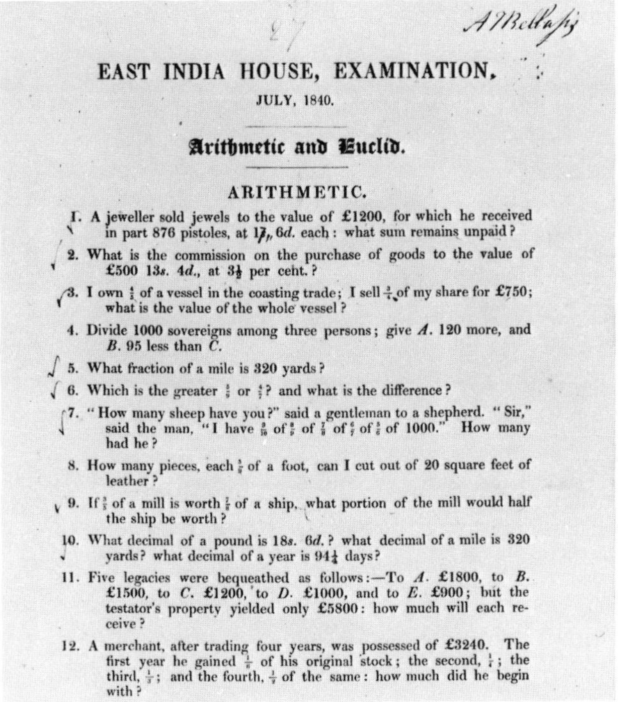

EAST INDIA HOUSE, EXAMINATION,

JULY, 1840.

Arithmetic and Euclid.

ARITHMETIC.

1. A jeweller sold jewels to the value of £1200, for which he received in part 876 pistoles, at 17s. 6*d*. each: what sum remains unpaid?
2. What is the commission on the purchase of goods to the value of £500 13*s*. 4*d*., at $3\frac{1}{2}$ per cent.?
3. I own $\frac{4}{5}$ of a vessel in the coasting trade; I sell $\frac{3}{4}$ of my share for £750; what is the value of the whole vessel?
4. Divide 1000 sovereigns among three persons; give *A*. 120 more, and *B*. 95 less than *C*.
5. What fraction of a mile is 320 yards?
6. Which is the greater $\frac{5}{9}$ or $\frac{4}{7}$? and what is the difference?
7. "How many sheep have you?" said a gentleman to a shepherd. "Sir," said the man, "I have $\frac{9}{10}$ of $\frac{8}{9}$ of $\frac{7}{8}$ of $\frac{6}{7}$ of $\frac{5}{6}$ of 1000." How many had he?
8. How many pieces, each $\frac{5}{8}$ of a foot, can I cut out of 20 square feet of leather?
9. If $\frac{3}{5}$ of a mill is worth $\frac{7}{8}$ of a ship, what portion of the mill would half the ship be worth?
10. What decimal of a pound is 18*s*. 6*d*.? what decimal of a mile is 320 yards? what decimal of a year is $94\frac{1}{4}$ days?
11. Five legacies were bequeathed as follows:—To *A*. £1800, to *B*. £1500, to *C*. £1200, to *D*. £1000, and to *E*. £900; but the testator's property yielded only £5800: how much will each receive?
12. A merchant, after trading four years, was possessed of £3240. The first year he gained $\frac{1}{8}$ of his original stock; the second, $\frac{1}{4}$; the third, $\frac{1}{3}$; and the fourth, $\frac{1}{9}$ of the same: how much did he begin with?

Indian Civil Service Examination paper from Haileybury College, July 1840. All nominees for the Service were required to spend two years at the College.

The British conquest and unification of India has been called a magnificent feat amounting to a miracle. After the collapse of the Moguls, and a century of war with France for imperial supremacy, British arms produced an Eastern empire in something like fifty years. Equally remarkable, in retrospect, was the orderly administration of this empire, containing something like one-fifth of the human race, by handfuls of civil servants and soldiers. The young recruits from Haileybury College or from the military school at Addiscombe relied on an enormous pyramid of subordinate Indian deputies and assistants; yet the mind boggles at the sheer sweep of their responsibilities.

It is proper to pay tribute to great men who commanded events, but the explanation of much British success lay in circumstance: in the divisions between rival groupings, south, centre and north-west, and the willingness of most of the Indian governing classes to collaborate with the British for a price. The country was a gigantic hodge-podge of caste distinctions and a cockpit of religious entities. By comparison, Canada or Australia, which are physically a little larger, contained only minute fringes of population, which were, moreover, entirely western European in culture. The Viceroy of India was in charge of an empire bigger than Rome's, an empire equal in extent to Europe without Russia, and containing quite as many different nations and races.

In some bewilderment, the historian J. R. Seeley asked himself how on earth such a mixture of colour, race, religion and history as represented by the British Empire could possibly make sense in Whitehall. How could Britain manage to be

despotic in Asia and democratic in Australia, be in the East at once the greatest Mussulman Power in the world and the guardian of thousands of idol-temples, and at the same time in the West be the foremost champion of free thought and spiritual religion, stand out as a great military Imperialism to resist the march of Russia in Central Asia at the same time that it fills Queensland and Manitoba with free settlers?

Britain was fortunate in her unique freedom after 1815 to extend her control with little or no opposition from outside powers. Nevertheless, the weight of responsibility in terms of foreign policy was immense. During the nineteenth century, she had to watch every move in the kaleidoscope of constantly shifting Eastern and Middle Eastern affairs, looking for signs of weakness in Turkey or Persia, French intrigues in Egypt, or Russian aggressions in Afghanistan. Any of these might invite a challenge or force an intervention. Possession of an Indian empire involved above all a mounting rivalry with Russia, whose phantom 'steam-roller' generated suspicion, fear and pugnacity; this public reaction often led to further extensions of British authority in the form of buffer states.

The maintenance in India of an effective administrative and military apparatus was bound to be expensive. By European standards the results justified the outlay, but such a calculation did little to relieve the feelings of Indian nationalists, who continued to accuse the British of draining away the wealth of their country. 'Animated with all the avarice of age, and all the impetuosity of youth,' charged an angry Burke in 1783,

they [the British merchants] roll in one after another, wave after wave; and there is nothing before the eyes of the natives but an endless, hopeless prospect of new flights of birds of prey and passage, with appetites continually renewing for a food that is continually wasting. Every rupee of profit made by an Englishman is lost forever to India.

It is difficult, even for unprejudiced statisticians, to make sense out of profits and losses, but it may be worth recalling that from Burke's day almost to our own time the possession of empire was not regarded as morally offensive, and the brutal exploitation of power was a familiar feature of Indian history long before the arrival of the Portuguese. The meeting and mixing of the twain – East and West – may not have been the best thing for peoples with long and civilized cultural traditions. But it happened, and even if 'the drain' in terms of gold and goods had been heavy, from a material point of view India gained

Famine, personified as a tiger, 'on the prowl'; a *Punch* cartoon of 1896.

from Europe more than she lost. During the nineteenth century, she acquired the techniques and equipment with which to begin to build the modern industrial state – at a cost in life, pain and labour probably a good deal less than that paid by the original operators and victims of the English Industrial Revolution.

Widespread poverty, starvation and sickness had been endemic over the centuries. Famine relief, first seriously tackled in the nineteenth century, remained a problem even after the coming of the railways. During the last quarter of that century, some 26,000,000 people were reported to have died, owing chiefly to drought and the fact that tillable land allowed an average of only an acre per person. These repeated human catastrophes were neither ignored nor forgotten in Calcutta or London; negligence and incapacity can never be entirely exorcized from the halls and huts of administration. But it is worth remembering that, by the beginning of the twentieth century, there existed in India 40,000 miles of canals, 23,000,000 acres of irrigated lands and a minimum reserve fund of £21,000,000 for emergency relief.

Yet cost accounting of this sort may appear trivial compared with the alleged cultural injury inflicted 'under the yoke' of the British Raj. Because 'empire' involved subordination, British rule implied in Asia or Africa the inferiority of non-white subject peoples. In India, there was a colour bar enforced in trains, restaurants, shops, clubs and within the public services. In all probability, no more than 10 per cent of the population were aware of the stigma, but a rule which engendered a sense of inferiority in the ruled, remarked Annie Besant, could have 'no living roots and must wither in the end'. All the genuine love for India manifested over the years by so many British civil servants, soldiers and missionaries, did not compensate for a lack of cultural sensitivity and an aloofness that sometimes hardened into arrogance.

The rulers of India were a projection of Britain; they refused to be absorbed. The whole system had come to be based on a separation of the races, not upon assimilation. Unlike the French, who looked on their subjects as potential Frenchmen, the British treated Indians as Indians and not as potential Britons. They conferred subjecthood, but withheld citizenship. To bridge the gap in personal relations between Indian and Englishman little existed apart from the material benefits of peaceful rule. Even in pre-Mutiny days, when the Raj appeared to be more powerful than ever before, some of the more thoughtful observers in high places were asking themselves where the goal lay, and whether the end might not be a rapid British withdrawal. Some twenty years after he gave up the Bombay presidency in 1827, one of the most astute governors in the history of the British Empire wrote:

The administration of all the departments of a great country by a small number of foreign visitors, in a state of isolation produced by a difference in religion, ideas and manners, which cuts them off from all intimate communion with the people, can never be contemplated as a permanent state of things.

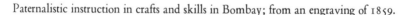
Paternalistic instruction in crafts and skills in Bombay; from an engraving of 1859.

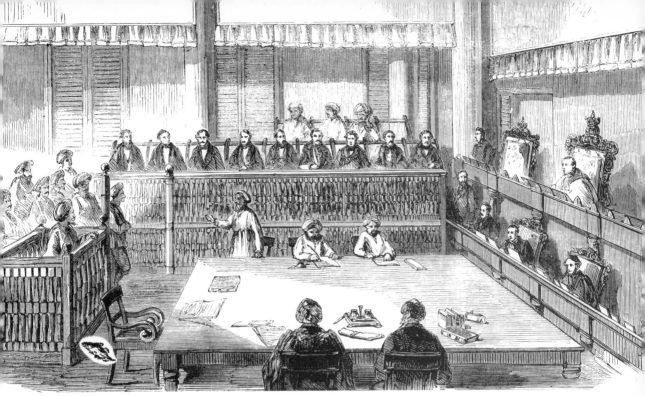

English judicial procedure transported to India: the supreme court of Madras in 1853.

Even during his period of office, Mountstuart Elphinstone felt that the education of Indians in matters of government must reach a stage when it would be impossible to confine them to subordinate employments. And if vents were not opened for their ambition and ability, he declared in 1822, 'we may expect an explosion which will overturn our government'. In his famous minute on Indian education (1835), Macaulay had written in similar fashion:

It may be that the public mind of India may expand under our system till it has outgrown our system; that by good government we may educate our subjects into a capacity for better government; that, having become instructed in European knowledge they may, in some future age, demand European institutions. Whether such a day will ever come I know not. But never will I attempt to retard or avert it. Whenever it comes it will be the proudest day in English history.

It was exactly a hundred years later that the recommendations of a British White Paper marked the fulfilment of Macaulay's hopes. Because India was willy-nilly reshaped and reinvigorated by the imposed political and linguistic structure of the conqueror, the long delay was a misfortune, and the consequences were almost tragic.

The Storming of Seringapatam, 1799.

The period between the Napoleonic Wars and the Mutiny was the great age of conquest and annexation. Paradoxically, it was also the period of greatest domestic resistance to further imperial expansion. When Warren Hastings left India in 1785, the East India Company held effective control over Bengal province and a few coastal trading depots like Bombay and Madras. During the half-century before the Mutiny, she extended her domain from a series of factory sites to the greater part of the sub-continent. The process of expansion involved almost continual conflict with native rulers, and under pressure of events the Company was forced into becoming a governing organization, more conspicuously after 1833 when its trading activities were ended.

With the final defeat of the persistent Marathas in 1817–18, the Company controlled nearly the whole of India proper except the Punjab and Sind. Under Lord Amherst (1823–28), parts of Burma were added for the sake of buffer security. In 1843, Sind was occupied, and six years later Lord Dalhousie was able to annex the Punjab. Confident of the benefits of British rule and contemptuous of 'the barbarism' and inefficiency of native states, Dalhousie enforced the doctrine of 'lapse', namely, that when a ruler died without children, the cherished custom of heir adoption was ignored and the Company was designated inheritor. Between 1848 and 1856 seven states, including Oudh, were so absorbed. British authority was now roughly conterminous with the future boundaries of India.

Dalhousie's reforms were far-reaching and beneficent, extending to education, agriculture, railways, postal services and telegraphs. The rapid rate of change and reconstruction inevitably created unrest, yet military precautions were neglected. All told, the entire British community in India, including Anglo-Indians, was under 100,000, and of these less than 37,000 belonged to British regiments. 'Our whole strength', wrote Sir Charles Metcalf, the Governor-General in 1835–36, 'consists in the few European regiments, speaking comparatively, that are scattered singly over the vast space of subjugated India. That is the only portion of our soldiery whose hearts are with us, and whose constancy can be relied on in the hour of trial.'

In retrospect, Henry Lawrence could say that after the Afghan disaster of 1842 (following the British army's retreat from Kabul, which only one man survived) the British position was discredited with the native soldiery. Certainly, the Mutiny appeared to be a military and not a popular rebellion; the educated classes seem to have been solidly pro-British. It was not a war of independence against a discredited Western invader. The violence was turned not so much against vulnerable British political supremacy as against the new order of things represented in part by Dalhousie's reforms. The pig-greased cartridges merely helped to touch off the explosion resulting from a growing anxiety, sometimes amounting to panic, over railway-building, public works, expansion of Christian missions, the doctrine of lapse, and the more subtle forms of interference with caste and culture. Eight days before the Mutiny, on 2 May 1857, the Governor-General, Lord Canning, wrote: 'until we treat natives, and especially native soldiers, as having much the same feelings, the same ambition, the same perception of ability and imbecility as ourselves, we shall never be safe'.

Sepoys at rifle practice using pig-greased cartridges, 1857–58.

Ruins at Lucknow after the Indian Mutiny; a photograph of 1857.

The Mutiny turned out to be a series of local outbreaks rather than a racial crusade. Not even the hostile ruler of Afghanistan, Dost Muhammad, intervened. Scarcely a third of the gigantic peninsula was affected, most of the native princes were loyal, and it is doubtful if more than a quarter of the sepoy army was disloyal to its British commanders. In many respects the panoramic scene was medieval – a war of forays and long marches by small columns through a dusty countryside that only wanted peace. It was a colonial war of handfuls against thousands, brutal and bloody; yet the issue was never in real doubt. The rebels had no organized plan of campaign; there was no national leader. The back of the insurrection was broken within four months, but the after-effects were long-lasting. The Mutiny was responsible for a long estrangement, and like the Boer War of some forty years later, it produced a legacy of bitter memories that fostered resentment through several decades. Before 1857 it had been generally assumed that the British stay in India would be short; after, it was generally assumed that it would be for a long time.

Lord and Lady Curzon in the State Procession, Delhi durbar, 1903.

When the East India Company was forced to resign its responsibilities in 1858, the Secretary of State for India, representing the India Office, became in practice the government of India, with actual administration under the control of the Viceroy and his exclusively British executive council. There was indeed a legislative council to which a few Indians were appointed, but as a subordinate extension of the executive council, it possessed little real independence. The first advance along the rough road towards self-government came in 1861, when the first Indian Councils Act instituted legislative assemblies for British India, both in the central government and in the provinces. Although members were nominated, half the membership was non-official and included a few Indians. A second Councils Act of 1892 introduced the principle of election, a minor revolution in government, significant as a precedent even though applied only to the non-official element.

Meanwhile, the agitation for complete self-government had taken on new impetus, supported as early as 1885 by the first Indian National Congress.

Gandhi outside his South African office, 1913.

Nehru as a boy.

With the retirement of Lord Curzon as Governor-General in 1905, the period of aggressive Indian nationalism had begun. To meet the new conditions, a scheme of reforms was produced in 1909. In a limited way, the resulting Act introduced the principle of representative institutions by making the privileges and composition of the legislative assemblies, central and provincial, more parliamentary in character, but did not surrender ultimate executive control.

There were, in fact, serious doubts in Whitehall and in Delhi as to India's capacity to advance safely towards independent nationhood. Lord Curzon, for example, did not believe that the Western parliamentary system could be made to work; to him, the dispensation of British justice was the best contribution the imperial power could make in a country deeply rent by schisms and feuds. In short, many British statesmen believed that the caste system and the Hindu-Moslem cleavage excluded the possibility of anything like a national sovereign entity.

But the First World War forced a revolution in much of British thinking. By her gifts and sacrifices of men and money, India increased her stature, and correspondingly her claims. The Imperial Conference statement of 1917, which recognized the Dominions as autonomous nations of an Imperial Commonwealth, included India 'as an important portion of the same'. And at long last, in August of the same year, the Secretary of State, Mr Montagu, informed the House of Commons that the policy of His Majesty's government was, 'the gradual development of self-governing institutions with a view to the progressive realization of responsible government in India as an integral part of the British Empire'.

The Montagu-Chelmsford Report, presented to Parliament and enacted in 1919, represented a substantial step in the education of India towards self-government. The period of transition was to be one of progress towards Indian rule, with the gradual passing away of British administrators. Meanwhile, a central council of state would remain responsible to the British government, empowered, in case of emergency, to override the vote of the elective legislative assembly. At the same time, a system of diarchy was introduced into the provincial assemblies. These were now vested with the power of controlling the executive, except in such reserved subjects as police and irrigation. 'Diarchy' was a unique innovation in the history of constitutional government, but the effects were tragically marred by the almost simultaneous passage of the Rowlatt Acts against sedition. These established Gandhi in his crusade of non-co-operation and civil disobedience, and marked the beginning of stormy agitations not unlike those preceding the grant of Irish Home Rule in 1922.

Urged on by extremists, the Congress Party clamoured for immediate parliamentary self-government as interpreted by Burke and Macaulay. Nationalism is too definite a word to explain the upsurge of popular feeling. It was by no means an anti-British movement; indeed, among the educated leaders it was combined with heroic concepts of English liberalism. The use of philosophic arguments based on Westminster precedent certainly made the British position vulnerable, and the ensuing wave of unrest was much more the result of British weakness than strength. Yet, understandably the British government hesitated before the awful responsibility of imposing, in one drastic stroke, a Western parliamentary system of democracy upon a vast conglomeration of regions and races, accustomed only superficially to the Western way of political life.

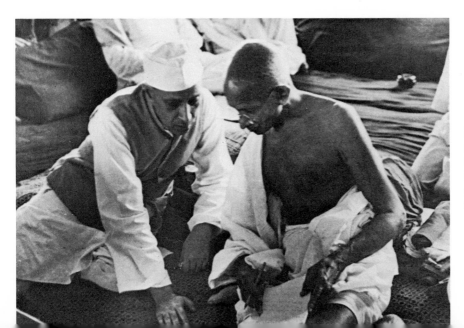

Nehru and Gandhi during the August 1942 session of the All India Congress Committee when the 'Quit India' resolution was adopted.

Another laboured investigation of the whole Indian problem was made by the Simon Commission, whose report appeared in 1930. But already it was clear that the vanguard of Indian nationalism had by-passed the route laid down by headquarters in Whitehall. Indian nationalists shouting 'Simple Simon' were now demanding not merely provincial, but national self-government, applied in an all-India federation which should include the Indian states as well as the British provinces. In response, a series of Round Table Conferences were held, lasting till 1933, which resulted finally in the draft of a new constitution embodied in the Act of 1935.

The grant of full responsible government to the provinces was inevitable; the guarantee of the domestic rights and privileges of Indian states was un-expected but sensible. Both British India and the Indian states were to be represented in a federal government and parliament, with Indian ministers responsible for all federal subjects except defence and foreign policy. In short, while the provinces were to enjoy the benefits and hazards of complete parlia-mentary government, the central government controlling the army was still in a position to intervene in case of emergency. The Act of 1935 marked an enormous advance along the road to self-government. Only the tragedy of internal dissension seemed likely to delay the grant of complete independence.

Unfortunately, fear of a Hindu-dominated, Congress-governed India aroused the Moslems, and their anxieties led them to demand more and more community safeguards, culminating in their insistence on a separate Moslem state to be called Pakistan. For nearly three centuries the unity of India had been preserved by British rule; now, in the middle of a world war for survival, it was natural that British statesmen should ponder the grave risks of civil strife on their own fortunes as well as those of India.

The Round Table Conference of 1931 was marked by Gandhi's strong opposition to Ramsay Macdonald's proposal of separate representation for the different Indian religious communities.

260

Independence Day, 1947: crowds watch the raising of the flag at Red Fort, Delhi.

Complete self-government was the basis of the Cripps offer of 1942, an invitation which inevitably depended on the willingness of the main Indian parties to co-operate. But the promise of such co-operation was not forth-coming. The Simla Conference of 1945 provided little more hope, for Hindus and Moslems failed to reach any kind of agreement. Notwithstanding, the British delegates drew up a series of proposals and, with the support of their government, offered to India in 1946 absolute independence, united or divided, within or outside the Commonwealth. The Independence Act was passed in August 1947; as a result of Moslem fears and Hindu intransigence the partition of India became a fact. The last Governor-General, Lord Mountbatten, may have cut the federal knot too abruptly. The ensuing madness and communal slaughter were reminiscent of the worst excesses of the Munity. Yet, however tragic the convulsion, and however sad the end of an historic unity, the executioner's masterstroke may have saved India from the bitter conflicts of civil war.

Epilogue

THE END OF THE BRITISH EMPIRE

In his learned *Survey of Commonwealth Relations*, Nicholas Mansergh pointed out that the process of Commonwealth evolution towards autonomy and equality provided the solid and indispensable foundation upon which the present indefinable association had been expanding. In short, whatever the Commonwealth is today in terms of composition, shape or lack of cohesion, it exists as an association, however fragile, whose basic character was achieved in the years past, and especially in the last fifty years.

If one accepts this thesis of continuing growth, it is not difficult to place Lord Durham's famous report of 1839 as the first milestone. By recommending the grant of local self-government, the American method of advance by revolution was avoided, and the way was open for a peaceful evolution towards 'dominion status' in the twentieth century. The movement in this direction was accelerated by the consolidation of groups of colonial units into national states – Canada between 1867 and 1873, New Zealand in 1876, Australia in 1901 and South Africa in 1910. Yet, the ultimate destination remained uncertain. Not until after the end of the First World War was it obvious that the trend was towards national independence. Indeed, the Great War, which appeared for a moment to have strengthened the old Empire and even to have revived the shattered dream of imperial federation, actually set in motion a train of events leading on an opposite course.

The first sign of approaching constitutional change was evident in 1917 with the meeting of the Imperial War Conference. At this conference, the Prime Minister of Canada, Sir Robert Borden, and General Smuts for South Africa, submitted a declaration of ends, which was endorsed by the conference without a dissenting voice. This *Resolution IX* placed on record the Dominions' view that after the war a readjustment of constitutional relations within the Empire would have to be made, and that such a readjustment,

◀ The new era: the raising of the Kenyan flag in Nairobi on Independence Day, 12 December 1963.

while thoroughly preserving all existing powers of self-government and complete control of domestic affairs, should be based upon a full recognition of the Dominions as autonomous nations of an Imperial Commonwealth, and of India as an important portion of the same, should recognize the right of the Dominions and India to an adequate voice in foreign policy and in foreign relations, and should provide effective arrangements for continuous consultation in all important matters of common Imperial concern. . . .

However imprecise and wistful in concept, it was a landmark in imperial history simply because it excluded finally the once-fashionable idea of federation, and implied condemnation of an even earlier vogue – separation. It was ambiguous and it was incomplete, but in general this Bill of Rights conceded everything short of independence – everything that any of the Dominions of that day could conceivably ask.

Resolution IX probably made it easier for Sir Robert Borden at the end of the war to take the initiative once again, and to insist, against the opposition of the United States' delegation, on membership of the peace conference. The

A lost dream of Empire: Cecil Rhodes speaking to Sir William Harcourt of the South Africa Committee, 1897.

separate signatures of the Dominion representatives on the Versailles Treaty preceded separate ratification by their parliaments. This hard-won international status was confirmed by the admission of the Dominions as members of the new League of Nations, along with the right of membership in the council. Dominion nationalism had finally emerged from the imperial cocoon and had asserted itself before the world.

Unhappily, with the coming of peace, the excessive national zeal stimulated by war began to evaporate and a kind of fatigue descended on both politicians and public in London and the Empire. No constitutional conference, such as had been recommended by *Resolution IX*, was called, and closer co-operation in imperial affairs represented little more than a policy of drift.

The danger of uncertainty was made evident in 1922 when the threat of war with Turkey, during the Chanak episode near the Dardanelles, led Lloyd George imprudently to ask the Empire for help. Only New Zealand responded wholeheartedly. The new Prime Minister of Canada, W. L. Mackenzie King, was shocked by the peremptory invitation, first knowledge of which he had obtained from newspapers. To him, the incident revealed the need to limit responsibility for the consequences of British foreign policy. Consequently, when, in 1923, a new treaty with Turkey was eventually negotiated, Canada declined to sign or ratify it, on the grounds that she had not been represented at the treaty conference. In 1925 none of the Dominions participated in the negotiations for confirming Germany's western boundaries under the Treaty of Locarno; and the final abandonment of a common foreign policy for the Empire revealed itself in the clause which specifically excluded the Dominions and India from the provisions, and in so doing recognized that a Dominion might adopt a passive role in any European conflict precipitated by obligations involving the mother country.

Therein lay 'the great dilemma', so eloquently publicized by Lionel Curtis. If there could no longer be a common foreign policy, what would happen to the unity of the Empire? For example, in matters of war and peace, could one group of the king's ministers (say, from Australia) advise him to go to war, and another group (say from Eire) advise him to the contrary. If national independence could only be guaranteed by separate foreign policies, could anything like an empire continue to exist? Until Eire proclaimed her neutrality in 1939, this delicate question remained unanswered.

On the other hand, none of the member Dominions in the 1920s wished to secede and the question was raised: could a formula – a principle – be found which would satisfy nationalist aspirations and at the same time meet the expressed wishes of the Dominions to remain within the old imperial fold. As it happened, at the Imperial Conference in 1926, a formula was discovered and

Rulers of Empire: Joseph Chamberlain and the colonial Prime Ministers at the Colonial Conference of June 1897.

translated by an Imperial Relations committee into a resolution which stated that the Dominions and Great Britain

are autonomous communities within the British Empire, equal in status, in no way subordinate one to another in any aspect of their domestic or foreign affairs, though united by a common allegiance to the Crown, and freely associated as members of the British Commonwealth of Nations.

By the skilful use of words, a beautiful equilibrium was established, satisfying everybody. It took a metaphysician like Lord Balfour to write a document of such subtlety, flexibility and ambiguity that Australia could be satisfied with a a crown indivisible, and South Africa with a crown divisible that permitted her people to pay homage not to a British king, but to the king of South Africa. Internationally, the Dominions could act as one, or as separate nations. All who acknowledged the crown as a common bond were to be 'equal in status', 'freely associated', 'in no way subordinate one to another' – and this included the United Kingdom. No one was pinned down in any way. In General Hertzog's view, even the right to secede was inherent in the resolution.

The Statute of Westminster of 1931 incorporated the essence of this resolution into law, recording in black and white the achievement of *de facto* independence under the British crown. In retrospect, it is easy to recognize that

And of Commonwealth: Queen Elizabeth, Harold Macmillan and Commonwealth leaders at the Commonwealth Conference of September 1962.

the statute was only another great milestone in evolution. At the time, it appeared as though a final synthesis was about to be achieved. But problems involved in the growth of living societies and living political organisms can have no final solutions. Certainly, what appeared to many observers in 1931 as a final solution of the problem of Empire turned out within a few years to be simply the beginning of a whole new set of problems.

It was the Second World War that upset the teetering edifice of Empire, accelerating political developments by forcing erstwhile backward races deeper into the complexities and passions of industrial civilization. Unlike the development of the old Dominions, the transition of the younger colonies towards independence was not gradual, because the driving force was a furious nationalism. Nationalism has always been a separative force; inflamed by Japanese conquests, feelings of national and racial self-consciousness shattered the old conceptions of empire in south-east Asia. Countries like Burma, India, Pakistan and Ceylon were metaphorically rocketed into independence.

It is well to remember, however, that this rapid diffusion of nationalist feeling did not by itself entirely undermine the foundations of the old imperial régime. The final and voluntary post-war surrender to the new nationalism embodied the changed political ethos in Britain. Admittedly, the will to maintain the old régime was to some extent sapped by the sacrifices involved in a long war, especially in the East against the Japanese; but more important were 'the winds of change' that affected both people and government. All told, there was little inclination to resist nationalist pressures in the surviving colonies. Public opinion was unable to stomach the imposition of indefinite rule by force of arms on unwilling populations. Perhaps Britain succumbed to the intense demands of nationalism prematurely; there might have been beneficent delays. Yet in the long run there was no alternative; self-government was at the end of the same old road of evolutionary constitutional development – the road roughly surveyed by Lord Durham in 1839, and thenceforward paved with good intentions and no mean achievements.

In 1947 the British government made precipitate arrangements for the complete independence of two Indian nations, as well as Ceylon and Burma, either within or outside the Commonwealth; and Burma did secede in circumstances of complete amity. In 1949, the United Kingdom recognized the secession of the newly created republic of Eire, although by legislative amendments citizens of this republic substantially retained all the rights and privileges of British subjects.

But the crucial constitutional turning-point was to be the invention of a formula which would enable the new Asian Dominion, India, to accept the idea of Commonwealth without accepting the obligation of allegiance to the crown upon which the original structure had been based. In 1949, the solution was to accept India as a republic, a republic acknowledging the king as head of the Commonwealth. It was a drastic and a startling admission, re-emphasized four years later by the decision of Pakistan to become a republic. But at least the new arrangement did recognize the unique position of the crown as the only institution essential to the Commonwealth relationship. The monarchy was to remain – even though in a diminished sense – a unifying symbol, and not just the royal emblem of territories peopled by British stock. None the less, the crown was no longer one juristic being and no amount of legal hair-splitting could alter the fact. Of even greater significance in its consequences, was India's decision to pursue a foreign policy of 'non-alignment'. However unrealistic, 'non-alignment', not constitutional independence, dealt the really damaging blow to Commonwealth links with India.

Yet, amicable settlements with India, Pakistan and Ceylon showed what might be accomplished in the future, and observers in Whitehall looked forward optimistically to an Africa which would share Asia's happy compromises. The outcome was not long delayed. Indeed, a single decade was to witness (with the exception of Portugal) almost the total withdrawal of European colonial rule in Africa. The process began smoothly enough when Ghana was given home rule and then declared herself a republic in 1957; it was completed eleven years later when the former protectorate of Swaziland in southern Africa gained its independence. As a result, seven-eighths of the Commonwealth now consists of Asian and African peoples; Asian and African states dominate the association's membership, ten of them with populations under a million, and more than half of them republics owing no allegiance to the queen. Such rapid and indefinite expansions of membership to include countries like Gambia and Malawi with insufficient resources to become viable states, makes a nonsense of independence and the ideal of equal partnership. With no little pungency, an astute Canadian political scientist depicted the new Commonwealth coach as 'oversized and under-powered, with too much play in the steering and too many hands on the wheel'.

Certainly, during the last few years, the Commonwealth has changed so rapidly in shape and substance that only an astrologer would dare to predict the future, and only a charlatan could be optimistic about it. Whether the event be called a 'transfer of power' or, in the sixties, a 'welcome dismissal' (sometimes with a 'prolonged golden handshake'), the introduction of indigenous govern-ments into under-developed countries recently under colonial rule, marked the final stage in the history of the British Empire. The historic path of evolution had been severed at last.

Such an end was not consciously predetermined; it was the growth, not the acquisition of Empire that came about almost, as J. R. Seeley had put it, 'in a fit of absence of mind'. For over 200 years imperial problems tended, naturally enough, to be assessed in the light of British experience; solutions were calcu-lated in terms of traditional formulas, regardless of their relevance to existing colonial conditions. Afro-Asian – even Caribbean – society is very different from British society. Yet British methods of parliamentary government were automatically introduced and implemented because of the conviction, as Lord Hailey once put it, 'that no other course would be consistent with British tradition . . .', and in later years because the educated inhabitants of British colonies would have disdained any alternative as a 'second best'.

Some 200 years ago, when the first British Empire was beginning to break up, Edmund Burke reiterated his faith in the abiding importance of the practical in government.

A statesman differs from a professor in a university; the latter has only the general view of society; the former, the statesman, has a number of circumstances to combine with these general ideas, and to take into his consideration. Circumstances are infinite, are infinitely combined; are variable and transient; he who does not take them into consideration is not erroneous, but stark mad – he is metaphysically mad. A statesman, never losing sight of principles, is to be guided by circumstances; and judging contrary to the exigencies of the moment, he may ruin his country forever. . . .

Whatever the obstacles, real or emotional, it is unfortunate that Burke's history lessons were not remembered and applied. In the twentieth century, a whole series of attempts was made to plant the Westminster parliamentary model – the product of time and the peculiar aptitudes of the British people – on races who had neither the temperament, the tradition, nor the training to make a success of it. Events of the last few years have demonstrated only too clearly that government is not a matter of abstractions open to solutions by formulas. No single design in the mechanics of government was likely to find lasting accept-ance in regions as remote from each other in time and place as seventeenth-century Massachusetts, eighteenth-century Bengal, nineteenth-century Upper Canada or twentieth-century Ghana.

On the other hand, nothing can alter the fact that British imperialism was for three centuries or more a vital phase of Asian, African and North American history. During that era, British political ideas and methods provided the underpinning for the actual self-governing structures of the colonies. Whatever the ills and prejudices engendered by colonial rule, whether the past was good or evil or a mixture of both, history has stamped a rough pattern of common interests, mingling language, commercial and legal practice, and many ordinary rules of life. Only time will tell whether the pattern will entirely fade in countries whose habits, laws and institutions are subject not only to the impulses of nationalism but to the static influences of geography and cultural back-ground.

Reduced in terms of internal coherence, and consequently in importance as a collective world power, the Commonwealth continues to exist as a fluctuating association of unequal partner states, whom accidents of history have thrown haphazardly together. Present collaboration is based on convenience and self-interest. Yet something nobler than self-interest will have to be kindled if it is to become more than an *ad hoc* coalition. Its benison to humanity must be founded on convictions more realistic, yet no less honourable, than the white-man's self-reproach for the brutalities of an imperial past and sensitivity to the appeals of the under-privileged.

In the old days, living elements, such as equality under the law and freedom of speech, were basic to the constitutional growth of the British Empire. In these unsettled times, the growing pains of nationalism are apt to mask the presence of such legacies. Yet it may be difficult for Commonwealth states to break completely from the ancient pattern, interwoven as it is with sentiment

The end of one story and the beginning of another: Julius Nyerere proclaims Tanganyika's independence in March 1961.

as well as habit. Much, of course, will depend on the strength, stability and prestige of the founder-member, on the capacity of the former mother country to withstand the threats and assaults of new barbarisms. Edmund Burke reminded his countrymen nearly 200 years ago:

As long as you have the wisdom to keep . . . this country as the sanctuary of liberty wherever men worship freedom they will turn their faces towards you.

Suggestions for Further Reading

General Works

Burt, A. L. *The Evolution of the British Empire and Commonwealth from the American Revolution* (Boston 1956)

Cambridge History of the British Empire, ed. Rose, J. H. and others (8 vols. Cambridge 1929–63)

Carrington, C. E. *The British Overseas: exploits of a nation of shopkeepers* (Cambridge 1950)

Dawson, R. M. ed. *The Development of Dominion Status, 1900–36* (2nd ed. London 1965)

De Smith, S. A. *The New Commonwealth and its Constitution* (London 1964)

Graham, G. S. *Empire of the North Atlantic* (2nd ed. London 1958)

Hancock, W. K. *Survey of British Commonwealth Affairs*, I *Problems of Nationality, 1918–36* (London 1937), II *Problems of Economic Policy, 1918–39* (2 pts. London 1940–42)

Knaplund, P. *The British Empire, 1815–1939* (New York and London 1942)

Britain, Commonwealth and Empire, 1901–55 (London 1956)

Knorr, K. *British Colonial Theories, 1570–1850* (Toronto 1944; reissued London 1963)

Koebner, R., Schmidt, H. D. *Imperialism: the story and significance of a political word, 1840–1960* (Cambridge 1964)

Mansergh, N. *Survey of British Commonwealth Affairs*, I *Problems of External Policy, 1931–39* (London 1952), II *Problems of Wartime Co-operation and Post-war Change, 1939–52* (London 1958)

Parry, J. H. *Europe and a Wider World, 1415–1715* (London 1949)

Rajan, M. S. *The Post-War Transformation of the Commonwealth: reflections on the Asian-African contribution* (London 1963)

Walker, E. A. *The British Empire: its structure and spirit, 1497–1953* (2nd ed. London 1953)

Wheare, K. C. *The Constitutional Structure of the Commonwealth* (Oxford 1960)

The Statute of Westminster and Dominion Status (5th ed. London 1953)

Williamson, J. A. *A Short History of British Expansion* (2 vols. London 1964)

The Empire before 1783

Adamson, J. H., Folland, H. F. *The Shepherd of the Ocean: a biography of Sir Walter Raleigh* (London 1969)

Alden, J. R. *A History of the American Revolution: Britain and the loss of the thirteen colonies* (London 1969)

Pioneer America (London 1966)

Andrews, C. M. *The Colonial Period of American History* (4 vols. 10th ed. New Haven and London 1964)

Andrews, K. R. *Drake's Voyages* (London 1967)

Bailyn, B. *The Ideological Origins of the American Revolution* (New York 1964)

Beer, G. L. *The Origins of the British Colonial System, 1578–1660* (New York 1908; reissued Gloucester, Mass. 1959)

Brebner, J. B. *The Explorers of North America, 1492–1806* (London 1955)

Bridenbaugh, C. *Vexed and Troubled Englishmen 1590–1642* (Oxford 1968)

Christie, I. R. *Crisis of Empire: Great Britain and the American Colonies, 1754–1783* (London 1966)

Dickerson, O. M. *The Navigation Acts and the American Revolution* (Philadelphia 1951)

Eccles, W. J. *Canada under Louis XIV, 1663–1701* (Toronto 1964)

Gipson, L. H. *The British Empire before the American Revolution* (10 vols. New York 1936–61)

Hansen, M. L. *The Atlantic Migration, 1607–1860* (Cambridge, Mass. 1940)

Harlow, V. T. *The Founding of the Second British Empire, 1763–93* (2 vols. London 1952–64)

Harper, L. A. *The English Navigation Laws* (New York 1939)

Jensen, M. *The Founding of a Nation: a history of the American Revolution, 1763–1776* (London 1968)

Labaree, L. W. *Royal Government in America* (New Haven 1943)

Mackesy, P. *The War for America, 1775–83* (London 1964)

Miller, P. *The New England Mind: the Seventeenth Century* (Cambridge, Mass. 1954)

Morison, S. E. *The Intellectual Life of Colonial New England* (New York 1956)

Newton, A. P. *The European Nations in the West Indies, 1493–1688* (London 1933)

Parks, G. B. *Richard Hakluyt and the English Voyages* (New York 1928; reissued New York 1961)

Ritcheson, C. R. *British Politics and the American Revolution* (London 1954)

Smith, J. M. *Seventeenth Century America. Essays on colonial history* (Chapel Hill 1959)

Williamson, J. A. *The Voyages of the Cabots and the English Discovery of North America* (London 1929)
Hawkins of Plymouth (London 1949)

Wright, L. B. *Religion and Empire: the alliance between piety and commerce in English expansion, 1558–1625* (Chapel Hill 1943)

Reese, T. R. *The history of the Royal Commonwealth Society, 1868–1968* (London 1968)

Robinson, K. *The Dilemmas of Trusteeship: aspects of British colonial policy between the wars* (London 1965)

Robinson, R., Gallagher, J. *Africa and the Victorians: the official mind of imperialism* (London 1961)

Schuyler, R. L. *The Fall of the Old Colonial System: a study in British free trade, 1770–1870* (New York 1945)

Shaw, A. G. L. *Convicts and the Colonies: a study of penal transportation from Great Britain and Ireland to Australia and other parts of the British Empire* (London 1966)

Thornton, A. P. *The Imperial Idea and its Enemies: a study in British power* (London 1959)

Young, D. M. *The Colonial Office in the Early Nineteenth Century* (London 1961)

THE EMPIRE AFTER 1783

1 *The United Kingdom*

Beloff, M. *Imperial Sunset,* vol. 1 *Britain's Liberal Empire, 1897–1921* (London 1969)

Bloomfield, P. *Edward Gibbon Wakefield: builder of the British Commonwealth* (London 1961)

Bodelsen, C. A. *Studies in Mid-Victorian Imperialism* (2nd ed. London 1960)

Bourne, K. *Britain and the Balance of Power in North America, 1815–1908* (London 1967)

Fieldhouse, D. K. *The Colonial Empires* (London 1966)

Garvin, J. L., Amery, J. *The Life of Joseph Chamberlain* (6 vols. London 1936–69)

Graham, G. S. *Great Britain in the Indian Ocean 1810–1850* (Oxford 1967)

Hancock, W. K. *The Wealth of Colonies* (London 1960)

Hanna, A. J. 'The British Retreat from Empire', *Britain and the Netherlands in Europe and Asia* (London 1968)

Heussler, R. *Yesterday's Rulers; the making of the British colonial service* (London 1963)

Hobson, J. A. *Imperialism: a Study* (London 1902)

Kendle, J. E. *The Colonial and Imperial Conferences, 1887–1911* (London 1967)

Knaplund, P. *Gladstone and Britain's Imperial Policy* (New York 1927)
James Stephen and the British Colonial System, 1813–47 (Madison 1953)

Langer, W. L. *The Diplomacy of Imperialism 1890–1902* (2 vols. 2nd ed. New York 1951)

McIntyre, W. D. *The Imperial Frontier in the Tropics, 1865–75: a study of British colonial policy in West Africa, Malaya and the South Pacific in the age of Gladstone and Disraeli* (New York 1967)

Manning, H. T. *British Colonial Government after the American Revolution* (New Haven 1933)

Mathieson, W. L. *Great Britain and the Slave Trade, 1839–65* (London 1929)

Mellor, G. R. *British Imperial Trusteeship, 1783–1850* (London 1951)

Miller, J. D. B. *Britain and the Old Dominions* (London 1966)

Morrell, W. P. *British Colonial Policy in the Age of Peel and Russell* (Oxford 1930)

Perham, M. *Lugard: I. the years of adventure, 1858–98* (London 1956), *II. the years of authority, 1898–1945* (London 1960)

Porter, B. *Critics of Empire* (London 1969)

2 *North America and the West Indies*

CANADA

Bracq, J. C. *The Evolution of French Canada* (New York 1924)

Brebner, J. B. *North Atlantic Triangle: the interplay of Canada, the United States, and Great Britain* (new ed. London and New York 1958)

Bruchesi, J. *Histoire du Canada* (new ed. Montreal 1959)

Brunet, M. *Les Canadiens après la Conquête, 1759–75* (Montreal 1969)

Burt, A. L. *The Old Province of Quebec* (London 1933)

Canadian Centenary Series. A history of Canada, ed. Morton, W. L., Creighton, D. G. (Toronto 1963–)

Careless, J. M. S. *The Union of the Canadas* (London 1968)

Cowan, H. I. *British Emigration to British North America: the first hundred years* (rev. ed. Toronto 1961)

Craig, G. M. ed. *Lord Durham's Report* (Toronto 1963)

Creighton, D. G. *John A. Macdonald* (2 vols. Toronto 1952, 1955)
The Commercial Empire of the St. Lawrence, 1760–1850 (new ed. Toronto 1956)
Dominion of the North: a history of Canada (2nd ed. London 1958)
Canada's First Century (Toronto and London 1970)

Easterbrook, W. T., Aitken, H. G. T. *Canadian Economic History* (Toronto 1956)

Eayrs, J. *In Defence of Canada: from the Great War to the Great Depression* (Toronto 1965)

Frégault, G. *Canada: the War of the Conquest* (Toronto 1969)

Galbraith, J. S. *The Hudson Bay Company as an Imperial Factor, 1821–69* (Berkeley and Los Angeles 1957)

Glazebrook, G. P. de T. *A History of Canadian External Relations* (Toronto 1950)

Graham, G. S. *A Concise History of Canada* (London 1967)

Hitsman, J. M. *Safeguarding Canada, 1763–1871* (Toronto 1968)

Innis, H. A. *The Fur Trade in Canada* (rev. ed. Toronto 1956)

Morton, W. L. *The Kingdom of Canada: a general history from the earliest times* (Toronto 1963)

New, C. W. *Lord Durham: a Biography of John George Lambton, First Earl of Durham* (Oxford 1929)
Lord Durham's Mission to Canada, ed. McCready, H. W. (Toronto 1963)

Rich, E. E. *The History of the Hudson's Bay Company, 1670–1878* (2 vols. London 1958–60)

Whitelaw, W. M. *The Maritimes and Canada before Confederation* (new ed. Toronto 1966)

Williams, G. *The British Search for the North-West Passage in the Eighteenth Century* (London 1962)

THE WEST INDIES

Augier, F.R. and others *The Making of the West Indies* (London 1960)

Burn, W.L. *The British West Indies* (London 1951)

Burns, Sir A. *History of the British West Indies* (London 1954)

Humphreys, R.A. *The Diplomatic History of British Honduras, 1638-1901* (London 1961)

Metcalf, G. *Royal Government and Political Conflict in Jamaica, 1729-83* (London 1965)

Murray, D.J. *The West Indies and the Development of Colonial Government, 1801-34* (Oxford 1965)

Parry, J.H., Sherlock, P.M. *History of the West Indies* (London 1956)

Ragatz, L.J. *The Fall of the Planter Class in the British Caribbean, 1763-1834* (Washington 1932)

3 Asia

GENERAL

Hall, D.G.E. *A History of South-East Asia* (London 1955)

Hoskins, H.L. *British Routes to India* (London 1928)

Irwin, G. *Nineteenth Century Borneo. A Study in diplomatic rivalry* (The Hague 1955)

INDIA, PAKISTAN AND CEYLON

Aziz, K.K. *Britain and Moslem India, 1857-1947* (London 1963)

Bearce, G.D. *British Attitudes towards India, 1784-1858* (Oxford 1961)

Cambridge History of India, The (6 vols. Cambridge 1922-32)

Das, M.N. *India under Morley and Minto: politics behind revolution, repression, and reforms* (London 1964)

Davies, C.C. *An Historical Atlas of India* (Oxford 1949)

De Silva, C.R. *Ceylon under the British Occupation, 1795-1833* (3rd ed. Colombo 1953)

Dilks, D. *Curzon in India*, vol. I (London 1969), vol. II (London 1970)

Edwardes, M. *British India 1772-1947* (London 1967)

Embree, A.T. ed. *1857 in India: Mutiny or National Uprising?* (Boston 1963)

Furber, H. *John Company at Work: a study of European expansion in India in the late eighteenth century* (Cambridge, Mass. 1951)

Gandhi, M.K. *Gandhi: an autobiography*, trans. Desai, M. (London 1948)

Gopal, S. *British Policy in India, 1858-1905* (Cambridge 1965)

Ludowyk, E.F.G. *The Story of Ceylon* (rev. ed. London 1967)

Marshall, P.J. *Problems of Empire: Britain and India 1757-1813* (New York 1968)

Mehrotra, S.R. *India and the Commonwealth 1885-1929* (London 1965)

Moon, E.P. *Gandhi and Modern India* (London 1968)

Pandey, B.M. *The Rise of Modern India* (London 1967)

Philips, C.H. *Historians of India, Pakistan, and Ceylon* (London 1961)

Spear, T.G.P. *India, Pakistan, and the West* (4th ed. Oxford 1967)

HONG KONG

Endacott, G.B. *A History of Hong Kong* (London 1958)

MALAYSIA

Bastin, J. *The Native Policies of Sir Stamford Raffles in Java and Sumatra: an economic interpretation* (Oxford 1957)

Chai, H.-C. *The Development of British Malaya, 1896-1909* (Kuala Lumpur 1964)

Cowan, C.D. *Nineteenth Century Malaya: the origins of British political control* (London 1962)

Mills, L.A. *British Malaya, 1824-67* (Kuala Lumpur 1966)

Parkinson, C. Northcote *A Short History of Malaya* (Singapore 1956)

Swettenham, F. *British Malaya: an account of the origin and progress of British influence* (rev. ed. London 1948)

Tarling, N. *Piracy and Politics in the Malay World* (Melbourne 1963)

Tregonning, K.G. *A History of Modern Malaya* (Singapore and London 1964)

4 Australasia and the Pacific

AUSTRALIA

Barnard, M. *A History of Australia* (2nd ed. Sydney 1964)

Burroughs, P. *Britain and Australia, 1831-1885: a study in Imperial relations and Crown lands administration* (Oxford 1967)

Clark, C.M.H. *A History of Australia* (2 vols. Melbourne 1962-68; others in preparation)

Crawford, R.M. *Australia* (London 1952)

Crisp, L.F. *Australian National Government* (3rd ed. Melbourne 1966)

La Nauze, J.A. *Alfred Deakin: A Biography* (2 vols. London and New York 1965)

Pike, D. *Dictionary of Australian Biography* (2 vols. Melbourne 1965-66; others in preparation)

Robson, L.L. *The Convict Settlers of Australia* (Melbourne 1965)

Shaw, A.G.L. *The Story of Australia* (rev. ed. London 1960)

Ward, J.M. *Earl Grey and the Australian Colonies, 1846-57* (Melbourne 1958)

Empire in the Antipodes: the British in Australasia, 1840-1860 (London 1966)

Ward, R.B. *The Australian Legend* (Melbourne 1958)

NEW ZEALAND

Beaglehole, J.C. *The Discovery of New Zealand* (2nd ed. Oxford 1961)

Burden, R.M. *The New Dominion: a social and political history of New Zealand, 1918-39* (Wellington and London 1965)

Cowan, J. *The New Zealand Wars* (2 vols. 2nd ed. Wellington 1955-56)

Rutherford, J. *Sir George Grey, 1812-98* (London 1961)

Scott, K.J. *The New Zealand Constitution* (Oxford 1962)

Sinclair, K. *The Origins of the Maori Wars* (London 1957)

A History of New Zealand (2nd ed. London 1961)

Wood, F.L.W. *New Zealand in the World* (Wellington 1940)

THE PACIFIC

Beaglehole, J.C. *The Exploration of the Pacific* (3rd ed. London 1966)

Legge, J.D. *Britain in Fiji, 1858-80* (London 1958)

Macdonald, A.H. *Trusteeship in the Pacific* (London 1949)

Morrell, W.P. *Britain in the Pacific Islands* (Oxford 1960)

Ward, J.M. *British Policy in the South Pacific, 1786-1893* (Sydney 1948)

Williamson, J.A. *Cook and the Opening of the Pacific* (London 1946)

5 Africa

GENERAL

Anene, J.C., Brown, G.N. *Africa in the Nineteenth and Twentieth Centuries* (Ibadan and London 1966)

Fage, J.D. *An Atlas of African History* (London 1958)

Gann, L.H., Duignan, R. *White Settlers in Tropical Africa* (London 1962)

Oliver, R., Fage, J.D. *A Short History of Africa* (2nd ed. London 1966)

Perham, M. *The Colonial Reckoning* (2nd ed. London 1963)

Perham, M., Simmons, J. *African Discovery: an anthology of exploration* (London 1948)

WEST AFRICA

Ajayi, J.F.A., Espie, I. *A Thousand Years of West African History* (Ibadan and London 1965)

Austin, D. *Politics in Ghana, 1946–60* (London 1964)

Ayandele, E.A. *The Missionary Impact on Modern Nigeria, 1842–1914* (London 1966)

Bourrett, F.M. *Ghana: the road to independence, 1919–57* (London 1960)

Burns, Sir A. *History of Nigeria* (5th ed. London 1955)

Curtin, P.D. *The Image of Africa: British Ideas and Action, 1780–1850* (London 1965)

Davies, K.G. *The Royal African Company* (London 1957)

Dike, K.O. *Trade and Politics in the Niger Delta, 1830–85* (Oxford 1956)

Fage, J.D. *A History of West Africa: an introductory survey* (4th ed. of *An Introduction to the History of West Africa*, Cambridge 1969)

Flint, J.E. *Sir George Goldie and the Making of Nigeria* (London 1960)

Fyfe, C. *Sierra Leone Inheritance* (London 1964)

Garley, H.A. *A History of the Gambia* (London 1964)

Hargreaves, J.D. *Prelude to the Partition of West Africa* ·(London 1963)

Kimble, D. *A Political History of Ghana: the rise of Gold Coast Nationalism, 1850–1928* (Oxford 1963)

Kingsley, M. *Travels in West Africa* (3rd ed. London 1965)

Newbury, C.W. *The Western Slave Coast and its Rulers* (Oxford 1961)

Wilks, I. *The Northern Factor in Ashanti History* (Legon 1961)

EAST AFRICA

Bennett, G. *Kenya, a Political History: the colonial period* (London 1963)

Bennett, N.R. *Studies in East African History* (Boston 1964)

Coupland, Sir R. *East Africa and its Invaders* (Oxford 1956)

Ingham, K. *A History of East Africa* (2nd ed. London 1964)

Low, D.A., Pratt, R.C. *Buganda and British Overrule, 1900–55* (London 1960)

Mungeam, G.H. *British Rule in Kenya 1895–1912* (Oxford 1966)

Oliver, R., Mathew, G. eds. *History of East Africa* vol. I (Oxford 1963), vol. II (Oxford 1965), vol. III in preparation

Sorrenson, M.P.K. *Origins of European Settlement in Kenya* (London 1968)

Taylor, J. *The Political Development of Tanganyika* (Stanford 1963)

CENTRAL AFRICA

Fagan, B. *A Short History of Zambia* (Nairobi 1966)

Gann, L.H. *A History of Northern Rhodesia: early days to 1953* (London 1964)

A History of Southern Rhodesia (London 1966)

Hanna, A.J. *The Story of the Rhodesias and Nyasaland* (2nd ed. London 1965)

Mason, P. *The Birth of a Dilemma: the conquest and settlement of Rhodesia* (London 1958)

Rotberg, R.I. *The Rise of Nationalism in Central Africa: the Making of Malawi and Zambia, 1873–1964* (Harvard 1966)

Wills, A.J. *An Introduction to the History of Central Africa* (2nd ed. London 1966)

SOUTH AFRICA

Furneaux, R. *The Zulu War* (London 1963)

Galbraith, J.S. *Reluctant Empire. British Policy on the South African Frontier, 1834–54* (Berkeley and Los Angeles 1963)

Goodfellow, C.F. *Great Britain and the South African Confederation, 1870–81* (Cape Town and New York 1966)

Hancock, Sir W.K. *Smuts: I the Sanguine Years, 1870–1919* (Cambridge 1962), II *the Fields of Force, 1919–50* (Cambridge 1968)

Keppel-Jones, A. *South Africa, a short history* (3rd ed. London 1961)

Kiewiet, C.W. de *A History of South Africa* (3rd ed. London 1956)

The Imperial Factor in South Africa (2nd ed. London 1965)

Kruger, D.W. *South African Parties and Policies, 1910–60* (London 1960)

Le May, G.H.L. *British Supremacy in South Africa, 1899–1907* (Oxford 1965)

Lockhart, J.G., Woodhouse, C.M. *Rhodes* (London 1963)

Macmillan, W.M. *Bantu, Boer, and Briton* (London 1929)

Mansergh, N. *South Africa, 1906–61: the price of magnanimity* (London 1962)

Marais, J. *The Cape Coloured People, 1652–1937* (London 1939)

The Fall of Kruger's Republic (Oxford 1961)

Muller. C.J.F. ed. *Five Hundred Years, A History of South Africa* (Pretoria and Cape Town 1969)

Thompson, L. *The Unification of South Africa 1902–10* (Oxford 1960)

Van Jaarsveld, F.A. *The Awakening of Afrikaner Nationalism* (Cape Town 1961)

Walker, E.A. *A History of Southern Africa* (3rd ed. London 1959)

The Great Trek (4th ed. London 1960)

Wilson, M., Thompson, L. eds. *The Oxford History of South Africa: Vol. I – South Africa to 1870* (London 1969)

BIBLIOGRAPHICAL AND RESEARCH AIDS

Flint, J.E. ed. *Books on the British Empire and Commonwealth: a guide for students* (London 1968)

Hewitt, A.R. *A Guide to Resources for Commonwealth Studies in London, Oxford and Cambridge* (London 1957)

Winks, R.W. ed. *The Historiography of the British Empire-Commonwealth* (Durham, N.C. 1966)

List of Illustrations

44 1st Skinner's Horse at a durbar. Anonymous water-colour, c. 1803. *National Army Museum, Camberley.*

46 Pineapple presented to Charles II by his gardener, John Rose. Painting attributed to H. Danckerts, c. 1675. *Collection The Dowager Marchioness of Chol-mondeley. Photo The Arts Council of Great Britain.*

48 The departure of an East Indiaman. Painting by Adam Willaerts, c. 1620. *National Maritime Museum, Green-wich.*

49 The *Delight*, East Indiaman, 1663. Watercolour by Edward Barlow. *National Maritime Museum, Green-wich.*

50 The *Custom House*, London. Engraving by John Harris, 1714. *Photo Science Museum.*

51 Petition to Oliver Cromwell, 1657. *India Office Library, London.*

East India House. Engraving from Briggs, *Relics of the East India Company. British Museum.*

52 Traders packing merchandise. Engraving from *New Map of the West Indies* by Robert Morden, 1700, in Herman Moll, *Atlas Royal. British Museum.*

53 The *Hearbe Cha.* Engraving from John Ogilby, *Embassy from the East India Company of the United Provinces to the . . . Emperor of China,* 1669. *British Museum.*

56 Second Earl of Halifax. Detail of pastel after Zoffany. *National Portrait Gallery.*

57 Broad Quay, Bristol. Painting by Peter Monomay, early 18th century. *Bristol City Art Gallery.*

58 Military architecture. Detail of engraving by Bowles and Carver, London, mid-18th century. *Fort Ticon-deroga Museum, New York.*

60 A Southeast View of Albany Factory. Watercolour by William Richards, possibly 18th century. *By per-mission of the Governor and Committee of the Hudson's Bay Company.*

61 Standard of Trade, from the Fort York account book, 1714–15. *By permission of the Governor and Committee of the Hudson's Bay Company.*

Beaver-hunting in Canada. Engraving from Charles Theodore Middleton, *A New and Complete System of Geography,* vol. II, 1778. *Metropolitan Toronto Central Library.*

63 Map of North America with Hudson's Bay and Straits by R. W. Seale, 1748. *By permission of the Governor and Committee of the Hudson's Bay Company.*

65 Prospect of the Coast from El Mina to Mowri. Detail of engraving from Jean Baptiste Labat, *A Voyage to Guinea,* 1745. *British Museum.*

Sugar plantation in the West Indies. Engraving from A. Manesson-Mallet, *Description de l'univers,* Paris 1683. *British Museum.*

Slaves working on a plantation. Engraving from I. Taylor, *Scenes in America,* London 1821. *Royal Com-monwealth Society.*

67 A view of the landing New England forces in ye expedition against Cape Breton 1745. Engraving by Brooks after Stevens. *Royal Ontario Museum, University of Toronto.*

68 Fall of Braddock, 1755. Engraving by C. Schuessele. *The Public Archives of Canada, Ottawa.*

A view of Fort Niagara. Engraving after a drawing by a member of the British force that captured it. Mid 18th century. *Webster Canadiana Collection, New Brunswick Museum, St John.*

76 'Sic transit gloria mundi.' Detail of etching by John Wilkes, September 1762. *By courtesy of Weinreb and Douwma, London.*

William Pitt the Elder. Detail from his monument in Westminster Abbey by John Bacon, 1784. *By courtesy of the Dean and Chapter of Westminster. Photo Mansell Collection.*

77 Map of North America in the eighteenth century.

78 A View of the Taking of Quebec, 13 September 1759. Anonymous engraving, c. 1790. *National Army Museum, Camberley.*

79 James Wolfe. Engraving from *Grand Magazine,* London 1760, after original drawing by Captain Harvey Smith. *Photo National Portrait Gallery.*

Battle of Quiberon Bay, November 1759. Painting by Dominic Serres. *National Maritime Museum, Greenwich.*

80 British officer in procession. Indian painting, end 18th century. *Victoria and Albert Museum.*

81 Officer of the East India Co. smoking. Detail of Indian painting by Dip Chand, late 18th century. *Victoria and Albert Museum.*

83 The Evacuations. Engraving by John Wilkes, December 1762. *By courtesy of Weinreb and Douwma, London.*

84 Shah Alam grants the *diwani* to Lord Clive, August 1765. Detail of painting by Benjamin West. *India Office Library, London.*

85 Warren Hastings. Painting by Sir Thomas Lawrence, 1811. *National Portrait Gallery.*

Edmund Burke. Painting from studio of Reynolds, 1771. *National Portrait Gallery.*

86 Interior of the Lutheran Church, York, Pennsyl-vania. Drawing by Lewis Miller, 1800. *Historical Society of York County Museum, Pennsylvania.*

90 Battle of Lexington, 19 April 1775. Contemporary engraving by Amos Doolittle. *New York Public Library.*

91 Cornwallis's letter to Washington, 17 October 1781. *The Pierpont Morgan Library, New York.*

93 Traders at Boston. Detail from *Political Electricity,* engraved by John Wilkes, 1770. *By courtesy of Wein-reb and Douwma, London.*

Planter selling tobacco. Engraving from Thomas Jefferys, *The American Atlas,* London 1776. *British Museum.*

Five pound bill, New York, 1758. *Numismatic Society, New York.*

shilling stamp, issued February 1858, Cape of Good Hope. 'Queen Victoria' one penny stamp, issued July 1853, New Zealand. 'Beaver' threepenny stamp, issued April 1851, Canada. *British Museum.*

129 Henry, third Earl of Bathurst. Painting by Sir Thomas Lawrence, *c.* 1816. *Reproduced by gracious permission of Her Majesty the Queen.*

Bust of James Stephen Jr by C. Marochetti, 1858. *National Portrait Gallery.*

130 Branding irons. *Wilberforce House, Kingston upon Hull County Museums.*

St Helena Slave Auction Bill, 1829. *Wilberforce House, Kingston upon Hull County Museums.*

131 Slave deck of *Albanoz.* Watercolour by Lt Francis Meynell (1821–70) from his logbook. *National Maritime Museum, Greenwich.*

Detail of a slave ship. Engraving from F. R. Walsh, *Notices of Brazil,* vol. II, London 1830. *By courtesy of Canning House Library.*

Model of the slave ship *Brookes* prepared for the Wilberforce Committee. *Wilberforce House, Kingston upon Hull County Museums.*

135 John Macarthur (1767–1834). Contemporary engraving. *Photo Australian News and Information Bureau.*

Leaving old England. Engraving from *The Graphic,* 18 December 1869. *Photo Australian News and Information Bureau.*

Sheep-shearing. Engraving from *Australian Sketcher,* 31 October 1874.

136 Bernardt Holtermann with the Beyers and Holtermann nugget, weighing 630 lb. Contemporary photograph by Beaufoy Merlin. *Mitchell Library, Sydney. Photo Australian News and Information Bureau.*

Forest Creek diggings at Mount Alexander, Port Phillip, Victoria. Engraving from *Illustrated London News,* 1852. *Photo Mansell Collection.*

137 Hyde Park, Sydney. Engraving by F. R. Ashton, late 19th century. *Photo Australian News and Information Bureau.*

Australian homestead, 1870s. Contemporary photograph by Beaufoy Merlin. *Mitchell Library, Sydney. Photo Australian News and Information Bureau.*

139 *Lord John taking the measure of the Colonies.* From *Punch,* 23 February 1850. *Photo Mansell Collection.*

140 *Cession of Matavai, Tahiti,* 1798. Engraving after original painting by Robert Smirke, commissioned by the London Missionary Society. *Congregational Council for World Mission.*

141 John Williams killed on the beach at Erromanga, New Hebrides, 1839. Engraving by Baxter. *Congregational Council for World Mission.*

143 New Zealand coast and Maoris. Engraving after Sydney Parkinson, *A Journal of a Voyage to the South Seas,* London 1773. *Photo Mansell Collection.*

144 Captain William Hobson. Contemporary watercolour by Mrs Musgrave. *National Library of Australia, Canberra. Rex Nan Kivell Collection.*

Baptism of the Maori chief Te Puni in Otahi Church, New Zealand. Governor Grey and his wife are present. Painting by C. D. Barraud, 1853. *National Library of Australia, Canberra. Rex Nan Kivell Collection.*

145 Auckland. Lithograph by V. Brooks from Charles Hursthouse, *New Zealand, The Britain of the South,* London 1857.

146 Missionary and his wife. Wood-carving by Haida Indians, Queen Charlotte Islands, British Columbia, mid-19th century. *British Museum.*

148 Victoria Railway Terminus, Bombay. Watercolour by A. H. Haig, 1878. *India Office Library, London.*

Royal Pavilion, Brighton, completed 1821. *Photo County Borough of Brighton.*

151 Captain Bulger, Governor of Assiniboia, Saskatchewan, and the chiefs and warriors of the Chippewa tribe at Red Lake, Ontario, in the Colony House, Fort Douglas, 22 May 1823. Watercolour by Peter Rindisbacher. *McCord Museum, McGill University, Montreal.*

153 *The Insurgents at Beauharnois, Quebec,* 1837. Detail of watercolour by Mrs E. Ellice. *The Public Archives Canada, Ottawa.*

First Earl of Durham. Mezzotint by T. Phillips. *The Public Archives of Canada, Ottawa.*

155 Burning of the Houses of Parliament in Montreal. Engraving from *Illustrated London News,* 19 May 1849. *The Public Archives of Canada, Ottawa.*

156 Adam Smith. Medallion by James Tassie, 1787. *National Portrait Gallery.*

157 *Dividend Day at the Bank.* Painting by G. E. Hicks, 1859. *By courtesy of the Bank of England.*

158 William Huskisson. Painting by R. Rothwell. *National Portrait Gallery.*

159 *West India Docks from the southeast.* Lithograph by W. Parrott, 1840s. *Port of London Authority. Photo Eileen Tweedy.*

161 *Papa Cobden taking Master Robert for a Free Trade Walk.* From *Punch,* 1845. *Photo Mansell Collection.*

Henry, third Earl Grey. *Photo Mansell Collection.*

162 Edward Gibbon Wakefield. Anonymous miniature. *National Portrait Gallery.*

163 Indian stand at the Great Exhibition, 1851. Lithograph by Dickinson after J. Nash from *Pages from the Great Industrial Exhibition. Victoria and Albert Museum.*

165 *Dragon Pagoda.* Lithograph from J. Moore, *Rangoon Views,* 1825–6. *India Office Library, London.*

166 *Signing of the Treaty of Nanking in the State Cabin of HMS Cornwallis,* 29 August 1842. Anonymous engraving. *Photo National Army Museum, Camberley.*

167 *Great Eastern* under construction in the naval dockyards at Millwall, 1857. *The Institution of Mechanical Engineers.*

279

Dr Mackinnon and J. Martin, the district commissioner, making a treaty with Chief Kamiri of the Kikuyu, Kenya, 11 August 1889. *Royal Commonwealth Society.*

217 Europeans surrounded by warriors and musicians in Borneo, late 19th century. *Photo Paul Popper.*

219 Diamond Jubilee Procession, London 1897. *Photo Radio Times Hulton Picture Library.*

221 Queen Victoria. Painting after Benjamin Constant in the Houses of Parliament. *Photo Ministry of Public Building and Works.*

223 P & O poster, *c.* 1930. *Peninsular and Orient Archives.*

225 *A Result of Free Trade.* Cartoon by J. M. Staniforth from *The Western Mail,* Cardiff, 13 January 1910.

226 Title-page of *The Imperial & Colonial Magazine & Review,* November 1900. *British Museum.*

228 Carriage of the Bombay, Baroda and Central India Railway. Engraving from *Illustrated London News,* 12 March 1864. *Photo Radio Times Hulton Picture Library.*

229 Loading a train in Uganda, *c.* 1890. *Royal Commonwealth Society.*

Drilling in the Niger delta by the British Petroleum Corporation, *c.* 1910. *Photo British Petroleum Co. Ltd.*

232 *So kind of John.* Cartoon by the Tariff Reform League. *British Museum.*

233 Trading ships in the Hooghly, Calcutta, 1890s. *India Office Library.*

235 *John Bull's Creditors.* Cartoon by Walter Crane, 1900.

236 The rebel chief Langalibalele and sons in Pieter-Maritzberg prison, 1879. *Photo National Army Museum, Camberley.*

237 Dr Jameson at the start of his raid, 1895. Contemporary engraving. *Photo Mansell Collection.*

Sir Alfred Milner. *Photo Radio Times Hulton Picture Library.*

President Paul Kruger. *Photo Director of Information, South Africa House.*

240 Lord Roberts planning the advance on Pretoria, at Kroonstadt, 1900. *Photo Radio Times Hulton Picture Library.*

Lord Kitchener and General Pole-Carew, 5 June 1901. *Photo Radio Times Hulton Picture Library.*

Christmas mail for the British forces, South Africa. *Photo Radio Times Hulton Picture Library.*

241 De Wet's commando crosses the Orange River. *Photo Director of Information, South Africa House.*

Three generations of Boers in 1900: P. J. Lemmer aged sixty-five, J. D. L. Botha aged fifteen, C. I. Pretorius aged forty-three. *Photo Radio Times Hulton Picture Library.*

243 Lord Roberts takes a slice of South Africa. German cartoon from *Klodderadatsch,* 1900. *British Museum.*

244 Celebrations in Fleet Street after the relief of Ladysmith, 1900. *Photo Radio Times Hulton Picture Library.*

245 Meeting of De Wet, General Botha, Lord Kitchener and Colonel Hamilton (front row) to discuss peace terms, 1902. *Photo National Army Museum, Camberley.*

247 First Cabinet of the Union of South Africa, 1910. *Photo Director of Information, South Africa House.*

249 Indian Civil Service examination paper from Haileybury College, July 1840. *India Office Library, London.*

251 *On the prowl.* From *Punch,* 5 December 1896. *Photo Mansell Collection.*

252 The David Sassoon Industrial and Reformatory Institution, Bombay. Engraving from *Illustrated London News,* 1859. *Photo Mansell Collection.*

253 Supreme court, Madras. Engraving from *Illustrated London News,* 1853. *Photo Mansell Collection.*

254 *The Storming of Seringapatam,* Fourth Mysore War, 1799. Engraving after R. K. Porter. *Photo National Army Museum, Camberley.*

255 Sepoys at rifle practice. Lithograph after drawing by Captain G. F. Atkinson from the Indian campaign, 1857-58. *Photo National Army Museum, Camberley.*

256 Ruins after the Indian Mutiny. Photograph by F. Beato, 1857. *Victoria and Albert Museum.*

257 Lord and Lady Curzon in the State Procession, Delhi durbar, 1903. *Photo Mansell Collection.*

258 Gandhi outside his South African office, 1913. *Photo Press Information Bureau, Government of India.*

Nehru as a boy. *Photo Press Information Bureau, Government of India.*

259 Gandhi and Nehru during a session of the All India Congress Committee, August 1942. *Photo Press Information Bureau, Government of India.*

260 Round Table Conference, London 1931. *India Office Library, London.*

261 Raising of the flag by Nehru at Red Fort, Delhi, on Independence Day, 15 August 1947. *Photo Press Information Bureau, Government of India.*

262 Raising of the flag in Nairobi, Kenya, on Independence Day, 12 December 1963. *Photo Keystone Press Agency.*

264 *A lesson in Empire making* with Cecil Rhodes. Sketch by Sydney P. Hall. *Photo Radio Times Hulton Picture Library.*

266 Colonial Conference, June 1897. From O. D. Skelton, *Life and Letters of Sir Wilfred Laurier,* vol. II.

267 Commonwealth Premiers Conference, September 1962. *Photo United Press International.*

271 Julius Nyerere, chief minister, proclaims Tanganyika's independence, March 1961. *Photo Keystone Press Agency.*

Index